CSR, Sustainability, Ethics & Governance

Series Editors

Samuel O. Idowu, London Metropolitan University, Calcutta House, London, UK

René Schmidpeter, Cologne Business School, Cologne, Germany

In recent years the discussion concerning the relation between business and society has made immense strides. This has in turn led to a broad academic and practical discussion on innovative management concepts, such as Corporate Social Responsibility, Corporate Governance and Sustainability Management. This series offers a comprehensive overview of the latest theoretical and empirical research and provides sound concepts for sustainable business strategies. In order to do so, it combines the insights of leading researchers and thinkers in the fields of management theory and the social sciences – and from all over the world, thus contributing to the interdisciplinary and intercultural discussion on the role of business in society. The underlying intention of this series is to help solve the world's most challenging problems by developing new management concepts that create value for business and society alike. In order to support those managers, researchers and students who are pursuing sustainable business approaches for our common future, the series offers them access to cutting-edge management approaches.

CSR, Sustainability, Ethics & Governance is accepted by the Norwegian Register for Scientific Journals, Series and Publishers, maintained and operated by the Norwegian Social Science Data Services (NSD)

Natalya Ketenci
Editor

Transition to the Circular Economy Model

The Case of Turkey

Springer

Editor
Natalya Ketenci
Yeditepe University
Atasehir, Istanbul, Türkiye

ISSN 2196-7075 ISSN 2196-7083 (electronic)
CSR, Sustainability, Ethics & Governance
ISBN 978-3-031-52699-2 ISBN 978-3-031-52700-5 (eBook)
https://doi.org/10.1007/978-3-031-52700-5

This Springer imprint is published by the registered company Springer Nature Switzerland AG
The registered company address is: Gewerbestrasse 11, 6330 Cham, Switzerland

Paper in this product is recyclable.

Preface

The circular economy is one of the few solutions to save our world from resources depletion. According to National Footprint and Biocapacity Accounts, people on average in the world use 1.75 times faster resources than the planet can generate. This number varies for different countries: for the USA, this number is 5.1; for Europe, on average, this number is about 3; and for Turkey, it is 2.1, which is above average. Turkey consumes twice more faster resources that the planet can generate and 2.6 faster resources the country can generate. Turkey behaves as it has 2.6 Turkeys; this number is less than numbers for the developed countries but higher than the average for the world. In addition to the lack of resources, the circular economy allows a significant decrease in the level of pollution by reusing resources several times without adding to waste. There are many laws developed in Europe to move production to the circular economy. Turkey is involved in the process of sustainability and the development of the circular economy; however, Turkey is still far away behind in standards that can decrease pollution and increase the efficiency of resource use.

Environmental degradation in the world has been one of the problems discussed in the literature for many decades. There are a lot of factors discussed that worsen our environment. Environmental degradation due to pollution from fossil fuels induces countries to decrease their use; however, until the productivity of renewable resources reaches the necessary level, countries continue to be highly dependent on non-renewable sources. Another important issue is increasing waste in all spheres of our life. One of the solutions for the environmental degradation slowdown is in circular economy. The circular economy aims to produce as little waste as possible by reusing materials in new productions. The circular economy is becoming part of many different sectors of an economy. This book aims to discuss and analyze different sectors that are starting to be involved in the circular economy process in Turkey.

Atasehir, Istanbul, Türkiye — Natalya Ketenci

About This Book/Conference

The Circular Economy Series (CES) – II International Conference, held on the 18th and 19th of November 2022, combined industry experts and researches to explore, share, and advance knowledge on transition of Turkey to the Circular Economy model. The conference was organized by the Management Application and Research Center of Yeditepe University (YUVAM), bringing together professionals from diverse sectors, including government, energy, glass, furniture, textile sectors, and international organizations. This book is a collection of chapters that are derived from best studies presented on the CES II conference.

The aim of this book is to analyze innovations in circular economy that may be applied to various sectors in Turkey. In addition, this book investigates cases from Turkey of transition to circular economy in different areas.

This book consists of 10 chapters that may be divided in several sections. The first part is related to a digital transformation on the way to the circular economy. This part consists of three chapters. The first chapter investigates digital and sustainable revolutions and attempts to find an answer of how digital transformation can be viewed through the lens of sustainability as a part of the circular economy. The next chapter considers artificial intelligence as a balance between institutions, environment, and society. This research explores how artificial intelligence can influence new substantial entrepreneurial trends, applications, and outcomes. It examines how this technology can increase and change the tasks associated with the idea of sustainability. This chapter provides a case study analysis of a multinational company headquartered in Turkey that cooperates with 41 companies. The final chapter of this part investigates snowballing danger related to electronic waste. Technology is developing with very high speed, where people prefer to have last technology models. The race for the latest technology significantly increases the consumption of electronic products generating enormous waste that is very harmful for the environment, human health, and natural life. This study examines the policies of companies of Turkey regarding the control and disposal of e-waste. The main concern of this chapter is an analysis of the e-waste sector in within the framework of the sustainable development goal (SDG) 12 – Responsible Production and Consumption. This study is the connection chapter between the first and the next part of this book combining studies on digital transformation and on Sustainable Development Goals.

The next part of the book is devoted to Sustainable Development Goals in the circular economy framework. The first chapter examines selected software companies to compare sectoral and economic growth opportunities in the context of the analysis of eighth Sustainable Development Goal – Decent Work and Economic Growth. The selected software companies are analyzed using the frequency analysis for the extent to which they meet the sub-targets according to the determined parameters. The next chapter presents the study in the framework of the fifth Sustainable Development Goal – Gender Equality. The logistics and transportation sectors are chosen by this study for being male-dominated for a long time. However, in the rapidly globalizing business world, it has become very important for women and men to have equal conditions in business life within the scope of SDG 5. In this research, 10 logistics companies listed in the BIST 100 index were accepted as a sample, and the annual sustainability, where human resources policy reports shared by the companies were examined. The main purpose of this research is to examine the logistics sector in Turkey from the perspective of gender equality and to present a projection of the current situation of the sector.

The next part of this book presents studies on consumer behavior within the framework of the circular economy. The two chapters of this part are devoted to fashion and luxury market consumption. The first chapter is examining secondhand fashion market. Through secondhand markets, product life can be extended. Therefore, fewer products can be produced. Secondhand clothing market is estimated to increase by threefold by 2025. The current size of the market in Turkey is 400 million TL. In this conceptual study, secondhand fashion consumption will be analyzed from the perspectives of sustainability and circular economy. The aim of this study is to investigate the evolution of circular consumption. It also aims to discuss the emerging digital secondhand fashion market strategies and fashion rental business. The next chapter's topic refers to secondhand consumption following the previous chapter, but this time secondhand consumption in the luxury fashion market is analyzed. Fashion is one of the industries criticized as causing the greatest harm to the environment; hence, the emergence of a circular economy perspective in that sector becomes vital. In that sense, this study aims to understand the circular economy practices of the secondhand luxury fashion segment as triggering the reusing of high- quality products in Turkey.

The next part of the book is focused on the green economy in different sectors. The first chapter investigates the adoption of green management practice in SMEs. The adoption of green management principles in a firm may depend on the support of the leadership team and the capabilities to create new resource combinations for the right environmental procedures, namely strategic flexibility. This study investigates the impact of leadership support and strategic flexibility to implement green management practices in SMEs. In line with the aim of the study, a survey was carried out on a sample of 214 SMEs that operate in chemical industries in Turkey. The findings revealed that leadership support contributed more than strategic flexibility to the adoption of green management practices of SMEs. However, the combined effect of leadership support and strategic flexibility was the greatest. The next chapter is related to green finances, where hedging clean energy equities with various hedging instruments, such as carbon, gold, oil, and the VIX, are investigated in a time-frequency space. The wavelet coherence and rolling-window analyses are employed to examine the frequency-dependent time-varying co-movements between green stocks and the potential hedging vehicles. The result of this study reveals that coherences at higher scales are stronger than those at lower scales, and alternative energy equities display a strong anti-cyclical relationship with the implied volatility index. This chapter further provides results of the study how hedging performances vary during the pandemic and documents improved performance after the pandemic, even though the hedging benefits are strongly dependent on wavelet frequencies. These results have significant implications for risk management and portfolio analysis.

The final part and chapter of the book finalizes with the analysis of environmental problems and its impact on the political protest movements. This chapter analyzes Kyrgyzstan as the case study. In Central Asia, infrastructure development poses real environmental, material, and cultural threats to local populations. These communities are often highly reliant on the environment for their livelihoods and well-being, and thus have a heightened understanding of what they stand to lose by not managing it carefully. Threats to the environment, whether they materialize or not, can create "relative deprivation" for local communities, generating local and specific grievances, which provide a general spur to activism. Despite lacking meaningful capital, poor groups can undertake resistance ranging from overt, confrontational behavior to subtle, everyday forms. This "environmentalism of the poor" is closely linked to the "environmental justice" movement. Several environmental mobilizations in Central Asia have been interpreted through an environmental justice lens.

Contents

About the Editor

Natalya Ketenci is a professor in Economics at Yeditepe University, Turkey, where she has been employed for the past 9 years. Since 2022, she is the director of the Management Application and Research Center at Yeditepe University (YUVAM). She received her PhD degree in Economics from the University of Reading, UK (2003), and an MSc in Mathematics from the Al-Farabi Kazak State National University (1996). At the same time, she is a member of the Centre for Euro-Asian Studies at the University of Reading's Henley Business School. Dr. Ketenci was assisting in the preparation of the Transition report 2001: Energy in transition in the European Bank for Reconstruction and Development, London (UK). Her works have been focused on international trade issues in the European Union and emerging countries. Her current research has a focus on energy issues in Turkey and on energy links between European and transition countries. She is one of the editors and authors of *Economics and Politics of Energy in the Middle East and Eastern Europe; and Turkish-Russian Relations: Prospects and Challenges* books published by Lexington Books in 2021 and 2019. The new book is published in 2022: *Circular Economy: Multidisciplinary Approach from Turkey*. Her publications include contributions to such journals as *Energy*, *Russian Journal of Economics*, *Empirical Economics*, *Economic Modeling*, and *Research in Economics*.

Contributors

Deniz Palalar Alkan is Associate Professor of Organizational Behavior at Yeditepe University. She has earned her baccalaureate degree from Florida Atlantic University majoring in International Business and Trade. She got her Master's Degree from Lynn University and PhD from Istanbul University. While attending Florida Atlantic University, she volunteered to work with students with disabilities. After obtaining her bachelor's degree, she started to work at several international banks, including Citibank N.A. and global insurance brokerage firms. She has been an instructor since 2011 and currently teaching courses including Leadership, Business Management, and Entrepreneurship at Yeditepe University. Her area of interest are organizational behavior, leadership, and diversity.

Burcu Arsan got her PhD degree in Management and Organization at Yeditepe University. Her dissertation title is "The Formation of CyberCulture in Learning Organizations," and her research focuses on digital transformation processes in organizations, cyberculture, industry 4.0, and lean thinking in organizations. Her research on those themes has appeared or is forthcoming in journals of management, digitalization, and social sciences. Her most recently published paper's title is "The future of artificial intelligence: how will emotions affect AI?". She holds a Master of Business Administration degree from Yeditepe University and a BA degree in Healthcare Management from Acıbadem University. She is a member of the Management Application and Research Center (YUVAM) at Yeditepe University.

Selçuk Bayraci is currently a data scientist and Data Analytics Unit Manager at Borusan Otomotiv. His research interests include financial econometrics, computational finance, econophysics, credit risk modeling, and big data analytics. He has published in prestigious journals, such as *Energy Economics* and *Technological Forecasting and Social Change*.

Sercan Demiralay is a senior lecturer in Finance at Nottingham Business School, Nottingham Trent University, UK. His research interests are in the fields of financial economics, sustainable finance, and alternative investments. He has articles published in leading economics and finance journals, such as *Energy Economics*, *Journal of Real Estate Finance and Economics*, and *Technological Forecasting and Social Change*.

Ayşe Gönül Demirel is a professor of Management and Strategy in the Department of Business Administration at Yeditepe University. She has earned her Baccalaurate degree from Bogazici University, Istanbul, majoring in Sociology; received a certificate in Marketing from the Chartered Institute of Marketing, UK; received her MBA in Management and Organizations from Yeditepe University, Istanbul; and PhD in Management and Organization from Yeditepe University in 2008 with a thesis on "An Exploratory Study on Developing and Testing Integrated Stakeholder Relationships Management Model" under the supervision of Prof. Dr. M. Atilla Öner. She has been teaching courses at the Department of Business Administration since 2004 in undergraduate, graduate and Doctorate level.

Her teaching experience includes courses such as organization theory and design, strategic management, business research methodology and data analysis, human resources management, and corporate governance. Her current research interests are stakeholder theory, managerial values, leadership, and corporate governance. Her recent research focuses on the influence of Big Data on management and organization issues. She has authored and coauthored several articles and international book chapters.

Yusuf Can Erdem has obtained his undergraduate Degree in Business Administration from Middle East Technical University, Ankara, Turkey. After graduation, he was honored with a state scholarship to get his graduate degree in the USA. Following his graduation from East Carolina University, NC, with an MBA degree, he has assumed sales and marketing responsibilities at local and multinational companies for 20 years. Following his retirement from professional business life, he has received his PhD in Business Administration from Yeditepe University in 2007. Ever since he has taught courses of E-Business, Supply Chain Management, Consumer Behavior, CRM, CXM, Marketing Research, International Marketing, and Marketing Strategy in both undergraduate and graduate schools of different universities. Many of his articles were deemed worthy of publication at local and international journal and congresses. Two of his books on "Customer Experience Management" have been published in the USA and Turkey. His current scholarly interest lies in CXM and the impact of circular economy on consumer behavior. He is currently a professor of Management at Yeditepe University, Istanbul, Turkey.

Hatice Gaye Gencer is a professor in Finance at Yeditepe University. Her main areas of research interest are financial economics, sustainable finance, and market integration. She has published a number of high-quality research outputs in reputable journals, such as *Empirical Economics*, *Bulletin of Economic Research*, and *Energy Economics*. She also has a great interest in the financial technologies and climate change.

Arzu Şar İçöz after receiving her MBA from Yıldız Technical University, she completed her doctorate courses in Business Administration at Yeditepe University and is preparing to take the qualifying exam. She has two publications titled "The Role of Generations in the Relationship between Organizational Culture and Entrepreneurial Orientation" and "The Role of Generation Y in the Relation between Hierarchical Culture and Entrepreneurial Orientation," which she prepared during her MBA process. In her work, she focused on the roles of generations in the sustainable entrepreneurial ecosystem and their relationship with organizational culture. She started her career as an assistant of the general coordinator in an international holding company, and in the following years continued working as a tourism guide, translator, and notary translator. In addition to her PhD studentship, she has been working as a lecturer in the English Preparatory School at Yeditepe University since 1996.

Rıfat Kamaşak is a professor of Management and Strategy at Yeditepe University, Istanbul, Turkey. He also holds board membership positions in several companies listed on Istanbul Stock Exchange. He worked in the food, confectionery, carpet, textile, aluminum, metal, retailing, trading, and consulting industries for nearly twenty years. Having completed his bachelor's degree in economics and a postgraduate diploma in international management at the University of Istanbul, he continued his graduate studies in the UK. Professor Kamaşak received his MA in marketing from Middlesex University London, MA in management from Durham University, and MSc in applied linguistics from the University of Oxford. He also has two individual PhD degrees: PhD in management studies from the University of Exeter (2014) and PhD in organization theory from the University of Istanbul (2004).

His primary interest areas are strategic management, knowledge and innovation, and equality, diversity and inclusion (EDI) at work. He has conducted field studies in Turkey and internationally, and his work is empirically grounded. His research is supported by international and national grants. He has published nearly 100 conference papers and over 50 papers in academic journals such as *Business Ethics: A European Review*, *Gender, Work and Organization*, *International Journal of Production Research*, *Knowledge Management Research and Practice*, *European Business Review*, *Journal of English for Academic Purposes*, *Management Research Review*, *Journal of Organizational Change Management*, and *Gender in Management*, among others. His book chapters have been published by Emerald Press, Cambridge University Press, Springer International Publishing, Palgrave Macmillan, Edward Elgar Publishing, and Information Age Publishing.

Özge Kirezli received her MA degree in Production Management and Marketing from Marmara University in 2010. In 2015, she received her PhD degree in Production Management and Marketing from Marmara University. She started her academic career as a teaching assistant at Business Administration Department of İstanbul Bilgi University in 2010 and worked till 2018. Since 2019, she is working as an assistant professor at Yeditepe University, lecturing marketing principles, marketing management, marketing research, and consumer behavior courses. She has articles in the *Journal of World Intellectual Property* and *Journal of Innovation Economics and Management* and book chapters about circular economy, sharing economy, green marketing, and corporate social responsibility in Lexington books, Global IGI books, and Routledge. Her research interests are consumer decision making and paradigm shifts in contemporary marketing.

Fulya Midilli Muskara is a PhD student in the Department of Business Administration at Yeditepe University. She got her MBA degree from the same university. She has two publications, "An exploratory study on Turkish consumers' attitude and purchase intention towards green products" and "A Literature Review on Understanding the Intention of Sustainable Food Purchasing with the Theory of Planned Behavior: Cultural Differences," which she prepared during her doctoral period. Her studies focus on consumers' attitudes towards sustainable products. Apart from her academic life, she has more than 13 years of sales experience in various sectors. She currently works as a Global Sales Manager in a company in the tobacco industry.

Yelnur Seitkozha Master of International Relations, Ablai Khan Kazakh University of International Relations and World Languages, 2022, Almaty

Bauyrzhan Simagambetov Master of International Relations, Academy of Public Administration under the President of the Republic of Kazakhstan, 2017, Astana.

Post-graduate programme «International Relations and European Integration», Estonian School of Diplomacy, 2018, Tallinn.

PhD Candidate, Al-Farabi Kazakh National University, Department of Political Science and Political Technologies, 2020–present time, Almaty.

The focus of his research "Features of political protests in contemporary society," is the development of theoretical and practical provisions on political protests as a social phenomenon.

Asli Tolunay is an associate professor of Marketing at the Business Administration Department of Yeditepe University (Turkey). She received her PhD in Marketing from Boğaziçi University, after working in multinational companies for 10 years in sales and marketing management positions. Her primary research interests are in the areas of consumer-brand relationship management and digital consumer behavior. She has publications in international (SSCI) and national peer-reviewed journals on these topics integrating several methodological approaches and has presented on various national and international conferences and received best paper awards.

Muteber Tuzcu is a research assistant at the Tourism Administration Department, at Boğaziçi University, İstanbul, Turkey, and a PhD student at Department of Management, Institute of Social Sciences, Boğaziçi University, İstanbul, Turkey. She received a bachelor's degree in Tourism Administration from Boğaziçi University. She has book chapters about circular economy and student's satisfaction in Lexington books and Global IGI books. Her research interests include services marketing, consumer behaviors, sharing economy, and sustainability.

Esin Yücel Karamustafa was born in 1983. She holds an economics degree from Kocaeli University ('05), and MBA degree from Yeditepe University ('16), and a PhD in Management and Organization from Yeditepe University ('20). She worked as a project assistant in Business Administration Department at Yeditepe University between 2014 and 2021; before that, she worked in various managerial positions for different global companies. Since 2021, she is working as an assistant professor at Altinbaş University, lecturing strategic management, advance organization theory, research methodology and business ethics, and organizational behavior and leadership.

The Convergence of Digital Transformation and Sustainable Revolution

Yusuf Can Erdem

1 Introduction

Digital transformation is the practice of transforming traditional business functions like marketing, sales, and customer service by using digital technologies both to generate new business procedures, new business culture, and customer experiences and to adapt the current ones in order to be able to meet ever-changing business and market expectations. In other words, all or parts of the businesses are redesigned in the age of digitalization. This transformation from paper-based practices to smart applications lets organizations to reimagine how to do business with the help of digital technology (Berman, 2012).

What is interesting is the fact that digital transformation is not only a technology issue since it cannot be succeeded without revised corporate culture, updated performance standards, adjusted management styles, and many other administrative regulations because the overall objective is still a better customer experience leading to customer loyalty. Even the plan to start a digital transformation project may be profoundly important for the customers because it may be perceived as a signpost by the customers that the company is about to embrace a new technology which will make it easier/enjoyable for both parties to operate, distribute, and consume the products/services.

Although digital transformation is a trendy topic, the concept of digitizing and digitalizing were introduced in the early 1990s and the 2000s. Many organizations have started their digital transformation journeys then, but the idea picked up pace dramatically with the rise of the Information and Communications Technologies (ICT) concept, that is, a broad term referring to all the infrastructure and

Y. C. Erdem (✉)
Yeditepe University, Istanbul, Turkey
e-mail: canerdem@yeditepe.edu.tr

N. Ketenci (ed.), *Transition to the Circular Economy Model*, CSR, Sustainability, Ethics & Governance, https://doi.org/10.1007/978-3-031-52700-5_1

components including computers, internet, cell phones, wireless networks, artificial Intelligence, social networking, video-conferencing, and other services and applications used by both organizations and individuals to access, regain, store, communicate, and use information in a digital form.

ICT has been characterized by technological improvements in time, from mainframe computers and mini-computers to personal computers with a crucial impact on almost all businesses in many different ways ever since 1945. ICT has also provided the platform for all functions of global logistics and communication to process huge amounts of data moving across the world at an ever-increasing speed so that both domestic and multinational companies will be more agile (Chandola, 2016).

Gartner forecasted that worldwide Information Technology (IT) expenditures will reach $4.2 trillion in 2021, which is 8.6% above the 2020 figure. Due to the Covid-19 pandemic, there has been a major increase in IT spending which has accelerated ahead of revenue expectations, according to Gartner. The respective IT expenditure growth rates were 0.9% in 2020 and 8.6% in 2021 and it is predicted to be 5.3% in 2022 (Costello & Rimor, 2021).

The easy accessibility of the Internet is the main facilitating factor for the Digital Transformation growth and the number of users accessing went up from 4.75 billion in January 2021 to 4.95 billion in January 2022. With an increase rate of 4.2%, the global internet penetration rate reached to 62.5% of the global population of 7.91 billion as of January 2022 (Kemp, 2022).

Mobile phones also made a major contribution for sharing, storing, and creating data for networking. The number of mobile users reached up to 5.31 billion (67.1% of the global population) as of January 2021. The growth rate over 1 year is 1.8%.

While digital transformation provides companies with new business models based on both existing and new digital technologies, it also requires a commitment to expand the customer base including the internal customers (employees), potential customers, and customers-to-be which are feasible thanks to the insights offered by social media. As of January 2022, the total number of social media users was 4.62 billion globally which is equal to almost 58.4% of the world's population. Also important is the growth rate of global social media user which was over 10% in 2021 (Kemp, 2022).

The digital transformation is neither limited to internet use nor social media membership but it can be defined as a holistic process including the whole organization to change products, bureaucratic and organizational culture and the relationships to stakeholders (Mergel et al., 2019).

According to the findings of a research by McKinsey, the major objective of transforming companies was to digitalize their operational systems and the successful ones were willing to use more sophisticated technologies, like artificial intelligence (AI), the IoT, and more progressive neural machine-learning techniques in the future (De la Boutetière et al., 2018). The major key success factors in digital transformation processes were listed by the researchers of McKinsey as follows: The right transformative leadership would both empower the internal customers to work in new ways by upgrading the routine work in digitalized means and generate competencies for the future workforce (Bahattarai, 2020). Despite all these efforts and investments, the research shows that the success rate of digital transformation projects in improving a company's performance and sustaining those gains is as low as 26% even at digitally sharp industries and much lower in traditional industries (Shooter, 2020). Nevertheless, this does not change the fact that organizations all around the world keep investing in holistic digital strategies for people, technology, data, processes, and governance. The forecast of International Data Corporation (IDC) for global digital transformation spending is above $10 trillion for the period of 2021 to 2031. The total spending of $2.8 trillion forecasted for 2025 is more than the double of amount allocated in 2020 (Shirer, 2021). Therefore, it can be concluded that the "digital transformation revolution" is here to stay since it has started a paradigm shift by taking an incorporated approach toward operations, sourcing, supply chain management, marketing, and other managerial functions of profit/non-profit organizations. The overall objectives are not only to improve traditional missions of cost savings, enhanced efficiencies, and facilitating customer satisfaction but also to design new ways of value creation and to continuously search for better ways of delivering value for both internal and external customers.

It can be said that the "digital transformation revolution" has dominated the last three decades and now it is time for a new societal paradigm shift, the sustainability revolution.

2 Sustainability

Recognition of "Sustainability" as an issue goes back to the 1960s. The year of 1969 was when the concept of "sustainable development", for the first time, was signed as a formal text by 33 members of the International Union for Conservation of Nature (IUCN). Also in 1969, the Environmental Protection Agency was established in the United States with a major impact on both theories and practice in global environmental policies.

In 1973, Haas (1973) wrote that all the organizations had major responsibilities for "pollution protection, charitable foundations, assistance to the disadvantaged and educational institutions" in addition to accomplishing their typical business missions. The findings of the research conducted with 500 companies by Ernst and Young in 1976 reported some social measurement confessions in the period between 1971 and 1973. Epstein (1977) was the first scholar who defined Social Accounting as the process of identification, measurement, checking, and recording of the economic and social impacts of institutions on the general public. He used the performance parameters of human physical resources, community involvement, and the contributions of services and products to the environment in general.

The term "sustainability" was defined for the first time in the Brundtland Report (Our common future) prepared by some member countries of the United Nations (UN) in 1987 as: "Sustainable development is development that meets the needs of the present without compromising the ability of future generations to meet their own" (Brundtland Report, 1987; Du Pisani, 2007).

In time, the notion of sustainability made huge progress with an expanding and evolving content. It is no longer referred to environmental considerations only but also anything from eco-friendly containers to all sorts of pollution including sound pollution, to green supply-chain solutions and many more.

In 2015, the UN settled 17 Sustainable Development Goals (SDG) in "the 2030 Agenda for Sustainable Development" which was approved by all 193 member states of the General Assembly (Transforming our world: the 2030 Agenda for Sustainable Development, 2015). Those goals can be grouped under five Ps:

- People (No Poverty, No Hunger, Good Health and Well-being, Quality Education, and Gender Equality).
- Prosperity (Affordable and Clean Energy, Decent Work and Economic Growth, Industry, Innovation and Infrastructure, Sustainable Communities/Cities and, Responsible Production and responsible Consumption and, Reduced Inequalities).
- Peace (Peace, Justice, and Strong Institutions).
- Partnership (Partnerships for the Goals).
- Planet (Climate Action, Life below Water, and Life on Land).

The broad and interdependent goals listed above were redefined with specific targets and indicators to measure the progress toward each target which were planned to be achieved between 2020 and 2030. Some of the stated goals refer to business environments like the SDG.12: "Ensure sustainable consumption and production patterns" and "encourage especially large and transnational companies to adopt sustainable practices and to integrate sustainability into their reporting cycle". Therefore, sustainability is not only an environmental, local, or social issue but in fact it is a revolution with a value system, worldview and consciousness and the depth of its change will be huge. Most of the dominant institutions in the world like the International Monetary Fund, the UN, G20 (The Group of Twenty), EU, and the Catholic Church are actively supporting sustainable revolution. More influential than the digital revolution, the sustainability revolution will be an exponential one which means the impact of it will be felt first gradually and then very suddenly.

The sustainability revolution already reshapes how we think about life and business for the next decades and its impact has already transformed fields like communication, finance (Global trade of commodities, environment protection funds), construction industry (solar energy, green buildings, recycled materials), transportation (hybrid cars, green transportation), pharmaceuticals, agriculture (organic foods), retail, and many others.

3 The Similarities of Two Revolutions

Although both sustainability and the digital revolutions promise to lead to major changes they have been underestimated at first by many c-level executives. In the beginning of the 2000s when digitalization was assumed to be the job of a web-developer, many short-sighted managers did not realize the fact that the "digital economy" was a whole new ballgame about to hit them. At first, many executives thought having a website with the photos of the board members was good enough but it was not even "digitization" which was all about transforming information from analog to digital. The second stage was to restructure the organizations to use digitized information in a simpler but more efficient way which is "digitalization". The same routine tasks were done faster and better with a more accessible data. On the contrary, "Digital Transformation" can be defined as "reimagining of the whole business by using digital technologies". This re-imagination may involve both creation of the new and modification of the existing business culture, processes, models, and customer experiences in order to adapt to the new requirements of both domestic and international markets. Unsurprisingly, many executives had difficulties to anticipate these progresses and ended up falling behind in competition and even being excluded from the market.

The same scenario is very communal today for sustainability. Many executives do not either grasp the urgency of the threat or misunderstand the risky consequences of not bearing in mind the sustainability revolution, but it is already with us (Birmingham, 2021). In the beginning, it was assumed to be a local climate change with a limited harm but in a short period, the real scope of the concept has been realized in a very costly way. Like in the case of the digital revolution, decision-makers both in companies and governments were slow in taking necessary measures to include sustainability into their agenda in the beginning. One of the reasons for this delay may be the ever-expanding ranges of both concepts. Like in digitalization, sustainability's scope is also growing to include many more environmental issues as well as social, administrative, cultural, and economic challenges – anything from gender rights to racial equity but the climate change is still the dominant and the frightening one because it affects almost everything from economic systems or trading modes to tourism and globalization. It designs cities, life expectancies, consumption patterns, and even social responsibility programs. Consequently, both political and socioeconomic implications of sustainability in general and of climate change in particular are more strategic and dangerous compared to the digital revolution.

The sustainable revolution, just like the digital revolution before it, is shifting the profit pools, and changing the high returns in certain sectors while discovering great prospects in others. Today, consumer demand for some sustainable products is skyrocketing. In 2019, total sales of plant-based meat reached 208 million units with a sales value of $5 billion and a growth rate of %18. The projection for the global fake meat sector in 2025 is worth over $7 billion (Bridgemen, 2020). An increasing number of customers are turning to vegetarian diets or are refusing animal ingredients entirely. Since they try to adapt a healthier lifestyle, consumers keep watching their nutrition to make sure it is also sustainable. The retail nutrition and wellness market is forecasted to grow to $50 billion by 2025 (Davis-Peccoud et al., 2020). One of the findings of the research conducted by Harvard Business Review in 2019 was that %50 of the increase in Consumer Packaged Goods (CPG) purchases by the US consumers between 2013 and 2018 came from sustainability-promoted products (Whelan & Kronthal-Saccohttps, 2019) Products with sustainability claims on their packages constituted 16.6% of the total market in 2018, up from 14.3% in 2013, and provided $114 billion in sales, up by 29% from 2013. What is more important is that the number of products marketed as sustainable grew 5.6 times faster than the ones that were not. In more than 90% of the CPG categories, products marketed with sustainability claims grew faster than their conservative equivalents (Whelan & Kronthal-Saccohttps, 2019).

In the automotive industry the change was more fundamental. The most influential cause of the drastic change in the popularity of electric vehicles was the fact that the European Union (EU) and the United States set some deadlines for the use of internal-combustion-engine vehicles for 2030 or 2035. The target is to increase the market share of electric vehicles (EV) min by 50% by 2030 (Davis-Peccoud et al., 2020).

As usual, some companies anticipated this change and acted before others, and they were rewarded by both investors and consumers. For instance, one of those early adopters, Unilever has been enjoying extreme growth rates in the sales of "purpose-led" brands, like Knorr, Dove, Ben & Jerry's, and Hellmann's. Compared to the rest of the portfolio, the sales of those sustainable living brands increased more than twice since 2014. In 2018, a total of 28 sustainable Unilever brands accounted for 75% of overall growth. Similar to what happened at the time of the digital transformation, some companies have already ridden the wave of the fundamental shift to consider sustainability in their business plans. These favorable returns in different businesses at different rates confirm the thesis that sustainable business can be both financially rewarding and ethical at the same time (Musaeva, 2021).

The global Covid-19 crises have accelerated both revolutions in a greater deal than expected. According to the findings of a recent global survey conducted by McKinsey in 2020 with 899 C-level executives from many industries, most of the respondents stated that their companies have speeded the digitization of both supply-chain and customer interactions and their internal operations by 3–4 years during the Covid-19 crises. They also asserted that the segment of digitally enabled or digital products in their portfolios has accelerated by almost 7 years mainly because of the increased demand by the customers. Not surprisingly, the respondents hope these changes to be long-lasting.

The same comment can be made for the sustainability revolution since the global pandemic has increased the vitality of some health-related issues for humankind; so, some of those environmental and social issues were included in the scope of sustainable development over the last 2 years (Gadiesh et al., 2021). In other words, Covid-19 has pulled back the curtain on our weakness to many universal risks and reminded us of more drastic ones yet to come.

Digital transformation also improves the sustainability aspects of businesses by optimizing raw material sourcing and usage which improves supply chain management by reducing energy consumption and by optimization of data and knowledge processing.

4 Convergence of Digital Transformation and Sustainability

"Digitainability" is a word created by combining the words "digitalization" and "sustainability" and it was generated for the project "digitainable" carried out by the Bonn Alliance for Sustainability research. Being one of the first projects, the aim of the digitainable project is to identify the relationship between sustainability and digitalization by systematically mapping the diverse facets of AI and digitalization on both sustainability strategies and 200 indicators of the UN Agenda 2030. The partners of the Bonn Alliance for Sustainability research group are Bonn International Centre for Conflict Studies, United Nations University, German Development Institute, University of Bonn, Hochschule Bonn-Rhein-Sieg University, Center for Development Research ZEF and they have started research to succeed the convergence of digital transformation and sustainability mission (Digitainable: Digitalization and Sustainability, 2019).

One of the recent studies was conducted in November 2020 with 4050 top-level executives from different industries in Europe, US, UK, Canada, China, Australia, Saudi Arabia, UAE, Singapore, and Japan by Accenture. The research company first measured companies' maturity in sustainable practices and their technology adoption. Then, all the respondent companies were classified on these two bases. The companies at the intersection of both dimensions were named as "Twin Transformers" and they were defined as the ones carrying out both sustainability and digital transformation at the same time. As expected, those companies are 2.5 times more likely to be among the businesses in the future according to Accenture. Some of the findings are below:

- European companies were the leading ones as far as discussing sustainability and technology-related topics in earnings calls with almost 50% in 2020 but only 5% of the companies discussed them concurrently and that rate was only 2% in 2018.
- European companies also took the lead in implementing the IT-based energy-saving measures and applying the criteria of sustainability in their sourcing decisions but when it comes to adoption of technology Europe is behind both the United States and Asia Pacific (APAC) countries. More companies (24%) from the Asia-Pacific region believe in the power of digital technologies in transforming their sustainable business practices while only 16% of the European companies believe in that. This may be because Europe is behind on the adoption of technology but 40% of the European companies claimed that they were making huge investments in technologies like Artificial Intelligence, and Cloud technologies.
- Most Twin Transformers (61%) generate more than 10% of their revenues from sustainability-driven models and 81% expect to do so in 3 years.42% of the global Twin Transformers believe in the significance of an eco-system business model for their future (Ollagnier, 2021).
- Today, nobody denies that digital transformation has become an essential necessity for organizations to stay pertinent in both the short and long term. However, this comment needs to be viewed through the lens of sustainability since it is

already a part of the social environment. Since the relationship between digital transformation and sustainability is defined as "interdependent", companies/organizations need to take sustainability and Corporate Social Responsibility (CSR) into consideration when they design their digitalization roadmaps. The first step on this road may be the right allocation of resources between two basic concepts accepting they are not mutually exclusive. In fact, C-suite managers should realize that the sustainability characteristic of a company is based on its digital intelligence (Susanto, 2021). Adding to the pressure, regulation has already shifted toward sustainability and will continue to do so. Consumers are increasingly aware of sustainability. The same is true for talent – unsustainable companies will find it hard to attract new employees and some will even lose the current ones.

- Over the next few decades, the digital revolution and the sustainability revolution will be interconnected: we'll put digital technology in place to achieve sustainability. The usual suspects, like big data, artificial intelligence, or the Internet of Things, will all do their bit here. Many companies will need to answer the dual challenge of the digital and the sustainability revolution with a dual strategy combining both because there's not enough time left to address these challenges one after the other (Columbus, 2020).

5 Building a Sustainable Customer Experience Strategy

Since sustainability characterizes the continuity of business not only today but also in the future, customer loyalty is a major concern for any organization with a sustainable vision. It is also true that loyalty is very much build upon satisfactory experiences in every stage of the customer experience, which is directly and indirectly shaped by the value systems of customers. Therefore, companies need to comprehend the ever-changing experiential expectations and value systems of both their actual and potential customers. The evaluation of those expectations and value systems in light of the company's total experiential goal is the essence of effective experiential design (Dente, 2017).

Managing "Customer Experience" is not solely about planning how customers can effortlessly flow through the company's value-delivery stages; rather, it is vital for creating outstanding customer experiences because it enables the company to be aware of every facet of what the customer is experiencing in relation to their brand. Obviously, the goal is to create loyal customers, but customers might become disloyal and leave a brand for a number of reasons: satisfaction level, perceived value, aftersales support problems, and so forth.

For years, more personalized services, and customization of both products and contacts were basic expectations of customers, and data-centric companies took advantages of all technological solutions based on digitalization to meet those expectations. But it is not sufficient anymore since one of the macro trends in the wish list of many customers is increased focus on sustainability today. According to a global research conducted by Cone Communications and Ebiquity in 2015, 91% of the respondents expressed their wish that companies should function not only on profitability but also in a socially and environmentally responsible way. Otherwise, 90% of the customers claimed to boycott the company because of irresponsible or deceptive business practices while 84% of them said they look for responsible products every time possible (Global CSR Study, 2015). A more recent finding of research done in the United States in 2018 by the same company is that 78% of Americans were certain that companies must positively influence society more than just making money. Also 77% of the respondents stated that they felt a stronger emotional link to Purpose-driven companies over traditional companies (Global CSR Study, 2018). Therefore, having sustainability as a part of the company culture is the first step in designing the customer experience strategy and digital transformation provides the best support in this process. It is all about how detailed information about the customers and their priorities is collected and how customized alternatives are presented to them so that their concerns for sustainability are removed. This is possible with creativity enabled by the right digital solutions. This collaboration can be implemented by empowering consumers to embrace sustainability. The key for this implementation is to use the lens of sustainability in every touch point with the customers. The consumer insights collected with use of right data collection techniques will inform the executives who are asking for more environmental-friendly or purpose-oriented choices like sustainable delivery options. A smart interactive website may be a good start to segment customers on their user profiles and to offer them the delivery options with their environmental implications. Secondly, customers can be segmented on various dimensions of sustainability and then they can be offered the selected products and services with respect to their sustainability priorities. This can even be carried out by the organization with a collaboration with other companies who also care about sustainability as a tool to enrich customer experiences they provide (Chorley, 2021). For example, if a customer purchases mainly organic cotton items from a brick-and-mortar store, the store can integrate that data into their database in order to send that customer info about the best organic food restaurants.

The biggest support on the way to design a sustainable customer journey anticipated to both attitudinal and behavioral loyalty comes from digitalization. All functions of Customer Relationship Management (CRM) and the research techniques based on this may be the most meaningful collaboration of digitalization and sustainability.

6 Conclusion

One of the most important skills of Homo sapiens is the accumulation of renewable knowledge and intellect.

Two hundred years ago, the Industrial Revolution radically changed civilization through a major accumulation of knowledge. The use of fossil fuels, steel, and steam power with the automation has led to inventions of machines and other labor-saving technologies with a major consequence of a hundredfold increase in productivity and at least for some people a meaningful wealth creation. The Industrial Revolution was also the beginning of both global society and the global economy with an unavoidable result of unequal distribution of wealth and Earth-system changes which turned out to be dramatic threats to human civilization in general. This era of rapid and dramatic change in history has been named the Anthropocene (Crutzen & Stoermer, 2000; Crutzen, 2005) which can be traced back to the analysis of air trapped in polar ice in the eighteenth century. Following the third civilization revolution, that is, the digital revolution in the twentieth century, the term "Digital Anthropocene was used for the first time in 2019 (WBGU-German Advisory Council on Global Change, 2019). Digital change risks further increasing resource and energy consumption and exacerbating damage to both the environment and the climate. The digital transitions disseminated and triggered, resource and greenhouse-gas-intensive growth patterns since technology has not yet been mobilized toward sustainability transformations. Moreover, uncontrolled digital change threatens to undermine important foundations of the democracies by destabilizing societies. The possible digital dynamics identified by WBGU in 2019 included disempowerment of individuals through authorization or totalitarianism, attacks to privacy, all-inclusiveness by automated decision-making systems, and disruption of labor markets. The increased empowerment of certain elite groups and dominance of some global companies based on digitalized opportunities and powerful database applications can also be added to the list of potential risky developments.

Yet, digital technologies can also empower a revolution toward, what is called, a Sustainable Anthropocene by enabling decarbonization across all industries, supporting shared economies through more efficient and sufficient energy systems and by watching and preserving ecological systems, and the guarding of the universal heritage. However, this does not occur automatically. Indeed, what has happened until now was just the opposite (Kriegler et al., 2018; TWI2050, 2019; Sachs et al., 2019). Therefore, as mentioned in all the reports prepared by the international research institutes like The International Institute for Applied Systems Analysis (IIASA) with National Member Organizations in Africa, the Americas, Asia, and Europe and the UN, fundamental changes have been listed to lessen the upsetting capacities of digitalization and generate paths toward sustainability. The report TWI2050 in Kriegler et al. (2018) listed Six Fundamental Transformations needed to achieve the 17 Sustainable Development Goals and long-term sustainability to 2050 and after: (i) Human Capacity & Demography; (ii) Consumption & Production; (iii) Decarbonization & Energy; (iv) Food, Biosphere & Water; (v) Smart Cities; and (vi) the Digital Revolution.

Among the six transformations listed above, the digital revolution will probably be the most significant one based on the ongoing advances in Artificial Intelligence, connectivity, digitized information, additive 3D printing, virtual reality, Internet of things, machine learning, block chain, robotics, quantum computing, and synthetic biology.

Sustainability is not a one-off goal, but something that we need to adjust at regular intervals. The digital revolution was not carried out in 1 day either, but has kept us busy for almost three decades so far – and is still way off crossing the finish line. Given current timeframes of the Paris Agreement, the European Green Deal, or Germany's Federal Climate Protection Act, the sustainability revolution is scheduled to blast off even faster than the digital revolution did.

Competing Interests The authors have no conflicts of interest to declare that are relevant to the content of this chapter.

References

Bahattarai, D. (2020). https://www.lftechnology.com/blog/digital-transformation/digital-transformation-mckinsey/#:~:text=In%20one%20of%20its%20 articles,deliver%20your%20product%20or%20service

Berman, S. J. (2012). Digital transformation: Opportunities to create new business models. *Strategy & Leadership, 40*(2), 16–24. https://doi.org/10.1108/10878571211209314

Birmingham, A. (2021). *Sustainability is the new digital, right down to the mistakes leaders make: Bain.* https://which-50.com/sustainability-is-the-new-digital-right-down-to-the-mistakes-leaders-make-bain/

Bridgemen, L. (2020). Plant-based meat: A brighter future for food?. https://sentientmedia.org/plant-based-meats/.

Brundtland Report, WCED 1987: 43.

Chandola, V. (2016). *Digital transformation and sustainability.* https://doi.org/10.13140/RG.2.1.3358.0567.

Chorley, J. (2021). https://www.forbes.com/sites/jonchorley/2021/08/05/customer-experience-reimagined-for-sustainability/?sh=5a46e9381b0d

Columbus, L. (2020). *10-reasons-sustainability-needs-to-be-part-of-your-digital-transformation--strategy.* https://www.forbes.com/sites/louiscolumbus/2020/11/08/10-reasons-sustainability-needs-to-be-part-of-your-digital-transformation-strategy/?sh=7dc1a2a7ef66

Costello, & Rimor. (2021). https://www.gartner.com/en/newsroom/press-releases/2021-04-07-gartner-forecasts-worldwide-it-spending-to-reach-4-trillion-in-202

Crutzen, P. J. (2005). Human impact on climate has made this the "anthropocene age". *New Perspectives Quarterly, 22*, 14–16. https://doi-org.lproxy.yeditepe.edu.tr/10.1111/j.1540-5842.2005.00739.x

Crutzen, P. J., & Stoermer, E. F. (2000). The anthropocene. *IGBP Newsletter, 41*, 17–18.

Davis-Peccoud, J., Van den Branden, J., Brahm, C., Mattios, G., & Joëlle de Montgolfier, J. (2020). *Sustainability is the next digital.* https://www.bain.com/insights/sustainability-is-the-next-digital/

De la Boutetière, H., Alberto Montagner, A., & Reich, A. (2018). https://www.mckinsey.com/business-functions/people-and-organizational-performance/our-insights/unlocking-success-in-digital-transformations#

Dente, C. (2017). https://www.artisenergy.com/sustainability/how-sustainability-increases-customer-experience/

Digitainable: Digitalization and Sustainability. (2019). https://www.bonnalliance-icb.de/en/bonn-alliance/research-education-transfer/projects/digitainable/

Du Pisani, J. (2007). Sustainable development – Historical roots of the concept. *Environmental Sciences, 3*(2), 83–96. https://doi.org/10.1080/15693430600688831

Epstein, M. J., Flamholtz, E., & McDonough, J. J. (1977). *Corporate social performance: The measurement of product and service contributions*. National Association of Accountants.

Gadiesh, O., Davis-Peccoud, J., & Mattios, G. (2021). Why sustainability revolution is the new digital?. https://www.bangkokpost.com/opinion/opinion/2059631/why-sustainability-revolution-is-the-new-digital.

Global CSR Study. (2015). https://www.conecomm.com/research-blog/2015-cone-communications-ebiquity-global-csr-study

Global CSR Study. (2018). https://www.conecomm.com/research-blog/2018-purpose-study

Haas, J. J. (1973). *Corporate social responsibilities in a changing society*. T. Gaus.

Kemp, S. (2022). https://datareportal.com/reports/digital-2022-global-overview-report

Kriegler, E., Messner, Nakicenovic, D., Riahi, K., Rockström, J., Sachs, J., Leeuw, S., & Detlef van Vuuren, D. (2018). *TWI2050 – The world in 2050. Transformations to achieve the sustainable development goals*. Report prepared by the World in 2050 initiative. International Institute for Applied Systems Analysis (IIASA). www.twi2050.org

Mergel, I., Edelmann, N., & Haug, N. (2019). Defining digital transformation: Results from expert interviews. *Government Information Quarterly, 36*(4) ISSN 0740-624X. https://doi.org/10.1016/j.giq.2019.06.002

Musaeva, G. (2021). *Unilever: Sustainability efforts create tangible value*. https://seekingalpha.com/article/4441169-unilever-sustainability-efforts-create-tangible-value

Ollagnier, J. (2021). *The European double-up*. https://www.accenture.com/_acnmedia/PDF-144/Accenture-The-European–Double -Up.pdf#zoom=50

Sachs, J., Schmidt-Traub, G., Kroll, C., Lafortune, G., & Fuller, G. (2019). *Sustainable development report 2019*. Bertelsmann Stiftung and Sustainable Development Solutions Network (SDSN).

Shirer, M. (2021). https://www.idc.com/getdoc.jsp?containerId=prUS48372321

Shooter, K. (2020). https://technologymagazine.com/data-and-data-analytics/mckinsey-unlocking-success-digital-transformations

Susanto, E. (2021). https://www.linkedin.com/pulse/digital-transformation-key-sustainability-edy-susanto/

Transforming our world: The 2030 Agenda for Sustainable Development. (2015). https://sdgs.un.org/2030agenda

TWI2050 – The World in 2050. (2019). *The digital revolution and sustainable development: Opportunities and challenges*. Report prepared by The World in 2050 initiative. International Institute for Applied Systems Analysis (IIASA). www.twi2050.org. Available at: pure.iiasa.ac.at/15913/ ISBN 10: 3-7045-0155-7 ISBN 13: 978–3–7045-0155-4. 10.22022/TNT/05-2019.15913.

WBGU-German Advisory Council on Global Change. (2019). https://www.wbgu.de/en/

Whelan, T., & Kronthal – Saccohttps, R. (2019). *Research: Actually, consumers do buy sustainable products*. https://hbr.org/2019/06/research-actually-consumers-do-buy-sustainable-products

The Impact of Artificial Intelligence on Substantial Entrepreneurial Orientation and a Case Study of a Multinational Company Headquartered in Turkey

Arzu Şar İçöz

1 Introduction

Despite the increasing ubiquity of both mechanical and cognitive automation, little has been written specifically on the sustainable entrepreneurship-artificial intelligence intersection (Liebregts et al., 2019; Obschonka & Audretsch, 2019; Townsend & Hunt, 2019; Nambisan & Baron, 2019; Fratini et al., 2019; Chalmers et al., 2021). This study aims to contribute to this need and will examine the relationship between these two phenomena in Turkey with a case study. The question of this research is about whether artificial intelligence influences substantial entrepreneurial orientations.

With the introduction of the concept of sustainability into our lives, this concept has not only remained as a concept related to the environment; from health to communication, from corporate to finance and cultural values. Since it has become used in all areas of life, some scholars, Yolles and Fink (2014), Fratini et al. (2019), and Haldar (2020), associated this concept with the intersection of two concepts: artificial intelligence and entrepreneurial orientations.

In circular economies with the principles of reduction, reusing, and recycling at their core, businesses are protected from negative factors such as resource scarcity and volatile prices, and new business opportunities and entrepreneurial trends emerge (Ghisellini et al., 2016). When sustainability emerged with the report by United Nations World Commission on Environment and Development in 1991, which touches on the differences between the beginning and the end of the twentieth century, it is stated that human activities, the effects of which were limited on a local

A. Ş. İçöz (✉)
Yeditepe University, Istanbul, Turkey
e-mail: arzu.icoz@yeditepe.edu.tr

N. Ketenci (ed.), *Transition to the Circular Economy Model*, CSR, Sustainability, Ethics & Governance, https://doi.org/10.1007/978-3-031-52700-5_2

scale for centuries, affect all entrepreneurial ecosystems at the global level today (Temizel, 1997). This research begins by putting forth how artificial intelligence is defined and evaluated then considers how technology will shape activities at a range of firm levels before turning to potential implications for substantial entrepreneurial outcomes.

Since technology and digitalization are becoming increasingly important topics for researchers in different disciplines, from economics and management to engineering and humanities, digital innovations such as the Internet, big data, cloud computing, artificial intelligence, and various digital technology-based platforms are impacting business initiatives and changing ways that go beyond entrepreneurial and innovation practices to influence culture, politics, and society. With the advent of the Information Age, legacy corporate attitudes and tactics are now envisioned in terms of success, innovation, and creativity, with artificial intelligence as a new approach to deal with the fast and volatile business environment (Townsend & Hunt, 2019; Muthukrishnan et al., 2020; Chalmers et al., 2021; Winecoff & Watkins, 2022).

Considering that the National Artificial Intelligence Strategy (UYZS) covering the years 2021–2025, which is Turkey's first strategy in this field, supports entrepreneurship and innovation to develop the artificial intelligence ecosystem, this study investigates the effect of artificial intelligence on entrepreneurial orientation and its implementations with a case study.

2 Literature Review

Today, the concept of success is conceived in terms of innovation, sustainability, and creativity with a forward-looking stance in circular economies. Therefore, an entrepreneurial spirit reigns where profit lies in finding new opportunities to develop new products, new services, and new relationships (Levis & Nicholas, 1995; Luu & Viet, 2019; Rostain, 2021). Sustainability awareness is important for evaluating and predicting systems at various levels, including professional organizational norms, organizational and meso-level networks, the natural environment, and macro-level societies that exist in the entrepreneurial ecosystem (Mc Kelvie et al., 2020).

In addition, theoretical understanding of artificial intelligence and broader processes of automation has been driven by economists who have taken a largely macro-level perspective to explore implications for employment, income, and policy (Acemoğlu & Restrepeo, 2018; Agrawal et al., 2019).

Turkey, the country where this study will take place, has its own characteristics. On the one hand, there is no strong infrastructure that supports the innovative and entrepreneurial spirit economically and culturally; on the other hand, it is seen that the economic dynamism, which is in a phase of transformation and development, pushes companies to a level of creativity and change that can compete with their competitors in developed countries. Therefore, it is important to consider and evaluate entrepreneurial orientations and to contribute to the literature of sustainable entrepreneurship projects that have gained a very steep upward momentum in Turkey recently.

Definitions of Artificial Intelligence

According to Kaplan and Haenlein (2019), artificial intelligence is defined as "a system's ability to interpret external data correctly, to learn from such data, and to use those learnings to achieve specific goals and tasks through flexible adaptation".

Wagner (2020) defined artificial intelligence as a three-dimensional system that encompasses a domain structure, general-purpose machine learning, and data generation. Zahra et al. (2023) posit that artificial intelligence possesses capabilities beyond those of humans, enabling the execution of tasks previously unattainable by human agents. This transformative capacity engenders a myriad of applications, ultimately culminating in enhanced performance and productivity across various domains.

Historical Development of Artificial Intelligence

The origins of artificial intelligence are the first example of the Analytical Engine developed by Ada Lovelace and Charles Babbage in the 1830s. Lovelace created what is considered the first operating program on Babbage's machine to calculate Bernoulli numbers, while creating the first prototype for contemporary artificial intelligence and machine learning systems. Lovelace addressed the issue of the Analytical Engine's potential to generate insights that the human mind could not but argued that the machine could not generate original ideas. This was discussed by British logician Alan Turing, one of the leading theorists in the development of modern computing, in his seminal article Computing Machines and Intelligence (Turing, 1950).

Five years later, Mihet and Philipon (2019) highlight that the concept was initialized through Allen Newell, Cliff Shaw, and Herbert Simon's, *Logic Theorist*, to mimic the problem-solving skills of a human and was funded by the Research and Development (RAND) Corporation that was considered to be the first artificial intelligence program and was presented at the *Dartmouth Summer Research Project on Artificial Intelligence* in 1956.

Obschonka and Audretsch (2019) add that from 1982–1990, $400 million dollars were invested with the goals of revolutionizing computer processing, implementing logic programming, and improving artificial intelligence. During the 1990s and 2000s, significant progress related to artificial intelligence had been made. In the early 2020s, artificial intelligence-based technologies received increasing attention as they began to be applied in many research areas related to the environment, sustainability, and innovation. Applications of artificial intelligence and other related technologies for sustainability are examples of technological "niche innovations" that can rise and spread rapidly after increased investment, regulatory compliance, and increased public and consumer interest (Galaz et al., 2021).

Artificial intelligence in sustainable development affects various dimensions of different sectors. For example, artificial intelligence is affecting global energy sectors, environmental outcomes, productivity, and other factors of society. It seems obvious that in the field of artificial intelligence, there has been an increase in the number of studies done by integrating artificial intelligence into many aspects of sustainability and solving such problems practically (Goralski & Tan, 2020; Kar et al., 2022). As to Turkiye the country where the case study was carried out, it has been reported that there are several organizations to raise awareness in the society. One of the most significant ones is Turkish Artificial Intelligence Initiative (TRAI) established in 2017 to develop the ecosystem in Turkiye. To date, it has held hundreds of events (TRAI Meet-Up, artificial intelligence seminars, artificial intelligence summits, demo-days) and directly contacted tens of thousands of people. The number of artificial intelligence initiatives in TRAI's ecosystem has increased to 248 as of April 2022.

Definitions of Entrepreneurial Orientation

While the act of entrepreneurship is literally expressed as "entreprendre" in French, "unternehmen" in German, one of the European languages, it is explained with the word "undertake" in English. Indeed, an entrepreneur takes all the responsibilities by arranging and managing the work in an organization, taking risks when necessary (Wickham, 1998).

According to the Turkish Language Institution, entrepreneurship in the literal sense. "*It is the act of designing the production process as a production factor by bringing together labour, capital and natural resources, organizing it and undertaking all its risks*" (tdk.gov.tr, 2022).

By many theoreticians, entrepreneurial orientation has been defined as "a firm strategic posture toward entrepreneurship" and it is a vibrant topic in entrepreneurship research (Covin & Wales, 2012; Andersen & Eshima, 2013; Gao et al., 2016; Covin & Wales, 2019; Singh et al., 2019; Villaseca et al., 2020).

Sustainable entrepreneurship is defined as "the examination of how opportunities will bring into existence future goods and services as discovered, created, and exploited, by whom, and with what economic, psychological, social, and environmental consequences" (Sarango-Lalangui et al., 2018).

During periods of uncertainty, entrepreneurial behaviours challenge the traditional business models because they encourage a collaborative and open approach to innovation with positive impacts on social and environmental sustainability (Di Vaio et al., 2022).

Historical Development of Sustainable Entrepreneurial Orientation

The Theory of Entrepreneurship was first put forward by Cantillon in 1734 (Thornton, 2008). Irish economist, Cantillon, while defining the entrepreneur, explained it as someone who buys or produces the product or service that he will sell at a future date for a price that has not yet been determined (Çetin, 1996).

In the early 1900s, Schumpeter argued that before his research, entrepreneurial behaviour included creating products and services that had not yet come to the market, entering new markets, adopting innovative production technologies, developing new raw materials, and implementing new ways of organizing business activities (Schumpeter, 1934; Wales, 2011). Between 1950 and 1970, economists who conducted studies evaluating the concept of entrepreneurship in the context of behavioural sciences emerged (Topkaya, 2013).

After economists such as Mc Clelland, Hagen, Lipset, and Bart, who are the theorists of the concept of entrepreneurship, entrepreneurial orientation research has its roots in the work of Mintzberg (1973). In his theorem on strategic decision-making, Mintzberg envisioned an entrepreneurial model of management characterized as an entrepreneur who actively seeks new opportunities in uncertain environments where gradual growth can occur to set an entrepreneurial strategy.

After 1985, entrepreneurship began to be seen as the process of establishing a new business, and its contribution to economic growth and employment was revealed. While evaluating Turkish entrepreneurship, it is mentioned that there was Turkish entrepreneurship based on the ahi-order organization during the Ottoman Empire, starting from the Seljuk State period, within the scope of the pre-Republican period. The industrial revolution that came after the Ahi order and the ever-increasing mass production that followed had difficulties in adapting to social and economic advances (Tutar & Küçük, 2003).

As for the period of the Ottoman Empire, since trade was under the dominance of Greek, Jewish, and Armenian communities, Turks among the existing ethnic communities were excluded from trade and encouraged to become soldiers, ulama or bureaucrats or to work on farms. As can be seen, a commercial infrastructure belonging to the Turks could not be established because the Turks were kept away from trade for about 40–50 years (Arslan, 2001; Karabat & Sönmez, 2010).

In the strategies implemented in Turkey between 1923 and 1929, establishing a national bourgeoisie structure and stockpiling money were the formations that led to private entrepreneurship. At the same time, when the identities of the entrepreneurs are examined in this period, it is seen that the high-level bureaucrats of the state have undertaken the entrepreneurship business. Based on this, it is possible to say that the first entrepreneurs of Turkey were statesmen (Öztürk, 2008).

Then in the 1990s, the research on sustainability mostly focused on entrepreneurial activities and its relationship with environmental problems and solutions, so the term was firstly discussed by Elkington (1997). Among the Digital Entrepreneur ecosystems that have started to appear in the literature since the early 2000s, the best-known example is Silicon Valley, which emphasizes the circulation of financial capital, technology, talent, and entrepreneurial projects in its internal environment (Isenberg, 2010).

It has also crossed geographical boundaries using practical approaches such as providing incubators. Thus, digital firms connect their internal and external elements such as digital entrepreneurs and digital entrepreneurship (Zahra et al., 2023). Some scholars, Maalaouhi et al. (2020) and Shi and Weber (2021), have identified the driving factors of entrepreneurial initiatives towards sustainable development in the frames of expanding and exploiting existing resources such as knowledge management, the ethical conscious, and the creation of business models to achieve economic, social, and environmental purposes.

Dimensions of Entrepreneurship

Following the original conceptualization by Miller (1983) and further elaboration of the entrepreneurial orientation by Covin and Slevin (1991), five dimensions were functionalized as innovation, proactivity, risk-taking, aggressive competitiveness, and autonomy.

The five dimensions have been useful for characterizing and distinguishing key entrepreneurial processes, a firm's entrepreneurial orientation (de Gennaro et al., 2016).

1. Innovativeness, regarding innovation, which is one of the dimensions of entrepreneurial orientation a relationship can be established with sustainability and artificial intelligence criteria. As entrepreneurship affects technology development, the increase in technological R&D can increase the innovation capacity of the region and further increase regional economic development. At this point, green entrepreneurship can be given as an implementing model which seeks to increase resource use and improve production methods through technological innovation, thereby reducing the environmental damage of production and recycling energy. To some extent, energy recycling can reduce production costs and unit input, which also supports economic growth (Wentao & Wang, 2022).
2. Proactivity, the authors Searle and Rooney (2013) claim that in many sustainability-relevant processes, organizations consider the proactivity of their employees in a remarkable level. For example, if a business has many talented and willing employees to be proactive, emerging problems are quickly identified, solutions sought and found. In addition, proactivity represents the future perspective, which encompasses the work carried out by companies to improve existing products or develop new products, anticipate changes and opportunities in the environment, encourage changes in tactics, and detect future market trends (Ruiz-ortega et al., 2018).

Furthermore, proactiveness shapes the strategic orientation of the new venture, encourages enterprises to develop new products and markets, promotes internal changes and organizational restructuring, to contribute to the growth of enterprise (Dumin & Smallboneb, 2019).

3. Risk Taking, Cantillon, the researcher who introduced the concept of entrepreneurship for the first time in 1734, explained that the reason why he keeps entrepreneurs apart from other employees is that they behave correctly in uncertain environments and take the risk (Lumpkin & Dess, 2001). The scandal of Volkswagen emission in Germany is an example of an illegal corporate risk taking resulted in destruction of environment and green-washing and put the society and firm sustainability at risk (Younas & Zafar, 2019).
4. Autonomy, entrepreneurial autonomy means being free to decide what, how and when entrepreneurial work is done to determine the strategic direction of the firm (van Gelderen et al., 2020). Regarding sustainable autonomy, Droz (2019) argued that environmental processes should be protected for four reasons, first, because the natural environment has meaning. Secondly, the global environment should be protected as an autonomous safety including other species. Third, independent of other people's judgments should be maintained as an independent, unbiased resource provider. Fourth, it must be preserved by virtue of its historical irreplaceability.
5. Competitive Aggressiveness defined as the propensity to engage in a sustained, diverse, or unique series of actions to challenge rivals and enhance their relative competitive position. It is a Gestalt-like sub-construct of competitive dynamics that is comprised of several sub-dimensions. While these sub-dimensions cannot measure unobserved variables such as propensity for risk taking, they are proxies for firm behaviours resultant from this orientation. Academics and managers have a similar interest in understanding the contributions of competitive dynamics to the field of strategy (Hughes et al., 2018). Competitive aggressiveness relates to how the company thinks about the future and strongly relates to the firm performances (Feichter et al., 2022).

The Definitions of Sustainability

The concept of sustainability corresponds to the Latin word "sustain". The transition of this concept to English has also been quite recent. According to Yolles and Fink (2014), this concept was first used by the online version of the Oxford Dictionary in the mid-1980s. In the dictionary, sustainability is pronounced as "to be maintained at a certain rate or level". Frechette (2010) tells us that sustainability drives long-term corporate growth, profitability, and corporate social responsibility. He also considers it to be future oriented, and to be often involved in fundamental organizational change.

Historical Development of Sustainability

The sustainability approach was first introduced in 1983 upon the request of the United Nations Secretary General and the Brundtland Report was prepared under the chairmanship of the Prime Minister of Norway by The World Commission on Environment and Development WCED with the title "Our Common Future" and presented at the United Nations General Assembly in 1987 with the participation of 20 different countries (Şen et al., 2018).

In 2012, 25 years after the first Rio Earth Summit, the United Nations Conference on Sustainable Development (UNCSD) was held. The conference focused on two themes in the context of sustainable development: a green economy and an institutional framework. As part of this new development roadmap, the UN approved the 2030 Agenda (SDGs), which are a call to action to protect the planet, end poverty and guarantee the well-being of people. Agenda 2030 has five overarching themes, known as the five Ps: People, Planet, Prosperity, Peace, and Partnerships (Mensah, 2019).

3 Methodology

For this study a case study of a multinational Holding headquartered in Turkey was conducted.

Model of the Research

Descriptive research was chosen as the design of the research. It is aimed to reveal the sustainability practices in the company as per the requirements of the monograph model, with the interviews held with the senior executives of the company and the documents obtained as it is the result of perspective in the research with the design of case study. Discovery and interpretation occur concurrently and are embedded in the context (Katz, 2015).

Data Collection

By observing the documents, the documents and reports containing the written and numerical information of the holding were examined. Another data collection tool chosen as an interview was the data collection method based on asking questions about the subject. In answering the questions, the holding's top managers in Turkey were interviewed face-to-face, and the manager of the company in Italy was interviewed via Skype. Since the interviewees supported what they said, it has been observed that there is a consensus with the documents belonging to the enterprise. It is thought that there will be no deviation in the results due to their personal beliefs, thoughts, and judgments.

Findings

As stated before, a field study was conducted in a Turkish-based global company to test the hypothesis that artificial intelligence has a significant effect on sustainable entrepreneurial orientations and to get the answer to the question of what kind of activities they do about sustainability. It would be beneficial to start the explanation of the findings by giving general information about the holding, which is the subject of the research.

The Organizational Structure of the Holding
The company, which was chosen as a case study, started its activities in 1937 with investments in the chemical industry. It started production in two different sectors, namely Forest Products Group in 1969 and Consumer Group in 1987. With nearly 17.000 employees, X Holding operates with 41 companies in different sectors such as in chemistry sector and in the wood-based panel sector. The holding's activities continue also in the port management sector, and construction and packaging. Under the umbrella of the Holding, 39 Turkish brands, produced with advanced technologies in 29 production facilities in 13 countries, serve customers around the world.

Examples to Implementations of Sustainability in the Holding
Based on the literature, it has been recognized many parallel projects to the concepts, artificial intelligence, entrepreneurial orientation, and sustainability within the group of companies studied in this research. The projects are as follows:

(a) *A Sustainability Report related to "Gasification of Waste Biomass and Renewable Clean Energy Production" R&D project.* In the research holding, energy management has been considered as one of the most important topics in the field of sustainability. It has been noted that the company, which has accelerated its work on energy efficiency in recent years, is positioned as a pioneer in the sector of energy efficiency with its TÜBİTAK-TEYDEB supported "Gasification of Waste Biomass and Renewable Clean Energy Production" R&D project. In the mentioned project, which includes the evaluation of biomass wastes and their clean disposal, the project provides gasification by using advanced technologies as an alternative to incineration.

    One of their top managers, who made statements about the project, emphasizes that they have the potential to prevent 15,000 tons of carbon dioxide emissions per year with the project.

(b) *A Sustainability Report related to Electrical Energy.* In the interview, one of the top managers also reminded that they produced an average of 1450 MWh of electrical energy per year with the Solar Power Plant, which was established on the roof of the MDF facility in Adana Organized Industrial Zone for the first time in 2016, another manager of the holding added that they are working on the conversion of the existing diesel fuel forklifts in the facilities to electric forklifts in order to ensure energy efficiency.
(c) *A Sustainability Report at its Facilities in Italy.* The company, which obtains the wood raw material used in production from 100% sustainable and renewable resources, procures raw materials from forests that have completed their life because of regeneration and maintenance activities in forests. They produce medium-density fibre from the recycling materials of waste furniture.
(d) *A Sustainability Report related to the Environment.* The company set an important example in cooperation with another company in industrial plantation forestry by planting 1.7 million saplings on 14,000 decars of land, approximately the size of 2000 football fields. Stating that they use 100% recycled raw materials in their facilities in Italy, they have become the "Biggest Turkish Investor".

4 Conclusions

The sustainability approach of the company, which is the subject of the case study for research, is as follows: to do their work with a responsible management approach, to be employee-oriented, to protect the natural balance, and to contribute to the society. While evaluating the results of this study, it demonstrates there is a significant relationship between artificial intelligence and sustainable entrepreneurial orientation. Based on the existing literature, the results of the case study support the research model. This study suggests that more research is needed into the more critical aspects of implementing circular economy strategies, in terms of the impact of artificial intelligence on sustainable entrepreneurial orientation.

Competing Interests The authors have no conflicts of interest to declare that are relevant to the content of this chapter.

References

Acemoğlu, D., & Restrepeo, P. (2018). *Artificial intelligence, automation and work.* National Bureau of Economic Research.
Agrawal, A., Gans, J., & Goldfarb, A. (2019). Economic policy for artificial intelligence. In *Innovation policy and the economy.*
Andersen, B. S., & Eshima, Y. (2013). The influence of firm age and intangible resources on the relationship between entrepreneurial orientation and firm growth among Japanese SMEs. *Journal of Business Venturing, 28*, 413–429.

Arslan, M. (2001). *İş ve Meslek Ahlakı*. Nobel Yayın Dağıtım.
Çetin, C. (1996). *Yeniden Yapılanma-Girişimcilik-KOBİ'ler ve Bunların Özendirilmesi*. Der Yayınları.
Chalmers, D., Mac Kenzie, N., & Carter, S. (2021). Artificial intelligence and entrepreneurship: Implications for venture creation in the fourth industrial revolution. *Entrepreneurship Practice and Theory, 45*(5), 1028–1053.
Covin, J. G., & Slevin, D. P. (1991). A conceptual model of entrepreneurship as behaviour. *Entrepreneurship Theory and Practice, 16*(1), 7–26.
Covin, J. G., & Wales, W. J. (2012). The measurement of entrepreneurial orientation. *Entrepreneurship Theory and Practice, 36*(4), 677–702.
Covin, J. G., & Wales, W. J. (2019). Crafting high-impact entrepreneurial orientation research: Some suggested guidelines. *Entrepreneurship Theory and Practice, 43*, 3.
De Gennaro, M. P., Wright, C. W., & Panza, N. R. (2016). Measuring entrepreneurial orientation in an assessment center: An individual level-of-analysis study. *The Psychologist-Manager Journal, 19*(1), 1–22.
Di Vaio, A., Hassan, R., Chabbra, M., Arrigo, E., & Palladino, R. (2022). Sustainable entrepreneurship impact and entrepreneurial venture life cycle: A systematic literature review. *Journal of Cleaner Production, 379*. https://doi.org/10.1016/j.jclepro.2022.134469
Droz, L. (2019). Redefining sustainability: From self-determination to environmental autonomy. *Philosophies, 4*(3), 42.
Dumin, Z., & Smallboneb, D. (2019). What affects nascent entrepreneurs' proactiveness. *Asia Pacific Management Review, 24*(4), 318–326.
Elkington, J. (1997). *Cannibals with forks: The triple bottom line of 21st century businesses*. Oxford.
Feichter, C., Moers, F., & Timmermans, O. (2022). Relative performance evaluation and competitive aggressiveness. *Journal of Accounting Research, 60*(5). https://doi.org/10.1111/1475-679X.12431
Fratini, C., Susse, G., & Jergensen, M. (2019). Exploring circular economy imaginaries in European cities: A research agenda for the governance of urban sustainability transitions. *Journal of Cleaner Production, 226*, 974–989.
Frechette, H. (2010). Definition: Sustainability. *Journal of Citizen Policy, 7, 265–274.*
Galaz, V., Centone, M., Callahan, P., Causevic, A., Patterson, T., Brass, I., Baum, S., Farber, D., Fischer, J., Garcia, D., McPherson, T., Jimenez, D., King, B., Larcey, P., & Levy, K. (2021). Artificial intelligence, systemic risks, and sustainability. *Technology in Society, 67*. https://doi.org/10.1016/j.techsoc.2021.101741
Ghisselini, P., Passarini, F., & Ruzzene, M. (2016). A review on circular economy: The expected transition to a balanced interplay of environmental and economic systems. *Journal of Cleaner Production, 114(7), 11–32.* https://doi.org/10.1016/j.jclepro.2015.09.007
Gao, Y., Ge, B., Lang, X., & Xu, X. (2016). Impacts of proactive orientation and entrepreneurial strategy on entrepreneurial performance: Empirical research. *Technological Forecasting and Social Change, 135*, 178–187.
Goralski, M., & Tan, T. K. (2020). Artificial intelligence and sustainable development. *The International Journal of Management Education, 18*(1). https://doi.org/10.1016/j.ijme.2019.100330
Haldar, S. (2020). Towards a conceptual understanding of sustainability – Driven entrepreneurship. *Corporate Social Responsibility Environmental Management, 26*(6), 1157–1170. https://doi.org/10.1002/csr.1763
Hughes, M., KalinKolev, M., & Mcnamarac, G. (2018). A meta-analytic review of competitive aggressiveness research. *Journal of Business Research, 85*, 73–82.
Isenberg, D. J. (2010). How to start an entrpreneurial orientation. *Harward Business Review, p. 1–15.*
Kaplan, A., & Haenlein, M. (2019). Siri, Siri, in my hand: Who's the fairest in the land? On the interpretations, illustrations, and implications of artificial intelligence. *Business Horizons, 62*, 15–25.

Kar, K., Choudhary, S., & Singh, K. (2022). How can artificial intelligence impact sustainability: A systematic literature review. *Journal of Cleaner Production, 376*. https://doi.org/10.1016/j.jclepro.2022.134120

Karabat, B. Ç., & Sönmez, A. Ö. (2010). The role of women entrepreneurship for the regional development. *3. Trakya Bölgesi Kalkinma ve Girişimcilik Sempozyumu.*

Katz, J. (2015). A theory of qualitative methodology: The social system analytic fieldwork, méthod(e)s. *African Review of Social Science Methodology, 58*, 224–235.

Levis, C., & Nicholas, D. (1995). The "adhocracy" as viewed by modernization theory. *International Journal of Political Economy, 25(3), 37–49.*

Liebregts, W., Darnihamedani, P., Postma, E., & Atzmueller, M. (2019). The promise of social signal processing for research on decision-making in entrepreneurial contexts. *Small Business Economics, 12*, 35–57.

Lumpkin, G. T., & Dess, G. G. (2001). Linking two dimensions of entrepreneurial orientation to firm performance. *Journal of Business Venturing, 16*(5), 429–451.

Luu, N., & Viet, L. (2019). Entrepreneurial orientation and social ties in transitional economies. *Long Range Planning, 52*(1), 103–116.

Maalaouhi, A., le Loarne-Lemaire, S., & Razgallah, M. (2020). Does knowledge management explain the poor growth of social enterprises. *Journal of Knowledge Management, 24*(7), 1513–1532.

Mc Kelvie, A., Chandler, G. A., de Tienne, D. R., & Johanson, A. (2020). The measurement of effectuation: Highlighting research tensions and opportunities for the future. *Small Business Economy, 54*(3), 689–720.

Mensah, J. (2019). Sustainable development: Meaning, history, principles, pillars, and implications for human action: Literature review. *Cogent Social Sciences, 5*(1). https://doi.org/10.1080/23311886.2019.1653531

Mihet, R., & Philipon, T. (2019). The economics of big data and artificial intelligence. *Disruptive Innovation in Business and Finance in the Digital World, 20*, 29–43. Emerald Publishing.

Miller, D. (1983). The correlates of entrepreneurship in three types of firms. *Management Science, 29*(7), 770–791.

Mintzberg, H. (1973). *The nature of managerial work.* Harper & York.

Muthukrishnan, S., Alajarmeh, S., & Kalaignan P. (2020) Analysing the factors influencing the adoption of sustainable manufacturing practices in SMEs. *Journal of Manufacturing Technology Management, 31*(5), 1021–1045. https://doi.org/10.1108/JMTM-12-2018-0400

Nambisan, S., & Baron, R. A. (2019). On the costs of digital entrepreneurship: Role conflict, stress, and venture performance in digital platform-based ecosystems. *Journal of Business Research, 21, 465–486.*

Obschonka, M., & Audretsch, D. B. (2019). Artificial intelligence and big data in entrepreneurship: A new era begun. *Small Business Economics, 19*(1). https://doi.org/10.1007/s11187-019-00202-4

Öztürk, İ. (2008). *İGİAD 2008 Girişimcilik Raporu* 9.

Rostain, M. (2021). The impact of organizational culture on entrepreneurial orientation: A meta-analysis. *Journal of Business Venturing Insights, 25*. https://doi.org/10.1016/j.jbvi.2021.e00234

Ruiz-ortega, M. J., Parra-requena, G., García-Villaverde, P. M., & Rodrigo-alarcon, J. (2018). Do relationships affect entrepreneurial orientation ? *Cuadernos de Economía y Dirección de La Empresa, 20*(3), 178–191.

Sarango-Lalangui, P., Santos, J., & Hormiga, E. (2018). The development of sustainable entrepreneurship research field. *Sustainability, 24*, 109–124.

Schumpeter, J. A. (1934). *The theory of economic development: An inquiry into profits, capital, credit, interest and the business cycle*. Harvard University Press.

Searle, B. J., & Rooney, J. (2013). In G. C. Avery & B. Hughes (Eds.), *Proactivity at work: A path to organisational sustainability*. Tilde University Press.

Şen, H., Kaya, A., & Alpaslan, B. (2018). Sürdürülebilirlik üzerine tarihsel ve güncel bir perspektif. *Ekonomik Yaklaşım, 29*(197), 1–47.

Shi, W., & Weber, M. (2021). The impact of entrepreneurs' prior experience and communication networks on perceived knowledge access. *Journal of Knowledge Management, 25*(5), 1406–1426.

Singh, S. H., Bhowmick, B., Eesley, D., & Sindhav, B. (2019). Grassroots innovation and entrepreneurial success: Is entrepreneurial orientation a missing link? *Technological Forecasting and Social Change, January* 1–17.

tdk.gov.tr. (2022). *Türk Dil Kurumu.*

Temizel, Z. (1997). *Yurttaşın yönetime karşı korunmasında bağımsız bir denetim organı: Ombudsman* (I.-E. International Union of local Authorities, Ed.). IULA Yerel Yönetimler Birliği Yayınları.

Thornton, M. (2008). *Richard Cantillon: İktisadi Teorinin Doğuşu, 2*(2).

Topkaya, Ö. (2013). Tarihsel süreçte girişimcilik teorisi: Girişimciliğin ekonomik büyüme ve İstihdam Boyutu. *Girişimcilik ve Kalkınma Dergisi, 8*(1), 29–32.

Townsend, D. M., & Hunt, R. A. (2019). Entrepreneurial action, creativity, & judgment in the age of artificial intelligence. *Journal of Business Venturing Insights, 11*. https://doi.org/10.1016/j.jbvi.2019.e00126

Turing, A. (1950). Computing machinery and intelligence. *Mind A Quarterly Review of Psychology and Philosophy, 236*, 435–437. https://doi.org/10.1016/j.jbvi.2019.e00126

Tutar, H., & Küçük, O. (2003). Girişimcilik ve Küçük İşletme Yönetimi. *Seçkin Yayınevi.*

van Gelderen, M., Shirokova, G., Shchegolev, V., & Beliaeva, T. (2020). Striving for entrepreneurial autonomy: A comparison of Russia and the Netherlands. *Management and Organization Review, 16*(1), 107–138.

Villaseca, D., Navío-Marco, J., & Gimeno, R. (2020). Money for female entrepreneurs does not grow on trees: Start-ups' financing implications in times of COVID-19. *Journal of Entrepreneurship in Emerging Economies, 09 Sep 2021, 13*(4), 698–720. Emerald Group Publishing Limited; Emerald. ISSN: 20534604. https://doi.org/10.1108/JEEE-06-2020-0172

Wagner, D. N. (2020). Economic patterns in a world with artificial intelligence. *Evolutionary and Institutional Economics Review, 17*(315) 11–131.

Wales, W. J. (2011). The measurement of entrepreneurial orientation. *Journal of Baylor University, 540*, 677–703.

Wentao, G., & Wang, J. (2022). Research on index construction of sustainable entrepreneurship and its impact on economic growth. *Journal of Business Research, 142*, 266–276.

Wickham, A. P. (1998). *Strategic entrepreneurship*. Pearson Education Limited.

Winecoff, A. A., & Watkins, E. A.: Artificial concepts of artificial intelligence: Institutional compliance and resistance in AI startups (2022).

Yolles, M., & Fink, G. (2014). The sustainability of sustainability. *Business Systems Review, 3*(2), 5–23.

Younas, Z., & Zafar, A. (2019). Corporate risk taking and sustainability: A case of listed firms from the USA and Germany. *Journal of Global Responsibility, 35*, 223–238.

Zahra, S. A., Liu, W., & Si, S. (2023). How digital technology promotes entrepreneurship in ecosystems. *Technovation, 119*, 102457.

The Impact of e-Waste Minimization on the Actualization of SDG 12: Responsive Consumption and Production

Burcu Arsan and Ayşe Gönül Demirel

1 Introduction

With the drastic effect of digitalization and economic growth, today manufacturers make unplanned production by ignoring natural resources, ecological balance, and carbon emissions. While some countries that are disadvantaged in terms of natural resources in the world have difficulty in meeting their basic needs, a culture of waste is dominant in some regions due to production and abundance of natural resources.

Today, humanity should be guided to make responsible production that is aware of natural resources, respectful of nature, humanity, and future generations. Otherwise, the principles of the linear economic model that follows the steps of "buy, consume, throw" will not be abandoned. E-waste, which is also defined as electronic waste, is considered a problem created by end-of-life products, even if it works with the development of technology.

Outdated technological products are replaced by newer ones without hesitation by consumers. The main reason for this is that there are many new product alternatives, and accessibility and repair costs are very high. Managing e-waste is just as important as its prevention. Because electronic devices are not disposed of as waste, which is a very complicated and dangerous process.

In unlicensed and unconscious hands, the toxic gases emitted by e-waste into the atmosphere during the melting and dissolution process can create very difficult results. For this reason, e-waste disposal is carried out only by competent, licensed processing centers. As much as the rapid cycle in the production of technological products, the fashion industry consumes resources very quickly. Due to the new season collections they release almost every 4 months, production is far beyond the

B. Arsan (✉) · A. G. Demirel
Yeditepe University, Istanbul, Turkey
e-mail: gonuld@yeditepe.edu.tr

N. Ketenci (ed.), *Transition to the Circular Economy Model*, CSR, Sustainability, Ethics & Governance, https://doi.org/10.1007/978-3-031-52700-5_3

needs of the society. Paint cartridges, sewing patterns, cutting tools, printing machines, etc. used during production are rapidly becoming outdated and most of them quickly become e-waste.

The "Regulation on the Management of Waste Electrical and Electronic Equipment" regulation, which came into force at the end of 2022, created awareness for the first time in Turkey. Also, businesses serving in various sectors have started to take precautions in the context of WEEE and become conscious about recycling and sustainability. Besides, our country, which is still considered a developing country, still lags behind many developed countries in recycling and waste disposal. The e-waste regulation that came into force in this context will serve as a guide for organizations and will also support the realization of responsible production and consumption, which is one of the sustainable development goals.

From this point of view, in this study, it is aimed to develop suggestions for the prevention and correct disposal of e-waste in the context of Responsible Production and Consumption, which is the 12th of the Sustainable Development Goals. Structured interviews were conducted with the managers of four textile manufacturers serving in many provinces in Turkey, and themes and sub-themes were set about e-waste management and responsible production.

2 Literature Review

E-Waste Management

Due to the rapid change in digital technologies, the lifespan of electronic devices is rapidly running out. This rapid transformation also reveals the result of e-waste that needs to be managed. The waste generated by technological devices that have a shortened lifespan is also called electronic waste or e-waste. Electronic waste is basically defined as products that are no longer preferred by the user for various reasons. These reasons may be that the product no longer works or is technologically outdated. Related devices are defined as Waste Electrical and Electronic Equipment; television, mobile phone, fax machine, computer, and washing/dishwasher (Ongondo et al., 2011).

The "Regulation on the Management of Waste Electrical and Electronic Equipment" published by the Republic of Turkey Environment, Urbanization, and Climate Change in December 2022 aims to protect the environment in a sustainable way, to apply circular economic principles, and to resource efficiency. The regulation, which entered into force at the end of last year, has been prepared in great detail and has a high inclusiveness.

The goal is basically to prevent the formation of electronic waste, and if it cannot be prevented, to dispose of it correctly and to minimize the generation of new waste. Finally, the related regulation has created an overarching responsibility for manufacturers of electrical and electronic goods (DeSA, 2013).

Companies that do not comply with the regulation will face certain penal sanctions in accordance with their responsibilities. According to the WEEE regulation, small household appliances, telecommunication and information equipment, lighting equipment, vending machines, and consumer equipment are included in e-waste control.

Nowadays, game consoles and smartphone models are renewed almost every year. While LCD televisions were a new technology just a few years ago, three-dimensional televisions are very popular today. The lifespan of the technological devices we use in our daily life is shortened due to their continuous updating. Nowadays, almost any user prefers to change their technological devices because they are broken.

According to the data shared in the Global E-Waste Monitoring Report published by the United Nations in 2020, individuals produce 7.3 kg of e-waste per person per year in their homes. The main reasons for this increase are the ease of access to electronic products, the increase in the production of new technological products, the decrease in their useful life, and the high repair fees (García-Sánchez et al., 2020).

Users prefer to replace their broken technological products with new ones instead of having them repaired. In the report shared by the United Nations, the amount of electronic waste, which was 44.4 megatons in total in 2014, is expected to increase to 74.7 megatons in 2030. Disposal process and correct management of the related wastes is very critical not only in terms of quantity, but also in terms of harmful contents such as cobalt, barium, or mercury.

It takes many years for electronic waste to dissolve in nature, so it is quite wrong to treat it as ordinary waste (Kang & Schoenung, 2005). Another report published by the United Nations shows that only 17.6% of e-waste is recycled correctly. How the remaining 82.6% of e-waste is recycled is not known by official records.

Also, the disposal of e-waste can be quite difficult. Many components that come out of an electronic product must be recycled at different temperatures. While some plastic parts release toxic gas fumes when exposed to high heat, the insulating sheaths in the same product require high heat in the recycling process. In this context, it is very critical to be conscious about waste management (Widmer et al., 2005).

In e-waste management, the most accurate guidance to users is to inform them that they should deliver their expired electronic products to authorized institutions (Perkins, 2014). In order to prevent the e-waste issue, the first step to be taken is to raise public awareness. Afterward, awareness should be raised that electronic waste is not an ordinary garbage and should be disposed of separately, even with other wastes. E-waste should only be delivered to municipal waste centers or licensed processing facilities (Lundgren, 2012). At the same time, the "bring the old, take the new one" campaigns, which are frequently applied by electronic product manufacturers today, are very environmentally friendly beyond saving money.

On the other hand, supporting projects implemented by institutions such as the Education Volunteers Foundation of Turkey (TEGV) will raise awareness in the society in terms of e-waste. TEGV aims to use outdated and unused technological tools in the education processes of young people in need in order to reduce the damage caused by e-waste to the environment in the "Don't Dispose" project. Since 2017, 450 tons of e-waste has been recycled through the related project (TEGV, 2020).

E-waste export can be considered as both the cheapest and the most profitable method of getting rid of hazardous waste. In underdeveloped/developing countries, especially women, children, and prisoners are employed under very serious health threats while recycling these wastes manually with cheap labor.

With the International Basel Convention in 1989, import and shipment of all toxic wastes from rich countries to poor countries has been prohibited since 1994. According to the treaty, all hazardous waste must be reduced and dissolved and disposed of within national boundaries (Smith et al., 2006).

Sustainable Development Goal 12: Responsive Consumption and Production

In 2015, 17 Sustainable Development Goals were adopted by 193 member countries of the United Nations (UN) in order to ensure sustainability in development until 2030 worldwide. Sustainable Development Goals consist of 17 main targets and 169 sub-targets related to these targets.

The steps prepared by the United Nations and targeted to be carried out by 2030 are "to fight toward inequalities between societies, end poverty and hunger, achieve gender equality, create peaceful and inclusive societies, ensure and protect human rights, and empower women and girls, ensuring inclusive and sustainable economic growth, lasting protection of the planet and natural resources, and, finally, creating prosperity and decent working conditions for all" (United Nations General Assembly, 2015).

The goals prepared by the United Nations are all interrelated. For example, while aiming to reduce poverty for societies directly contributes to healthy living, healthy living also increases participation in education (Tsalis et al., 2020). The Sustainable Development Goals present goals in order to make the world a better, equal, fair, and livable place, and provide a common language for sustainable development (Schramade, 2017).

While the world population continues to increase rapidly, natural resources are also rapidly depleted. Since production and consumption are directly based on the use of natural resources, both institutions and individuals have responsibilities in the effective use of scarce resources. With the business world's focus on Responsible Production and Consumption, one of the United Nations' Sustainable Development Goals, individuals have also started to prefer environmentally friendly brands (Kanie et al., 2017).

In particular, the "SDG 12 Responsible Production and Consumption" objective, which aims to "provide sustainable production and consumption examples, draws attention to the role of the business world in sustainable development" (Stewart et al., 2018).

The primary sub-goals of the responsible production and consumption target are as follows: (1) It aims to develop circular models that focus on the use of renewable and sustainable energy. (2) To carry out studies to increase the consciousness and awareness of consumers in the context of sustainability, to encourage them, and to include them in sustainable development (Gunawan et al., 2020). (3) Donation of unsold products by manufacturers from different sectors to those in need. (4) Consuming and managing natural resources efficiently, minimizing food losses that may occur during supply chains, managing the disposal of chemical wastes in the most accurate way, reducing waste generation, and providing information to all segments of society about sustainable lifestyles (KPMG, 2018).

3 Methodology

Qualitative methods were used in the model of the research. Textile company executives were chosen as the sample. Structured interviews were conducted with the managers of four textile companies operating in Turkey. The main reason for choosing the textile industry as the sample is the rapid development of production technologies and the large scale of production since it serves the fashion industry. Another significant reasons for selecting the textile sector as a sample are that they respond very quickly to technological developments and are one of the leading sectors in the country's economy.

Textile companies were included in the analysis by being coded as Textile Company 1/Textile Company 2/Textile Company 3 and Textile Company 4. During the structured interviews, the managers were asked what kind of projects they produced for the e-waste processes of their institutions and what transformations they made. Because what they should accomplish, and their absolute targets are specified by the related regulation.

The data obtained in the light of the interviews with the managers are analyzed by the MAXQDA package program. In the qualitative data analysis performed through MAXQDA, the Statistics of Subcodes analysis was applied for frequency analysis of themes and sub-themes. Afterward, Code Theory Model Analysis, which is one of the MAXMaps methods, was utilized, and then Code Map Distance Matrix analysis was also adopted.

In the context of the 12th Sustainable Development Goals, responsible production and consumption, e-waste management has a vital place. How companies will manage the relevant processes more effectively and how they will raise awareness to their employees will be on the agenda in the future.

One of the main purposes of this research is to evaluate what kind of policies the leading companies of the textile sector, which is rapidly developing and has a great impact on the country's economy, follow in the context of e-waste and responsible production.

4 Findings

The qualitative data of the research were analyzed with the MAXQDA 2020 package program, and the frequency results were determined with the subcode analysis statistics. Then, visual distributions were determined by Code-Theory Model and Code Map Distance Matrix analysis among MAXMaps analyses. During the interviews with Textile Company Managers, structured interview questions titled "e-waste management of textile companies" were asked, and five themes and two sub-themes were found.

In the Code-Theory Model analysis, which is illustrated in detail in Fig. 1, five themes and two sub-themes were found and the most mentioned theme by the textile sector managers was determined as "Extending the Life of Technological Products". All the managers who contributed to the research emphasized that they aim to increase the lifespan of the technological products they use, both in accordance with the regulations brought by the sustainability departments established in their institutions and by raising awareness on behalf of the environment.

Afterward, the most emphasized theme by the managers was "Licensed E-Waste Disposal Centers". The main reason why the related theme is given importance by the managers is the "Regulation on the Management of Waste Electrical and Electronic Equipment", which came into force on December 26, 2022. Because the WEEE regulation has serious and deterrent penal sanctions. Thereafter the most

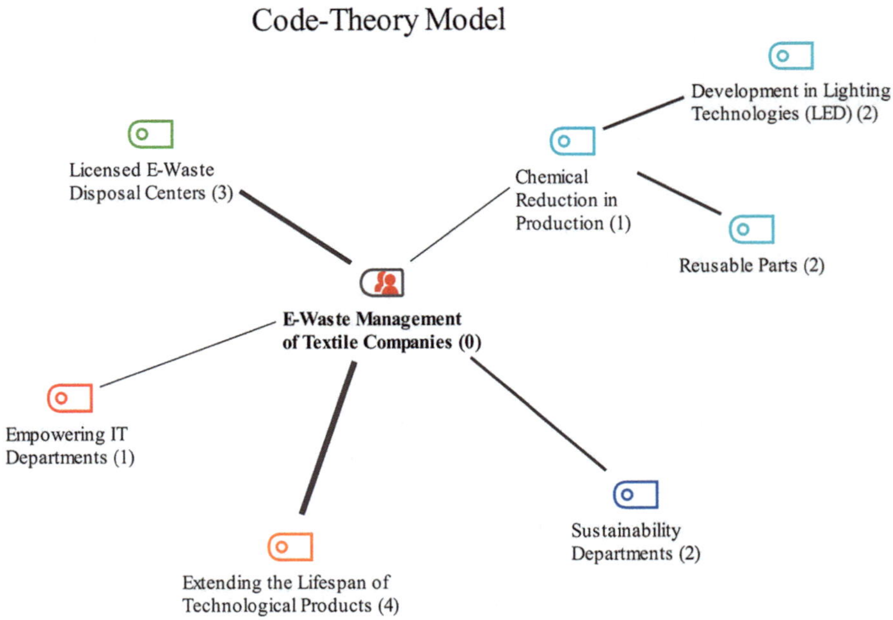

Fig. 1 Code-theory model for E-waste management of textile companies. (Source: The figure is prepared by authors)

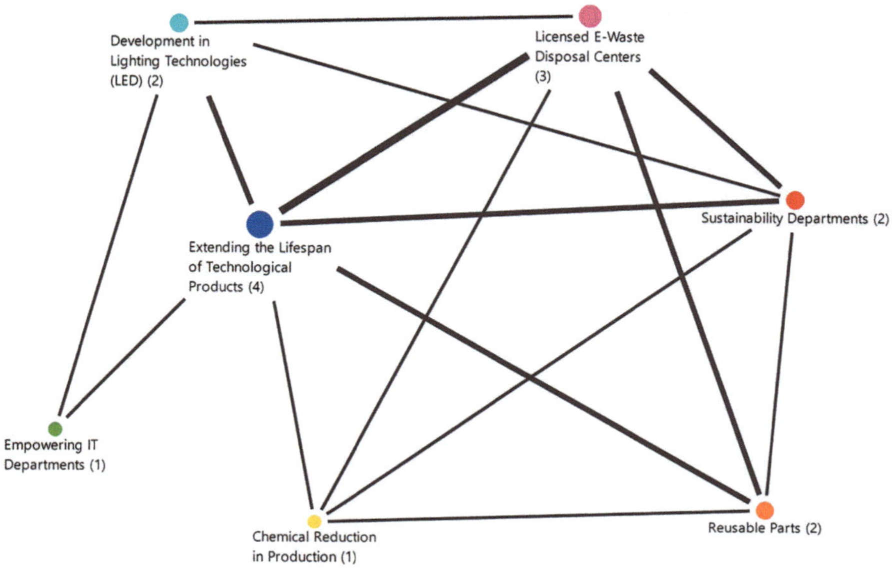

Fig. 2 Code map distance matrix analysis results. (Source: The figure is prepared by authors)

emphasized themes and sub-themes were "Sustainability Departments" and "Development in Lighting Technologies (LED)".

Code Map Distance Matrix Analysis, which is visualized in detail in Fig. 2, shows the connections between themes and sub-themes according to the decoded interview texts. As seen in the figure, the relationship between the "Extending the Lifespan of Technological Products" theme and the "Licensed E-Waste Disposal Centers" theme was found to be stronger than the others, in line with the responses of the managers.

In the sub-code statistics given in Table 1, the frequency distribution was formed in line with the themes and sub-themes emphasized by the administrators. The highlighted theme or sub-theme is marked with an "X" by the MAXQDA app in response to statements from each company executive.

5 Discussion and Suggestions

The economic growth and the uncontrolled increase in production with the direct effect of digitalization have affected the ecological balance and increased the carbon footprint. Efficient consumption of our common natural resources and disposal of toxic wastes and electronic wastes also serve this purpose. In this context, it is very important to raise awareness and encourage businesses, industries, and most importantly consumers about reducing waste and recycling until 2030. Despite all the

Table 1 Statistics of Subcodes for E-Waste Management of Textile Companies. Source: The table is prepared by authors

	Textile Company 1 ($N = 1$)	Textile Company 2 ($N = 1$)	Textile Company 3 ($N = 1$)	Textile Company 4 ($N = 1$)
E-waste management of textile companies				
Sustainability departments	X	X		
Chemical reduction in production	X			
Reusable parts	X		X	
Development in lighting technologies (LED)		X		X
Extending the lifespan of technological products	X	X	X	X
Empowering IT departments				X
Licensed E-waste disposal centers	X	X	X	

technological and economic developments, a considerable part of the world's population has few resources that cannot meet their basic needs.

Irresponsible production prevents the equal distribution of services and goods around the world. Responsible production and consumption, which is the 12th of the Sustainable Development Goals, aims to warn individuals and institutions to act more consciously. The linear economic model principles that proceed as "Buy, consume, dispose" consume natural resources, reduce biodiversity, harm sustainable principles, and change the ecosystem.

With the unstoppable speed of digitalization, production technologies, and autonomous devices, digital goods are replaced with new ones before they reach the end of their useful life. Technological devices that do not have any working problems yet and work regularly are changed only because a newer model is released. In this context, it is very important for our world that both technology companies and consumers have awareness.

While there are young people who have never seen a smartphone, tablet, or computer in one part of the world, it is completely against the principles of responsible consumption that there are consumers who renew their smartphones every 6 months in another part of the world.

The textile sector also produces uncontrollably as much as the technology and informatics sector. Under the name of fashion, brands present their new collections to their consumers every 4 months and consume natural resources rapidly. The production, which is far beyond the needs of the consumers, is carried out strictly according to the linear model. Machines used in the production phase wear out rapidly, electronic paint cartridges and sewing machines used in production often become waste. The extent of the damage to nature and natural resources caused by e-waste that is not disposed of correctly is quite large.

Related businesses should consider the issue of waste and e-waste by adopting and applying the circular production and economy model. Contrary to popular belief, the circular economy can create great opportunities rather than hinder the growth of organizations. McDonough of Stanford University describes the circular economy as a great business opportunity. Today, businesses should be aware of the limited resources and make planned production (Doppelt, 2017).

They should ensure that the products they produce are longer lasting and of high quality, by increasing their sales fees if necessary. Manufacturers should focus on R&D studies in order to achieve this goal. Extending the product life, usage area, and life cycle is also among the production principles of the circular economy. Product designs should be developed so that waste products can serve a new purpose and become suitable for reuse.

This research has been conducted with the aim of projecting a snapshot of how e-waste disposal processes are managed in Turkey. However, research was carried out only from the perspective of the textile industry and the managers of four different companies were interviewed, and the development process in terms of other sectors could not be conveyed. Although it has been 8 months since the WEEE regulation came into force, textile companies have made efforts to support sustainable development goals. In the future, studies on the e-waste disposal management process of different sectors in different time periods can contribute to the literature. For further studies, conducting research on e-waste disposal management process in different time periods and in different sectors will contribute greatly to the related literature.

Competing Interests The authors have no conflicts of interest to declare that are relevant to the content of this chapter.

References

DeSA, U. N. (2013). *World population prospects: The 2012 revision* (Vol. 18, pp. 620–626). Population Division of the Department of Economic and Social Affairs of the United Nations Secretariat.

Doppelt, B. (2017). *Leading change toward sustainability: A change-management guide for business, government and civil society*. Routledge.

García-Sánchez, I.-M., Aibar-Guzmán, B., Aibar-Guzmán, C., & Rodríguez-Ariza, L. (2020). "Sell" recommendations by analysts in response to business communication strategies concerning the Sustainable Development Goals and the SDG compass. *Journal of Cleaner Production, 255*, 112. https://doi.org/10.1016/j.jclepro.2020.120194

Gunawan, J., Permatasari, P., & Tilt, C. (2020). Sustainable development goal disclosures: Do they support responsible consumption and production? *Journal of Cleaner Production, 246*, 118989. https://doi.org/10.1016/j.jclepro.2019.118989

Kang, H. Y., & Schoenung, J. M. (2005). Electronic waste recycling: A review of U.S. infrastructure and technology options. *Resources, Conservation and Recycling*, Cilt 45, Sayı 4, s. 368–400.

Kanie, N., Bernstein, S., Biermann, F., & Haas, P. M. (2017). Introduction: Global governance through goal setting. In N. Kanie & F. Biermann (Eds.), *Governing through goals: Sustainable development goals as governance innovation* (pp. 1–28). The MIT Press.
KPMG. (2018). *How to report on the SDG: What good looks like and why it matters*. https://assets.kpmg/content/dam/kpmg/xx/pdf/2018/02/how-to-report-on-sdgs.pdf (Erişim Tarihi: 10.02.2023).
Lundgren, K. (2012). *The global impact of e-waste: Addressing the challenge*. International Labour Organization.
Ongondo, F. O., Williams, I. D., & Cherrett, T. J. (2011). How are WEEE doing? A global review of the management of electrical and electronic wastes. *Waste Management, 31*(4), 714–730.
Perkins, D. N. (2014). E-waste: A global hazard. *Annals of Global Health*, Cilt 80, Sayı 4, s. 286–295.9.
Schramade, W. (2017). Investing in the UN sustainable development goals: Opportunities for companies and investors. *Journal of Applied Corporate Finance, 29*(2), 87–99. https://doi.org/10.1111/jacf.12236
Smith, T., Sonnenfeld, D., & Pellow, D. (2006). *Challenging the chip: Labor rights and environmental justice in the global electronics industry*. Temple University Press.
Stewart, R. M. M., Fantke, P., Bjørn, A., Owsianiak, M., Molin, C., Hauschild, M. Z., & Laurent, A. (2018). Life cycle assessment in corporate sustainability reporting: Global, regional, sectoral, and company-level trends. *Business Strategy and the Environment, 27(8), 1751–1764.* https://doi.org/10.1002/bse.2241
Tsalis, T. A., Malamateniou, K. E., Koulouriotis, D., & Nikolaou, I. E. (2020). New challenges for corporate sustainability reporting: United Nations' 2030 agenda for sustainable development and the sustainable development goals. *Corporate Social Responsibility and Environmental Management, 27*(4), 1617–1629. https://doi.org/10.1002/csr.1910
Türkiye Eğitim Gönüllüleri Vakfı (TEGV). (2020). *Atma Bağışla Projesi*. https://tegv.org/atma-bagisla-projesi
United Nations General Assembly. (2015). *Resolution adopted by the General Assembly on 25 September 2015 (A/RES/ 70/1)*. https://documents-ddsny.un.org/doc/UNDOC/GEN/N15/291/89/PDF/N1529189.pdf?OpenElement (Erişim Tarihi: 25.07.2022).
Widmer, R., Oswald-Krapf, H., Sinha-Khetriwal, D., Schnellmann, M., & Böni, H. (2005). Global perspectives on e-waste. *Environmental Impact Assessment Review, 25*(5), 436–458.

How Can the Circular Economy Contribute to the Achievement of SDG 8: Decent Work and Economic Growth?

Esin Yücel Karamustafa, Burcu Arsan, and Deniz Palalar Alkan

1 Introduction

The mechanized mass production methods that developed after the direct impact of the Industrial Revolution forced the economic models to evolve. Especially after the Second World War, many countries made industrialization their economic policies in order to develop. However, in the long term, the mentioned industrialization method has brought with it challenging environmental problems. On the other hand, the mentioned environmental problems and pollution are not only created by the production processes. Consumers also have a considerable share in the formation of environmental problems. In order to put an end to this dark course, the "World Commission on Environment and Development" was established by the United Nations in 1993.

The Commission also introduced the concept of sustainable development, which we actively use today. They defined the related concept as meeting the needs of current generations without affecting the possibilities of meeting the needs of future generations. Then, in 2015, the United Nations and World leaders agreed on 17 key goals to ensure the prosperity and continuity of the world by 2030.

These goals are designed not only about environmental issues and sustainable production models but also about employee well-being, fair wages, equality, and inclusiveness. One of these 17 goals, "SDG 8: Decent Work and Economic Growth", aims to reduce poverty around the world by aiming at decent, fair wages and stable

E. Y. Karamustafa (✉)
Altinbas University, Istanbul, Turkey
e-mail: esin.karamustafa@altinbas.edu.tr

B. Arsan · D. P. Alkan
Yeditepe University, Istanbul, Turkey
e-mail: deniz.alkan@yeditepe.edu.tr

N. Ketenci (ed.), *Transition to the Circular Economy Model*, CSR, Sustainability, Ethics & Governance, https://doi.org/10.1007/978-3-031-52700-5_4

employment. Especially in the dimension of decent work, gender equality between men and women, salary and promotion according to competency, equal access to educational opportunities, and the evaluation of in-house diversity as wealth are emphasized.

In this study, it is aimed to examine how the circular economy approach can contribute to the realization of SDG 8. Five IT companies that are listed on the BIST 100 and that are actively traded were selected for examination. Through the human resources and sustainability reports that these companies publish regularly, the parallelism to the related targets and sub-targets was examined, and as a result, suggestions were made to the IT sector.

2 Literature Review

Circular Economy

Ellen MacArthur Foundation, who introduced the idea and concept of the circular economy, mentions and emphasizes that altering the current system requires changing everything and everyone. Governments, businesses, products, and individuals are also included to this transformation (Ellen MacArthur Foundation, 2020). The most distinctive feature that distinguishes circular economy principles from others is that, contrary to other views, it does not connect the concept of growth to the consumption of natural resources. One of its top priorities is to design models that aim to exclude waste and, most importantly, pollution from the system. Circular economy aims to maximize the lifetime of any material or product within the system. Also, it aims to renew and improve the environment and natural systems.

There are many accepted definitions of circular economy in the literature. But one of the most fundamental among them is the definition made by the Commission in 2015. In the European Union Commission, the circular economy is explained as an economic model in which the values of resources, products, and materials are kept as long as possible in the economic structure and the amount of waste is minimized (European Commission, 2015). Circular economic thinking is an economic model that focuses on protecting the environment, based on continuity from the production process to waste generation. It exists with the principles of "Reduce-Reuse-Recycle" instead of the "Buy-Build-Dispose" process of the linear and traditionally accepted economic model. In today's world, linear economy does not work effectively for some reasons (Catlin & Wang, 2013).

Primarily, access to basic resources such as clean water, fossil fuels, and food is becoming increasingly difficult, biodiversity is declining, and financial systems are collapsing around the world. On the other hand, the circular economy concept is founded on an industrial economy that corrects system failures, prevents waste, reduces the use of toxic chemicals in production, and transitions to renewable energy (MacArthur, 2013).

The circular economy focuses on three key elements to find solutions to both resource and system problems: to optimize sustainable resource efficiency, to develop and protect natural resources and capital, and to maintain the efficiency of the economic system (Antikainen et al., 2018). The abbreviation "3R" is used to describe the fundamental system of the circular economic model. The concept of 3R, which defines the processes of the circular economy, comes from the initials of the concepts Recycle, Reuse, and Reduce (Liu et al., 2017). The concept of recycling is defined as the evaluation of the end-of-production wastes or the functionalization of the recycling of existing wastes.

Sustainable Development Goals

Sustainable development as a concept is established on three moral imperatives: to achieve global social equality, to meet human needs, and to be respectful of environmental boundaries (Holden et al., 2014). The most common definition is to meet today's needs globally without compromising the capability and autonomy of future generations to meet their own needs (Pitelis, 2013).

In this context, it is clear that it aims to develop from an ecological, social, and economic perspective in order to ensure the continuity of humanity in the global sense. In general, the sustainable development strategy aims to increase the harmony between people and nature, as well as between people (Gedik, 2020).

The concept of sustainable development was formed by bringing together the words "development", which is an economic definition, and "sustainability", which is related to the environment. By the 1980s, the environment and economy were not defined as opposite concepts and more inclusive definitions were started to be made, and the concept drew the attention of academics first and then the business world.

On the other hand, about 8 years before the "United Nations Brundtland Report" (1987), in which the concept of "sustainable development" was introduced, the famous economist Passet (1979) mentioned the need for a development model that would not adversely affect the entire universe (Brunel, 2004).

In 1987, the report titled "Our Common Future", prepared by the United Nations World Commission on Environment and Development, was published (Keeble, 1988). Afterward, with the Agenda 21 text, which was shaped by the United Nations Rio de Janeiro Conference in 1992, the foundations of future sustainable development policies were laid. In the following years, environmental summits were held in various countries by the United Nations at regular intervals (Dow, 1992). However, in 2015, the sustainable development goals that we all know, which are described as a global call to action, were emerged (PalalarAlkan & Kamasak, 2023).

The related goals are identified as the roadmap of everything that is aimed to be achieved for all humanity and the world by 2030. It consists of 17 comprehensive universal goals and 169 targets in total, also called sustainable development targets. On the other hand, since the related goals all concentrate on global problems, they are directly related to each other. To measure the progress made in achieving the targets, the United Nations Statistical Commission has established a general measurement framework. In order to measure the achievement of 169 goals, 230 indicators were constructed (GBD 2015 SDG Collaborators, 2016).

Three hierarchical steps stand out in achieving the Sustainable Development Goals. The first is to reach a state of social agreement in terms of sustainability. This state of agreement can only be achieved by determining ethical goals. In the second step, the main issues agreed upon are turned into targets. In the last step, intensive studies are initiated toward the related targets (Klauer, 1999). This hierarchical arrangement, which was put forward by Klauer in 1999, was also effective in the setting of the targets in 2015.

"Decent work and economic growth", the eighth of the Sustainable Development Goals, supports productive and inclusive employment and provides fair wages and opportunities to everyone globally (Hák et al., 2016). At the summit held by the United Nations in 2015, the promotion of entrepreneurship and technological innovations was emphasized as the key to the realization of the related target. Besides, decent work also includes vocational training programs that will support equal employment and productivity for male and female employees.

The International Labor Organization announced that there were 204 million unemployed individuals in 2015. Therefore, while global economic growth slows down, the rate of increase in the number of unemployed individuals is accelerating. Especially natural resources, which are decreasing day by day, cause a raw material crisis in many sectors and cause them to become smaller. Therefore, the principles of linear economic models such as produce, consume, and reproduce negatively affect the realization of this goal (European Commission, 2015).

Besides, in the United Nations Environment Program in 2010, it was emphasized that almost worldwide female workers were paid 25% less than males and the younger generations had difficulties in finding a job. By signing the "social memorandum", large-scale companies around the world have promised to give more importance to gender equality, fair salary principle, transparent taxation, and inclusiveness of vocational training programs compared to the past, within the scope of SDG 8 (Rai et al., 2019).

Some objectives of SDG 8 are as follows: (1) By evaluating national conditions, maintaining per capita economic growth, and ensuring 7% development on a yearly basis. (2) Increasing economic efficiency by developing technological development and innovation in a sectoral sense. (3) Aiming for the growth of medium-sized companies by increasing policies that support creativity and innovation. (4) Ensuring the participation of young people in productive employment until 2030, with the principle of inclusiveness, without discrimination between the disabled and men-women. (5) Increasing employment-oriented training programs until 2020 and including young people in these trainings. (6) Strengthening national financial institutions by providing individuals with access to insurance, banking, and other financial services. (7) Protection of the rights of migrant workers and their inclusion in employment within the principle of inclusiveness. (8) Also, it is aimed to end all forms of abuse by 2025, such as the prevention of modern slavery, forced labor, and youth labor (Kreinin & Aigner, 2022).

3 The Circular Economy and Its Potential Constructive Impact on SDG 8

As the interest and importance given to the Sustainable Development Goals increased, it became clear that linear economic principles were not sufficient, and thus the circular economic model emerged. Through the Circular Economy, principles such as reducing the amount of resources used, recycling, and saving have come to the fore, and these principles directly support sustainable development goals. Besides, it has been realized that it will not be sufficient for the producers to participate in the circular economy alone. Thus, changing the behavior of consumers will make it easier to reach the related goals.

Numerous goals set by the United Nations directly emphasize circular economic principles. For instance, the production process, which begins with the fair acquisition of raw materials, continues with the correct processing of the related resources, transforming them into products or services and delivering them to the waste management system appropriately after they are delivered to the consumer. This process brings together both sustainable development goals and circular economy on a common ground. Besides, contrary to popular belief, the circular economy does not only concentrate on tangible materials or raw materials. It also contributes to factors that directly affect all sectors such as business plans, employment models, and training & development.

For instance, (1) the problem of hunger can be prevented with the circular economy model in order to prevent the inefficient use of basic resources and waste in the food sector. (2) In terms of resource efficiency, raw materials can be prevented from exiting the system by keeping them within the production cycle. In this way, the waste of resources is largely avoided. Besides, the consumption of energy and water resources is controlled. (3) Decent job opportunities and economic growth will be achievable due to green cities that have been re-designed within the framework of the circular economy principles. (4) As cities that are planned properly will generate less damage to nature, the negative effects on both aquatic and terrestrial life will decrease. The separation of agricultural areas and industrial zones in green cities is also of great importance for creating healthy societies. (5) In light of all these developments and transformations, changing the existing incorrect thought models will enable the emergence of institutions based on justice, peace, and egalitarianism.

When the five basic principles of the circular economy listed above are evaluated separately, the parallels between them and the 17 titles of the sustainable development goals are noticed. It is an indisputable fact that the circular economy will be a successful model in achieving the relevant goals (Schroeder et al., 2019).

4 Methodology

In this research, five IT companies listed in BIST 100 were selected for analysis. The human resources and sustainability reports published annually or semi-annually by companies within the scope of the three sub-targets of Sustainable Development Goal 8 were systematically examined between July 2022 and July 2023. BIST 100 is the main indicator used to measure the performance of the 100 highest-valued stocks in terms of market and trading volume traded on Borsa Istanbul.

The three sub-objectives of SDG 8 included in the research are explained below: 8.3 (Increasing policies that support job creation and business growth), 8.5 (By 2030, ensure that all women and men, including youth and persons with disabilities, have access to full and productive employment and decent work, and full adoption of the principle of equal pay for equal work), 8.6 (Supporting the employment of young people and their general and vocational education).

In particular, the reason for choosing these three targets is that they are more likely to be supported more effectively by the main goals and functions of the circular economy. The IT companies included in the research were coded as IT1, IT2, IT3, IT4, and IT5. As a result of examining the reports of five related IT companies, themes, and sub-themes were created and analyzed through the MAXQDA package program. During the data analysis performed through MAXQDA, the Statistics of Subcodes analysis was used for frequency analysis of themes and sub-themes. Afterward, Hierarchical Code-Theory Model Analysis, one of the MAXMaps methods, was utilized.

The main reason for selecting the informatics sector as the sample is that, it is developing and transforming very rapidly by nature and has a male-dominated perception. The main reason for selecting the informatics sector as the sample is that, it is developing and transforming very rapidly by nature and has a male-dominated perception.

Employees who cannot adapt to the rapid technological developments in the related sector or who cannot keep up with the speed have a high probability of staying out of the system. For this reason, it is very vital for companies in the IT sector to have awareness and follow the right policies in order to realize SDG 8. For this purpose, the reports of the related companies were examined and their parallels with the sub-targets of SDG 8 were determined.

5 Findings

The qualitative data of the research were analyzed through the MAXQDA package program, and the frequency results were determined by the statistics of subcodes analysis. Afterward, visual distributions were determined with the Hierarchical Code-Theory Model among the MAXMaps analyses.

When the reports of the five IT companies for Sub-Target 8.3, the most emphasized sub-theme was "Searching for innovative products and solutions" as shown in Fig. 1. The related sub-theme was emphasized 44% more in the four company reports compared to the others. Afterward, other sub-themes mentioned by the companies were determined as "Increasing the capability of existing products" and "Project and product development". As can be seen in Table 1, two of the five IT companies emphasized the sub-themes listed above with 22%. Finally, a company emphasized the "Total Quality Management" sub-theme with 11%.

As seen in Fig. 2, "Equal opportunity in employment" and "Inclusion and Diversity" were the most emphasized sub-themes in the semi-annual and annual reports published by five IT companies when evaluated from the SDG 8.5 perspective. Afterward, according to the Statistics of Subcodes analysis results seen in Table 2, "Inclusion and Diversity" and "Equal opportunity in employment" are the concepts most emphasized by institutions, with a rate of 33%. Afterward, the most mentioned sub-theme is "Fair Salary" with 22%.

As seen in Fig. 3, when the semi-annual and annual reports published by five IT companies are evaluated from the perspective of SDG 8.6 sub-goals, "Support for vocational training" was found to be the most emphasized sub-theme. The next most emphasized sub-theme is "Investment in Education and Scholarship Support". Afterward, as can be seen in Table 3, according to the results of the Statistics of Subcodes analysis, the most focused sub-theme with 33% is "Support for vocational training".

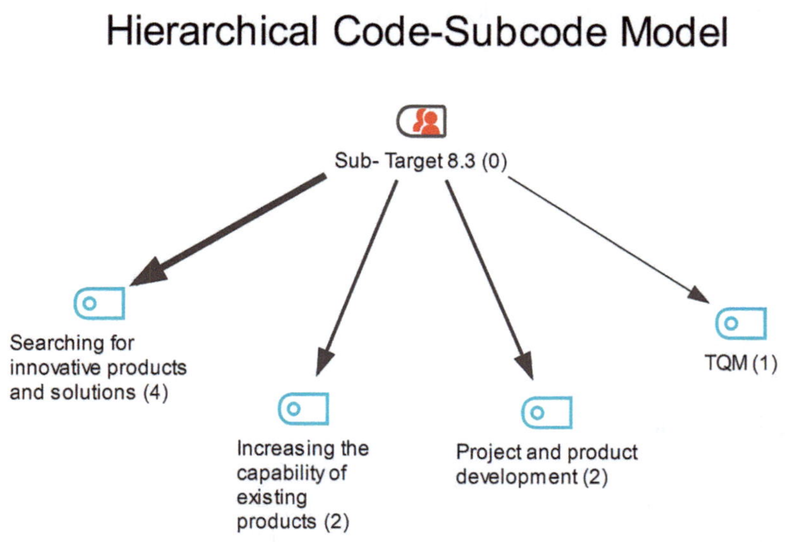

Fig. 1 Hierarchical code-theory model for sub-target 8.3. (Source: The figure is prepared by authors)

Table 1 Statistic of subcodes for sub-target 8.3

Sub-target 8.3/statistics of subcodes	Sections	Percentage
Increasing the capability of existing products	2	22.22
TQM	1	11.11
Project and product development	2	22.22
Searching for innovative products and solutions	4	44.44
TOTAL	9	100.00

Source: The table is prepared by authors

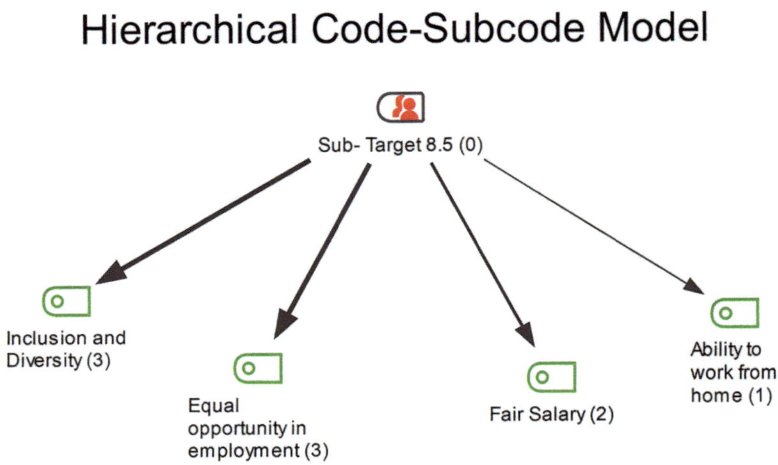

Fig. 2 Hierarchical code-theory model for sub-target 8.5. (Source: The figure is prepared by authors)

Table 2 Statistics of subcodes for sub-target 8.5

Sub-target 8.5/statistics of subcodes	Sections	Percentage
Inclusion and diversity	3	33.33
Fair salary	2	22.22
Ability to work from home	1	11.11
Equal opportunity in employment	3	33.33
TOTAL	9	100.00

Source: The table is prepared by authors

6 Discussion

Private sector action will be essential to realize the potential benefits of the circular economy (CE). It is becoming increasingly apparent that circular economy business models can be lucrative, and many companies, including small and medium-sized enterprises, intend to adopt such models globally. This manuscript aims to investigate the question: "To what extent are circular economy practices relevant to the

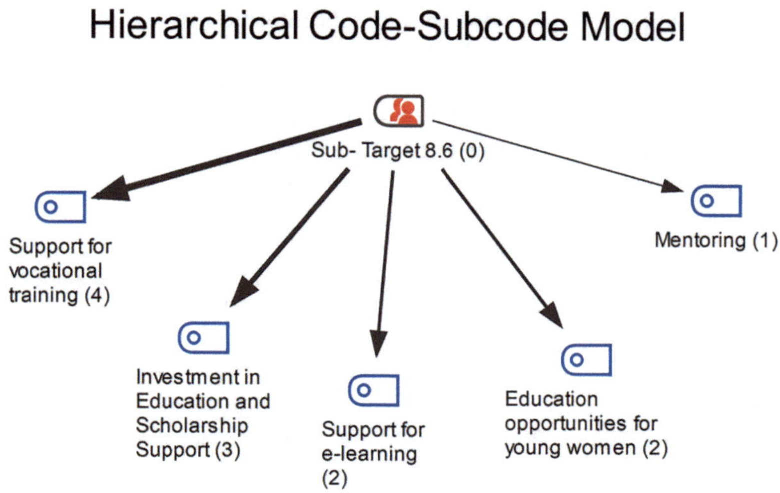

Fig. 3 Hierarchical code-theory model for sub-target 8.6. (Source: The figure is prepared by authors)

Table 3 Statistics of subcodes for sub-target 8.6

Sub-target 8.6/statistics of subcodes	Sections	Percentage
Support for vocational training	4	33.33
Support for e-learning	2	16.67
Education opportunities for young women	2	16.67
Mentoring	1	8.33
Investment in education and scholarship support	3	25.00
TOTAL	12	100.00

Source: The table is prepared by authors

Sustainable Development Goals, in particular Sustainable Development Goal 8 and its' sub-targets". We aimed to investigate the interplay between circular economy and Sustainable Development Goal 8 using a qualitative approach. This paper explored how the circular economy approach can contribute to achieving SDG 8, "Decent work and economic growth", designed to facilitate productive and inclusive employment and ensure fair wages and opportunities. SDG 8 has numerous objectives aimed at increasing the well-being of societies through mechanisms such as increasing youth employment, minimizing the gender pay gap, and promoting innovation.

There is a positive relationship between the global adoption of CE practices and progress on SDG 8. An examination of the semi-annual public reports of five information technology companies operating in Turkey was conducted to determine whether CE practices contribute to adopting the Sustainable Development Goals

(SDGs). This study examines how the selected companies integrate the SDG 8 target, including the sub-targets of SDG8: SDG8.3, SDG8.5, and SDG8.6.

Our analysis shows that companies are oriented toward "searching for innovative products and solutions", incorporated within the sub-target of SDG 8.3. It corresponds with CE practices for waste reduction and recycling. Moreover, the study results indicate that companies are firmly focused on improving the capabilities of existing products, thereby reducing the need for new products, which is one of the core principles of circular economy practices.

Specifically, our analysis shows that companies adopt talent management practices to reduce gender pay gaps, aiming to increase employee engagement and fair recruitment. For the sub-target 8.6, which is related to youth employment and promoting vocational education, company report results show that companies place great emphasis on the importance of continuing vocational education. According to this result, talent retention aligned with CE practices to reduce redundancies is paramount. The heightened focus on such practices is critical to an industry characterized by employee attrition and turnover.

Following the findings of this study, there is a positive relation between the adoption of CE practices that inevitably contribute to adopting the Sustainable Development Goals, such as SDG 8, and its sub-targets to promote economic growth and job creation. The SDGs can facilitate the promotion of CE practices as much as CE can contribute to achieving many SDG targets. Given the limitations of this study, we recommend further investigation to generate more empirical evidence concerning the link between CE and the Sustainable Development Goals.

Competing Interests The authors have no conflicts of interest to declare that are relevant to the content of this chapter.

References

Antikainen, R., Lazarevic, D., & Seppälä, J. (2018). Circular economy: Origins and future orientations. In H. Lehmann (Ed.), *Factor X, challenges, implementation strategies and examples for a sustainable use of natural resources* (pp. 115–129). Springer.

Brunel, S. (2004). Le développement durable, Paris, PUF, collection Que-sais-je?', Développement durable & territoires.

Catlin, J. R., & Wang, Y. (2013). Recycling gone bad: When the option to recycle increases resource consumption. *Journal of Consumer Psychology, 23*(1), 122–127.

Dow, K. (1992). Exploring differences in our common future(s): The meaning of vulnerability to global environmental change. *Geoforum, 23*(3), 417–436.

Ellen MacArthur Foundation. (2020). Financing the circular economy: Capturing the opportunity. https://www.ellenmacarthurfoundation.org/financing-the-circular-economy-capturing-the-opportunity

European Commission. (2015). Communication from the Commission to the European Parliament, the Council, the European Economic and Social Committee and the Committee of the Regions—Closing the loop—An EU action plan for the circular economy.

GBD 2015 SDG Collaborators. (2016). Measuring the health-related sustainable development goals in 188 countries: A baseline analysis from The Global Burden of Disease Study 2015. *The Lancet, 388*(10053), 1813–1850.
Gedik, Y. (2020). Sosyal, Ekonomik Ve Çevresel Boyutlarla Sürdürülebilirlik Ve Sürdürülebilir Kalkınma. *Uluslararası Ekonomi Siyasetİnsan Ve Toplum Bilimleri Dergisi, 3*(3), 196–215.
Hák, T., Janoušková, S., & Moldan, B. (2016). Sustainable development goals: A need for relevant indicators. *Ecological Indicators, 60*, 565–573.
Holden, E., Linnerud, K., & ve Banister, D. (2014). Sustainable development: Our common future revisited. *Global Environmental Change, 26*, 130–139.
Keeble, B. R. (1988). The Brundtland report: 'Our common future'. *Medicine and War, 4*(1), 17–25.
Klauer, B. (1999). Defininig and achieving sustainable development. *International Journal of Sustainable Development & World Ecology, 6(2), 114–121.* https://doi.org/10.1080/13504509909470000
Kreinin, H., & Aigner, E. (2022). From "decent work and economic growth" to "sustainable work and economic degrowth": A new framework for SDG 8. *Empirica, 49*(2), 281–311.
Liu, L., Liang, Y., Song, Q., & ve Li, J. (2017). A review of waste prevention through 3R under the concept of circular economy in China. *Journal of Material Cycles and Waste Management, 19*(4), 1314–1323.
MacArthur, E. (2013). *Towards the circular economy, economic and business rationale for an accelerated transition*. Ellen MacArthur Foundation.
PalalarAlkan, D., & Kamasak, R. (2023). The practice of "SDG washing" in developing countries. In *6th international academic conference on management and economic*. Oxford, UK.
Passet, R. (1979). *L'économique et le vivant (Economics and the Living). Paris, Petite Bibliothèque Payot, 287 p.*
Pitelis, C. (2013). Towards a more ethically correct governance for economic sustainability. *Journal of Business Ethics, 118*(3), 655–665.
Rai, S. M., Brown, B. D., & Ruwanpura, K. N. (2019). SDG 8: Decent work and economic growth – A gendered analysis. *World Development, 113*, 368–380.
Schroeder, P., Anggraeni, K., & Weber, U. (2019). The relevance of circular economy practices to the sustainable development goals. *Journal of Industrial Ecology, 23*(1), 77–95.

Sustainable Development Goal 5: Gender Equality – A Study on the Logistics Sector

Esin Yücel Karamustafa

1 Introduction

Since the beginning of the twentieth century, female employees have begun to take part in the employment and labor market worldwide as never before. Especially the global transformation and change experienced in the last 30 years has brought along the diversity of jobs, labor usage, and occupations for female employees (Urhan, 2016).

Şentürk's research conducted in 2016 revealed that female employees in Turkey are at a disadvantage compared to male employees in terms of salary and education in almost every sector. Another result of the same research is that female employees have difficulties being managers for this reason (Şentürk, 2016).

Beyond the perception in Turkey, the logistics industry is interpreted as a "no place for women" all over the world (Turnbull, 2013). Also, Women in Supply Chain Group (2010) explained that the reason for the masculinization of the logistics industry is that companies prefer male employees. Contrary to what is known, the population of women who have studied the related departments and are ready to join the workforce is quite high. The research conducted by Lynagu in 1996 explained one of the most fundamental problems in the sector is the exclusion of women from vocational training and the inability to provide equal opportunities.

The main reason for selecting the logistics sector as the sample in this study is that it has been developing rapidly in the last 20 years and it is crucial to move away from the male-dominated perception. Besides, in line with the global action call made by the United Nations, one of the goals to be achieved by 2030 is Gender

E. Yücel Karamustafa (✉)
Altinbas University, Istanbul, Turkey
e-mail: esin.karamustafa@altinbas.edu.tr

N. Ketenci (ed.), *Transition to the Circular Economy Model*, CSR, Sustainability, Ethics & Governance, https://doi.org/10.1007/978-3-031-52700-5_5

Equality. Raising awareness in all male-dominated sectors and managers in order to achieve SDG 5 is one of the main objectives of this research.

In order to achieve the above-mentioned purpose, 6 logistics companies listed in BIST 100 were selected as a sample, and the HR and sustainability reports published by the companies on a semi-annual and annual basis were examined in detail and systematically. Thus, by projecting the current situation to the related sector, deficiencies and aspects that are available for development were revealed.

The results of the research show that the first six companies that are traded with high value in the logistics sector demonstrate policies in favor of training their female employees in the context of information technologies. Because the development of female employees in terms of information technologies and digitalization will directly benefit the institutions they work for.

Also, when the reports are analyzed in line with the sub-objectives of SDG 5, it is seen that the need for manpower has decreased and many processes have been automated with digitalization in the logistics industry, which still does not have policies on discrimination between men and women. The main reason for this inference is that there are still managers at the head of logistics companies who have the perception that the industry is male-dominated.

2 Literature Review

Sustainable Development Goal 5: Gender Equality

In the years when awareness about global climate change has not yet developed and many technologies that pollute the environment have emerged, it has been realized that the world will not be able to withstand this order for another 100 years. At the United Nations Environment Conference held in the same period, an eco-development policy was developed, and the protection of the resources of future generations and human-centered sustainable development came to the fore.

In the following years, the importance given to the related concept increased and during the Brundtland Commission (World Commission on Environment and Development) held in 1987, the report "Our Common Future" was published in order to protect the continuity of the world and the sustainable welfare of human beings. For the first time in this report, concepts such as equality, environmental problems, and poverty were discussed together and the definition of sustainable development was made.

Afterward, at the "Earth Summit" held in Rio de Janeiro in 1992, the concept of sustainability was accepted as a global development strategy. In the following years, Sustainable Development ceased to be a definition and became a global productivity strategy (Akgül, 2010).

Thereafter, targets were set and progress was made in areas such as climate change, protection of nature, efficient use of natural resources, inequality, and poverty. However, unfortunately, the achievements in this process were not found to be sufficient on a local or global basis (Turkish Ministry of Development, 2012).

Subsequently, in 2000, principles such as human dignity, well-being, and equality at the global level, which are the common responsibility of all societies, were also considered as a part of development thought. The Millennium Declaration consists of eight main principles that are aimed to be realized by 2015. These targets cover topics such as climate problem, resource efficiency, poverty and hunger, gender equality, and maternal health (The Millennium Declaration, 2000).

At the next United Nations Environment Commission, 17 Sustainable Development Goals were determined to be achieved by 2030, with the acceptance of 169 countries, including Turkey (United Nations Department of Economics and Social Affairs, 2016). At the same time, the above-mentioned new global agenda highlights the principle of "equal rights for all people in all parts of the world" by 2030 and expects countries to shape their policies and plans accordingly (Social Benefit Summit, 2016).

The new global goals are policies that do not ignore social, humanitarian, and economic needs while centered on the idea of sustainability. The reason why it is considered more successful than the targets set in the past is that it is more inclusive and holistic. Gender equality, which can be defined as "the equal participation of women and men in all aspects of social life", is one of the most focused goals of the United Nations. Discriminations resulting from gender roles imposed by society limit the development and right to life of women.

The related goal aims to prevent all kinds of discrimination and inequality against girls and women. Working actively within the United Nations, the Women's Unit strives to bring gender equality into the mainstream all over the world. Besides, it is obvious that in societies where women and girls are empowered, their presence creates a multiplier effect and accelerates economic growth and development.

For example, a study conducted by the EU in 2017 showed that female workers are paid 24% less than men. This inequality causes women to not have access to education, health, and social services as easily as men, and to fall into the second place in global competition. Thus, within the scope of sustainable development goals of the United Nations, countries and organizations aimed to close the existing gap between women and men and to ensure equality until 2030. Because almost all over the world, despite working more, women receive less wages, have employment problems, and face many obstacles in reaching working conditions befitting human dignity.

The United Nations has set sub-targets to end discrimination and all kinds of unequal attitudes toward women, and to eliminate all kinds of abuse and violence in public and private spheres. In this context, informing boys about gender equality from an early age and teaching respect for the opposite gender is the most important goal at the micro level.

Logistics Sector in Turkey

Due to its location, the logistics sector is at the center of all transformations within production and consumption and is updated every day. In the global context, the logistics industry is expected to reach a value of 12 trillion dollars by 2025. Likewise, the rapidly growing logistics sector in Turkey is expected to reach 400 billion dollars.

Today, every item used in the home or workplace is definitely included in the logistics system, is stored, transported in trucks, and reaches individuals. Turkey, which is of great geopolitical importance, is of vital importance for Europe and the region both in terms of production and distribution. Because, every day in Turkey, approximately 450 thousand trucks carry loads. More than 400 warehouse companies and more than 200 shipping sites/truck garages support Turkey's logistics ecosystem (Arslan, 2021).

Turkey is in a key position in line with commercial dynamics due to the potential of the region it is in the center of, especially in Central Asia and the Black Sea Region (Bayramoğlu, 2014). The logistics sector also has strategic importance in the context of the development of Turkey's economy. In the report published by YASED in 2012, opportunities are increasing day by day with its suitable geographical location, manpower potential, and cost structure. More than 500 thousand people are employed in the developing sector, including the sub-markets (Afatoğlu, 2013).

The transportation and logistics industry has traditionally been defined as male-dominated (Turnbull, 2013) and it is mentioned by the Women in Supply Chain Group (2010) that male employees are preferred because it is a sector that requires strength and endurance. This rate is 22% on average in European Union countries. In the report published by Wilat, Turkey is one of the countries with the highest gender gap among OECD countries. Another comment by Wilat is that with 46%, male leaders support male talents rather than female talents. Besides, 38% of women employees on maternity rest find it difficult to find a place in the sector after leaving their jobs.

3 Methodology

In this research, six logistics companies listed in BIST 100 were selected to examine policies and practices in line with Gender Equality. The main reason for choosing the logistics industry as a sample is that it is considered male-dominated. In addition, it has been examined which policies the institutions focus on to achieve SDG 5, one of the sustainable development goals.

Annual and semi-annual human resources and sustainability reports prepared by the human resources departments of logistics companies for publication on the Public Disclosure Platform (KAP) were systematically examined in detail for 1 year (August 2022–August 2023). BIST is the abbreviation of Borsa İstanbul. It is the stock market formed by the combination of the Istanbul Stock Exchange (ISE), the Futures and Options Market (VOB), and the Istanbul Gold Exchange (IAB), where stocks are traded.

The three sub-objectives of SDG 5 included in the research are explained below: 5.1 (End all forms of discrimination against all women and girls everywhere), 5.5 (Ensure women's full and effective participation and equal opportunities for leadership at all levels of decision-making in political, economic, and public life), 5.6.b (Enhance the use of enabling technology, in particular information and communications technology, to promote the empowerment of women).

In particular, the main reason for selecting these three sub-targets was to evaluate the perception of companies serving in the logistics sector in the context of gender equality. The logistics companies included in the research were coded as LOG1, LOG2, LOG3, LOG4, LOG5, and LOG6.

The sustainability and human resources reports of the six logistics companies included in the research were examined in detail, and by making frequency analysis, which sub-target was emphasized the most and the missing aspects were revealed. The main reason for choosing the logistics sector as the sample in this study is that it has a male-dominated perception by nature. Thus, it aims to set an example for other sectors by raising awareness.

4 Findings

The Sustainability and Human Resources reports published on the Public Disclosure Platform (KAP) of the six logistics companies included in the research were evaluated in terms of SDG 5 Gender Equality. In light of the frequency analysis conducted, below are the sub-targets that each logistics company concentrates on, Table 1.

Besides, sub-targets that companies do not have any project on are also highlighted with the title "the company has no policy on this matter". The six logistics companies selected as the sample are the first six companies of the Logistics sector in Turkey that are traded with the highest value in BIST 100. Thus, it should be noted that a meaningful projection of the sector is presented.

SDG 5.1 "End all forms of discrimination against all women and girls everywhere" is supported and emphasized by 50% of the six logistics companies within their published reports. The remaining three logistics companies did not mention that there is a policy or project to prevent gender discrimination in their organizations.

In continuance, SDG 5.5 "Ensure women's full and effective participation and equal opportunities for leadership at all levels of decision-making in political, economic and public life" was emphasized more with 67%, and 4 of the logistics companies emphasized that female employees can work in any position in their institutions.

Table 1 Frequency analysis results: Policy distributions of logistics companies according to SDG5

Logistic companies	5.1. End all forms of discrimination against all women and girls everywhere	5.5. Ensure women's full and effective participation and equal opportunities for leadership at all levels of decision-making in political, economic, and public life	5.6.b. Enhance the use of enabling technology, in particular information and communications technology, to promote the empowerment of women
LOG1	The company has no policy on this matter.	The company has no policy on this matter.	X
LOG2	X	X	X
LOG3	X	X	X
LOG4	The company has no policy on this matter.	X	X
LOG5	The company has no policy on this matter.	The company has no policy on this matter.	The company has no policy on this matter.
LOG6	X	X	X

Source: The table is prepared by the author

Finally, the most emphasized sub-goal of the research by logistics companies is SDG 5.6.b. (Enhance the use of enabling technology, in particular information and communications technology, to promote the empowerment of women). 83% of the evaluated institutions emphasized the importance of utilizing communication technologies and training for the empowerment of female employees.

5 Discussion

Logistics activities have a very vital function for today's businesses because they are effective in terms of both customer satisfaction and cost reduction. Great efforts are made to ensure that the logistics service continues uninterruptedly, both in our country and in the world. With the importance that the logistics sector has gained in production activities, it has started to attract the attention of different academic disciplines. Similarly, with the increase observed in the number of female employees and managers in this sector, which is actually defined as a male-dominated field, the number of studies with a gender perspective on the sector has also started.

In this context, the related study is significant in terms of determining the deficiencies of women working in the logistics sector in the context of gender equality, one of the sustainable development goals. Although the logistics sector is a disadvantageous sector for women, the increasing level of education of women in the sector and the developments in the business world regarding human rights have led to the employment of more female workers in this sector.

Besides, in the sector where female employees are considered as disadvantaged group, countries and organizations have great responsibilities. In the context of gender equality, it is a fundamental responsibility to achieve 17 development goals signed by 169 countries, including Turkey, by 2030. In the related research, the three most basic sub-targets of SDG 5, which institutions should focus on in order to achieve gender equality, were selected and the current situation was revealed in order to achieve each of them until the targeted year.

As a result of the analyzed reports of the six logistics companies included in the research, it has been observed that most of the institutions do not actively produce projects and policies in order to prevent discrimination between men and women employees. Ensuring equality of opportunity in the logistics sector, which is defined as male-dominated, and enabling women to reach their full potential directly affects the success of the sector.

When SDG 5.5 is analyzed, it is seen that only four of the six logistics companies produce policies. In the context of gender, it is very important for women to work in all positions in organizations and to prevent the glass ceiling. Institutions should ensure that women's role models are formed for the future of the sector and that they set an example for young people.

A study conducted by BI Norwegian Business School with the participation of 3000 managers revealed that women are more suitable for managerial positions than men, and they have superior leadership qualities. Managers were examined in five categories, including initiative and clear communication, openness to different ideas and ability to innovate, sociability and supportiveness, systematic management, and ability to set goals. In four of the five categories, female managers were found to be more successful than men.

When the SDG 5.6.b sub-target is analyzed, it is seen in the reports that five out of six companies show an educational approach to the sector's information and communication technologies in order to empower women. Interestingly, companies that aim to develop female employees for the benefit of their organizations do not work as actively when it comes to women's leadership and gender equality.

Women have a major role in today's workforce, especially in other sectors. The fact that sectors with a male-dominated perception, such as logistics, are deprived of the leverage effect created by women, essentially harms the logistics sector itself. In order to eliminate this disadvantage and to make women role models in the sector more visible, the recommendations listed below should be taken into account by institutions and managers.

(1) Guidance and training should be planned for female employees to adapt to sectoral digitalization and new technologies, and employees should be supported accordingly. (2) Foreign language, time management, and specialization are the most vital skill needs in the logistics sector, and universities and vocational schools need to develop their curricula on these subjects. (3) Organizations in the logistics sector should cooperate with universities or vocational schools to develop the skills of their female employees. (4) Making gender equality a fundamental part of the business strategy, equal pay for women and men, and applying a flexible work schedule to mothers can be considered as the first steps to achieve gender equality.

In this study conducted by Gallup (2015), 41% of employees with female managers and 35% of employees with male managers were highly committed to their managers. The positive impact of women leaders in business life should be taken into account. Today, with digitalization, the power-based ways of doing business in the logistics industry have been shelved. At least as much as male managers, female managers can be active in the information and technology-based logistics sector.

One of the primary purposes of this research is to highlight that women employees in the logistics sector, which has started to work based on technology, will be at least as successful as male employees. Because today, the industry is no longer dependent on manpower and is no longer male-dominated. In the context of gender equality in their companies, they should be aware of this fact early, and their organizations should review their human resources and sustainability policies. Otherwise, it is inevitable that they will not be able to keep up with the sectoral change and transformation.

Competing Interests The authors have no conflicts of interest to declare that are relevant to the content of this chapter.

References

Afatoğlu, A. (2013). Lojistiğin 2013 Atılımı. Turkishtime, Mayıs 1–25.

Arslan, A. (2021) Dijitalleşmeyle Birlikte Nakliye Sektöründe Artık Eskisi Gibi Olmayacak 9 Alışkanlık. Medium.

Akgül, U. (2010). A.Ü. Dil ve Tarih Coğrafya Fakültesi Dergisi. Sürdürülebilir Kalkınma: Uygulamalı Antropolojinin Eylem Alanı. Sayı: 24.

Bayramoğlu, K. (2014). Lojistik Sektörü Devlet Politikaları ile Desteklenmeli-Nilgün Keleş ile Röportaj. Ekovitrin, Ocak, 136–141.

Gallup (2015). WIN/Gallup International's Global Survey Shows Three in Five Willing to Fight for Their Country.

Millennium Declaration. (2000). http://www.un.org.tr/includes/files/Binyil02.pdf

Social Benefit Summit. (2016) İstanbul; Sürdürülebilir Kalkınma İçin Küresel Hedefler. http://www.sgsistanbul.org/surdurulebilir-kalkinma-hedefleri

Şentürk, B. (2016). Türkiye'de Kadın Emeğine Genel Bir Bakış. *Akademik Sosyal Araştırmalar Dergisi, 4*(31), 194–209.

United Nations Department of Economic and Social Affairs. (2016). *Transforming our world: The 2030 agenda for sustainable development.* https://sustainabledevelopment.un.org/post2015/transformingourworld).

Turnbull, P. (2013). *Promoting the employment of women in the transport sector–Obstacles and policy options.* International Labour Organization, Working Paper (No. 298).

Türkiye Kalkınma Bakanlığı. (2012). Türkiye'de Sürdürülebilir Kalkınma Raporu: Geleceği Sahiplenmek. Ankara.

Urhan, B. (2016). Kadın Emeği ve Toplumsal Cinsiyet, Toplumsal Cinsiyet Tartışmaları (der.) F. Sayılıgil, 121–152, Dipnot Yayınları: Ankara.

Women in Supply Chain Group. (2010). *The unseen gender in transport and logistics: Making women-visible.* Erişim Adresi. https://twfhk.org/sites/default/files/u21/TheUnseenGenderInLogisticsAndTransport.pdf

YASED. (2012). 2023 Hedefleri Yolunda Bilgi ve İletişim Teknolojileri. Eylül 1–168.

A Touch of Circular Economy on Luxury Fashion Industry: Analyzing the Second-Hand Luxury Fashion Rental Platform in Turkey

Özge Kirezli and Muteber Tuzcu

1 Introduction

The fashion industry is one of the largest contributors to environmental degradation, with its unsustainable practices and excessive waste production (Niinimäki et al., 2020). Not only the fast fashion industry (Bick et al., 2018; Pal & Gander, 2018) but also the luxury fashion industry (Joy et al., 2012) adopts the linear economy principles, which can cause irreversible changes in the environment. The linear economy model adopts the principle that raw materials are extracted from their sources and used in production, and then disposed of without recycling (Ellen MacArthur Foundation, 2015). It mostly focuses on unsustainable business models such as overuse of environmental resources, environmental waste, and unhealthy production practices as well (Bocken & Short, 2021). These practices depend on take-make-consume-waste principles. The circular economy model, on the other hand, is seen as the system solution to eliminate the degradation of the linear economy model (Ellen MacArthur Foundation, 2015). The circular economy is a model that consists of the actions of reducing the use of raw materials, reuse of waste materials, and recycling (Liu et al. 2017). The approach is also based on three fundamental principles – reduce, reuse, and recycle – by extending the lifetime of products (Faria et al., 2020; Kirchherr et al., 2017). The most basic way to define a circular economy is maximizing environmental, societal, and economic benefits by minimizing waste (Murray et al., 2015). Depending on this definition, there is a high correlation

Ö. Kirezli (✉)
Yeditepe University, Istanbul, Turkey
e-mail: ozge.kirezli@yeditepe.edu.tr

M. Tuzcu
Boğaziçi University, Istanbul, Turkey
e-mail: muteber.tuzcu@bogazici.edu.tr

N. Ketenci (ed.), *Transition to the Circular Economy Model*, CSR, Sustainability, Ethics & Governance, https://doi.org/10.1007/978-3-031-52700-5_6

between sustainable consumption and circular economy practices. These two constructs cannot be separated because underlying notions are related to each other (Pieroni et al., 2019).

A growing interest in the second-hand fashion industry market might be the base for the transition to circular economy practices (Persson & Hinton, 2023). Academicians have not stood idle to the transaction and its business models, its impacts, and its reflection on customers. Most of the research focuses on mainly opportunities and barriers of second-hand fashion products, consumer behavior, and disposal activities, while few studies have tried to understand a circular economy approach in the non-brand-new luxury fashion business models (Weber, 2018). The paper aims to explore second-hand luxury fashion rental services' business models in Turkey via the Ecocanvas model. The chapter continues with a literature review, which narrows down from circular economy and sustainability practices in the fashion industry to second-hand markets and eventually how innovative approaches in the luxury second-hand market evolve the existing business models. Then, the methodology is delineated. Findings are designed under three parts: a general look at the second-hand luxury fashion industry in Turkey, the overall process of second-hand luxury fashion rental platforms, and an application of The "Ecocanvas" (Circular Business Canvas Model) analysis of second-hand luxury fashion rental platforms. Lastly, the chapter closes with a comprehensive conclusion.

2 Literature Review

Circular Economy and Sustainability Practices in Fashion Industry

The concept of circular economy and sustainability has gained momentum in both academic and non-academic environments (Geissdoerfer et al., 2017; Pieroni et al., 2019). The United Nations defines sustainability as *"meeting the needs of the present without compromising the ability of future generations to meet their own needs"* (https://www.un.org/en/academic-impact/sustainability). Three dimensions of sustainability are economic, social, and environmental (Purvis et al., 2018). Circular economy practices reinforce the limit of environmental sustainability by emphasizing innovative business models, creating trustable relationships with business ecosystems and profit (Jia et al., 2020). The fundamental and crucial common point of these two concepts is their motivation, which is decreasing environmental pollution through innovative business models with the cooperation of actors in the ecosystem (Geissdoerfer et al., 2017). In recent years, the fashion industry has increasingly embraced circular economy and sustainability practices. This trend has become prevalent in the field (Charnley et al., 2022).

Niinimäki et al. (2020) refer to the circular economy approach in the fashion industry, as aiming to expand the use of products and develop a more sustainable and circular system. Circularity includes concepts such as sharing, renting, repairing, renovating, and recycling existing products for as long as possible. With this approach, the life cycle of products is extended; so waste is minimized. Similarly, Jia et al. (2020) emphasize the need for collaborative relationship development including all the related stakeholders to ensure circular economy practices and sustainability in the fashion industry.

Second-Hand: As Sustainable and Innovative Business Models in Fashion Industry

Increasing concern for the environmental issue makes humanity search for different business models to be part of innovative solutions (Faria et al., 2020). Customer awareness, community, and competitor pressure also make companies more sensitive to offering sustainable business practices (Jia et al., 2020). In addition to these, new business models for circularity and sustainability are crucial to achieving and maintaining competitive strategy (Pieroni et al., 2019). Creating a sustainable business model involves outlining how an organization delivers value to customers and stakeholders while maintaining natural, social, and economic resources beyond its limits. This approach aims at communicating the company's commitment to sustainability while ensuring it captures economic benefits (Schaltegger et al., 2015, Campos Franco et al., 2019) and social well-being (Yawar & Kuula, 2021). Furthermore, previous research indicated that reusing textile products has more advantages than recycling (Farrant et al., 2010; Zamani et al., 2017; Charnley et al., 2022).

Pieroni et al. (2019) identified different innovative business models in the circular economy and sustainability business ecosystem. Access-based consumption, industrial symbiosis, and alternative ownership methods are innovative solutions to help companies to be part of a sustainable environment (Pieroni et al., 2019).

Moreover, Fernandes et al. (2018) studied the differences and similarities between circular and collaborative business models in the second-hand fashion industry. They classified business models based on how customers acquire textile products from these companies. Two types of models were analyzed: renting and reselling. They also indicated that renting activities are mostly circular business activities while reselling practices are collaborative business activities. The authors claim that collaborative consumption is one of the sub-practices of the circular economy business. These two business models play crucial roles in minimizing the usage of natural resources by increasing the product life cycle (Fernandes et al., 2018).

Second-hand fashion mobile applications and their business model were also investigated by Faria et al. (2020). Selling, buying, and borrowing are the main activities of circular economy platforms. The scholars identified key barriers to shopping and loaning activities on such platforms. Low demand for these second-hand businesses is one of the main obstacles. In addition, the barrier, social, and environmental considerations are not taken into account in the prices (Faria et al. 2020).

Additionally, Charnley et al. (2022) identified prospects in the second-hand fashion industry as heightened consciousness about environmental issues, efficient product categorization, and attractive deals while avoiding deceitful item descriptions. Furthermore, innovative shopping encounters and offering assurances for products were highlighted as further possibilities to explore in this industry.

Luxury Second-Hand Markets: As Innovative Business Solution

The reason for changes in consumers' behavior and fancy prices of luxury brand new products makes the second-hand luxury market attractive. Thus, the second-hand luxury market has been booming. Frequent fashion item turnover also supports luxury resale or renting markets (Kessous & Valette-Florence, 2019).

The luxury fashion industry has been criticized because of its harmful manufacturing practices on animals and the environment, engaging factory worker abuse, and unethical marketing tactics as unsold stock (Kerr & Landry, 2017). Such unsustainable practices in this industry challenge the three pillars of sustainability. On the other hand, luxury items are associated with high quality (Campos Franco et al., 2019) which makes them be used longer than fast fashion textile products. This characteristic can contribute positively to sustainability by adopting a value-creation model that is centered on the principles of circular economy (Dominguez & Bhatti, 2022) when owners of these products no longer want to use them, these people can resell or rent them online platforms because their high quality enables to give them a second chance. Also, new owners would prefer to choose them because of psychological and fulfillment needs including social climbing and status-seeking, eco-friendly consumption habits, and brand heritage and vintage fashion trends (Kessous & Valette-Florence, 2019).

Business Model Canvas in the Circular Economy Perspective: Emergence of Ecocanvas

Osterwalder and Pigneur (2013) introduce the Business Model Canvas, which is a tool for contemporary businesses to be guided following innovation in the competitive business environment (Pollard et al., 2023; Murray & Scuotto, 2016). It includes fundamental elements named as key partners, key activities, key resources, value proposition, customer relationships, customer segments, communication channels, cost structure, and revenue streams (Murray & Scuotto, 2016; Teece, 2010, Chesbrough, 2004, Zott & Amit, 2010; Magretta, n.d.). Richardson (2008) mentioned that these fundamental elements are grouped into three value categories:

value proposition including value proposition, customer segments, and relationships, creation and delivery including key activities, key resources, channels, and key partners, and capture including cost structure and revenue.

Dominguez and Bhatti (2022) believe that the conventional business model canvas should be expanded to encompass sustainability and social considerations as vital components of a company's operations. Visualization of the Business Model Canvas in the circular economy ecosystem could also bring several benefits such as identifying which pre-used material is reusable or not, showing the circularity of materials and interactive relation among such materials properly (Nußholz, 2018).

The Business Model Canvas is also issued in terms of circular economy context (Pollard et al., 2023; Braun et al., 2021; Uçar et al., 2020; Manninen et al., 2018; Urbinati et al., 2017; Lewandowski, 2016). Some studies among them also targeted the expansion of the traditional model business canvas (Manninen et al., 2018; Lewandowski, 2016). However, a visual representation of the Business Model Canvas in the related literature has not been presented in previous studies (Nußholz, 2018). Pollard et al. (2023) proposed a new Business Model Canvas for the electrical and electronic manufacturing sector in the circular economy context. Circular Economy Business Model Canvas is directed at electrical and electronic business advantages for value proposition, creation, and capture (Pollard et al., 2023). Uçar et al. (2020) focused on a new business canvas with three Rs approaches: reduce, reuse, and recycle. They highlight that the innovative canvas in a circular economy context is enabled and triggered by digital technologies to have accurate value propositions, key resources, and revenue streams (Uçar et al., 2020).

Lewandowski (2016) has attempted to expand the traditional Business Model Canvas for fitting into circular economy practices. The take-back system and adoption factors were added to the new canvas. For example, some fashion companies employ a take-back system as reverse logistics. In addition to this, due to easier transformation to circular economy principles requires adoption factors both internally and externally (Lewandowski, 2016).

The term eco-canvas was introduced in the related field by Daou et al. (2020). The new term is built on three triple perspectives: economic and legal, environmental, and social dimensions. Ecocanvas consists of 12 blocks: Environmental Foresight, Social foresight, Needs and Challenges, Customer Segment, Circular Value Chain, Key Resources, Cost Structure, Stakeholders Relationship, Communication and Sales, Unique Circular Value Proposition, Revenue Streams, and Circular Business Model & Innovation. Each of these blocks is explained according to Daou et al.'s (2020) study. Environmental and Social foresight act as upcoming trends in these areas which might have a substantial influence on the business. Needs and challenges arise from both micro-environmental and macro-environmental forces that the business tries to fulfill these gaps in the industry. The customer segment refers to the main characteristics of the clients served by the company (Osterwalder & Pigneur, 2013). The circular value chain clarifies whoever will be affected by the business, as the main stakeholders. Key resources are identified as the total set of tangible and intangible resources in the business processes, starting from the raw material to the disposal step (Garcia et al., 2012; Osterwalder

& Pigneur, 2013). Cost structure refers to all kinds of costs incurred in the necessary operations. Stakeholders' relationships try to dissolve the nature and dynamics of the relationships with the stakeholders. Communication and sales indicate the alternative methods and mediums to relate to the stakeholders in terms of communication and sales channels. The unique circular value proposition clarifies what a consumer acquires by choosing the company's offering (Osterwalder & Pigneur, 2013). Revenue streams identify the probable sources of cash for the business. Lastly, the circular business model and innovation define the key features of the circular business model (Daou et al., 2020).

3 Methodology

This study adopted a qualitative research design to deepen the understanding of alternative luxury second-hand fashion business models and companies' sustainability communication patterns. We believe that as an emerging country, Turkey is in its initial phases of experiencing and adopting novel circular economy business models, that's why studying this phenomenon requires a qualitative research plan rather than a quantitative one (Yin, 2018; Eisenhardt & Martin, 2000). As for the research approach, a multiple case study methodology is preferred. The reason for that choice can be justified, as cited in the literature, multiple cases are beneficial to provide a more reliable and comprehensive look rather than single cases, aiding to detect the unique value propositions among different business models (Eisenhardt, 1989; Yin, 2018).

A purposive sampling strategy is utilized to deliberately select cases (platforms) to visualize different business models (such as renting or selling) to include all aspects. For that study, global luxury fashion manufacturers are neglected. All the selected cases provide luxury fashion renting or second-hand selling as their only business model.

4 Findings

In that section, the second-hand luxury fashion industry in Turkey is to be analyzed as giving birth to new business models, thanks to the circular and sharing economy perspective. The findings are presented in three headings. First, a general look at high-end fashion is provided, as to how the novel shift in non-linear practices is affecting the whole eco-system. Then, the overall process of second-hand luxury fashion rental platforms is examined, as we believe the perfect fit for sharing economy's effect on this industry. Last, the Daou et al.'s (2020) "Ecocanvas" Analysis: Circular Business Canvas Model Analysis of Second Hand Luxury Fashion Rental Platforms is performed, which is a renewed form of Osterwalder and Pigneur's

(2013) Business Canvas Model. The Ecocanvas is analyzed under 12 dimensions; Environmental Foresight, Social foresight, Needs and Challenges, Customer Segment, Circular Value Chain, Key Resources, Cost Structure, Stakeholders Relationship, Communication and Sales, Unique Circular Value Proposition, Revenue Streams and Circular Business Model & Innovation.

A General Look to Second-Hand Luxury Fashion Industry in Turkey

Second-hand markets are not a new trend in the fashion industry, but up to recent years, consumers were used to considering second-hand fashion items only for special occasions, like weddings and prom. However, the sharing economy principle also triggered customers' and entrepreneurs' attention to applying this item to luxury fashion. In that manner, new business models emerged in second-hand luxury fashion, which either focused on reselling or renting high-end fashion items.

In the last 3 years, the fashion industry has shown great interest in circular and sharing economy practices. One driver can be attached to economic downturns, which leads consumers to consider the monetary value of their possessions. Another driver is the new generation's renewed understanding of second-hand markets. In other words, a "second-hand item" might be used to accuse the items of not being new, but the new trend of "pre-loved item" indicates a strong emotional bond, especially with luxury possessions, whereby emotional value is highlighted. Although no genuine act was visible in the Turkish market, global luxury fashion producers, such as Selfridges, the British store chain serving the luxury segment, sell vintage second-hand products with its "RESELLFRIDGES" project (Yorulmaz Ozsumer, 2021). The luxury giant Kering Group, which includes brands such as Gucci, Alexander McQueen, and Balenciaga, has acquired a 5% stake in French high-end vintage sales platform Vestiaire Collective, as well (Yorulmaz Ozsumer, 2021).

Although luxury fashion brands are relatively more hesitant about sharing economy practices, several new ventures emerged in luxury fashion, which symbolizes the industry's enthusiasm. Due to the scale of operations, the most successful ones can be counted as Davet Cok Elbisem Yok (DCEY), Authentic Seconds, Seasons & Stories, Original Seconds, Peony, Unomoi, and Modaloop. Although they might be serving the same customer need, of acquiring second-hand luxury fashion items at affordable prices in an environmentally sustainable way, these platforms differ on several bases. The main differentiative points are stated as: item provision mode (in three forms; re-selling, renting, and both), product ownership (taking inventory or no inventory), distribution channel (online platform only, online platform, and physical store), and revenue streams (subscription or commission based).

All the platforms are contributing to the core aim of supporting an alternative to buying a brand new item, such as buying second-hand luxury fashion items, renting them on a stated time frame, or a combination of offering both items for reselling or renting. Some platforms are holding an inventory of products, which comes with a considerable cost, whereas peer-to-peer lending is another approach by only serves as a medium to meet two parties. Most of these practices are doing business in online platforms; however, an increasing trend is seen as having at least one showroom to offer users to physically see and try on items. Among all these dimensions, we believe the most dramatic point is about revenue streams. In the subscription-based revenue system, companies request a monthly fee from the users, to rent a stated number of items. In the commission-based revenue system, the user pays the price per item and the lender sets the price, but gets %50–60 of the price, on average.

The Overall Process of Second-Hand Luxury Fashion Rental Platforms

We believe that sharing economy practice best fits with second-hand luxury fashion rental platforms for two reasons. First, both re-sell and renting extend the life cycle of the items; however, it is the renting mode that increases the full utilization of the item by different users, which is sharing it with the others. The second reason is the more complicated and interesting business model, renting platforms have, is noteworthy to examine in detail.

The platforms offer its beneficiaries a full service – starting with the choice of fashion items to lending these items in a neat form to other users. These platforms manage the whole operation and users don't have to deal with anything. If the products to be rented are suitable for display on the platform, professional photo shooting is done and uploaded to the website. When the users make the reservation for renting, processes such as dry cleaning, tailoring, and delivery to the next user, belong to the platform. However, there exist two major differences: product ownership and revenue streams. One wave of the platforms takes ownership of the products, from the previous owners and lists these items in the platforms, by controlling the authenticity of the items, professionally photo shooting, dry cleaning, tailoring, setting the price, and delivering the items. The other wave is requesting the listing of the items from the lenders and either directly sending the items to new users or the platform. All extra burdens, like dry cleaning, tailoring, and delivery charges, are fulfilled by the platforms, like the first type.

As for the second differentiating factor, revenue streams are considerably different. The first approach is commission-based. The users are charged for the item they select. The platform gets the whole payment in both cases, but if the ownership of the items belongs to other users, 40–50% of the total price is deducted as commission and the earned fee is deposited to the lender. Table 1 illustrates the "Ecocanvas" analysis.

Table 1 The "Ecocanvas" analysis: circular business canvas model analysis of second-hand luxury fashion rental platforms

Environmental foresight	Circular value chain	Needs/challenges	Unique circular value proposition	Stakeholder relationship	Customer segments	Social foresight
Traditional textile industry's detrimental effect on the environment	Consumers as product providers OR Platform offering products Consumers as beneficiaries Carriers & Delivery companies Dry cleaning service providers Tailors Professional photographers	Need to come up with sustainable solutions for the fashion industry by using sharing economy principles, but not forcing people to give up a particular lifestyle – growing awareness and demand for sharing economy practices in other industries (carpooling, room sharing, swapping)	Reflecting the desire for innovation and variety in consumers' wardrobes with a proactive and sustainable philosophy without compromising the joy of luxury fashion	Trustworthy and close relationship with consumers prioritizing customer retention Direct and transparent relationship with carriers and delivery firms, dry cleaning services, and tailors as collaborators	People who favor sustainable fashion practices, but not giving up their passion for luxury fashion as well. The target segment is a perfect combination of sustainability-conscious and luxury fashion variety-seeking consumer	Consumers being more sensitive and demanding to industry's sustainability practices Consumers have a prejudice against the second-hand fashion industry due to hygiene-related issues A growing trend towards leaner lifestyles such as frugalists.
	Key resources			*Communication & sales*		
Environmental impact	High-end & Premium fashion items Platform to meet providers and beneficiaries Payment processing and order taking like technological infrastructure Encouraging consumers to participate in collaborative consumption practice through the website and social media Effective communication and coordination with collaborators (carriers and delivery firms, dry cleaning services, and tailors)			Social media engagement (Instagram and LinkedIn posts) Press releases (Co-founders interviews on sustainable fashion movement and practices Website blogs (either on sustainable fashion topics or user experiences and photos)		*Social impact*

(continued)

Table 1 (continued)

Environmental foresight	Circular value chain	Needs/challenges	Unique circular value proposition	Stakeholder relationship	Customer segments	Social foresight
Less textile waste Extended use of items. Decreased carbon footprint	*Cost structure*		*Revenue streams*			Consumers find value through sharing not buying. Being a part of a like-minded community
	Fixed costs (labor, rent, and administrative costs) Variable cost (carriers and delivery, dry cleaning, photo shooting, tailors, ironing)		Commission-based (%40–50 of the item's price) OR Subscription-based (monthly fees)			
	Circular business model and innovation					
	Consumers share their wardrobes and enjoy high-end fashion items by not paying the full price and extending the life cycle of the items by creating less textile waste.					

Source: The table is prepared by the authors

Environmental Foresight

The fashion industry, as one of the most pollutant industries, is forming a huge burden on nature (Dissanayake et al., 2019; Goworek, 2011; Birwistle & Moore, 2007). Hence, the fashion industry's environmental effects need to be realized twofold. The first one is on the production processes. The industry is held responsible for producing 8–10% of global CO_2 emissions, which corresponds to 4–5 billion tons annually (Ninnimaki et al., 2020; UN, n.d.; Quantis, 2018). Also, industrial water pollution from treatment and dyeing is stated as the reason for oceanic microplastic pollution (Ninnimaki et al., 2020; Kant, 2012). The second one focuses on the post-consumption phases, turning to textile waste either to be burned in landfills or unsold, more than 92 million tons per year (Ninnimaki et al., 2020; Goworek, 2011). It's also estimated that $190 million worth of clothing ends up in landfills each year (https://modaloop.co/surdurulebilir-moda/). The 2016 McKinsey report explains that three-fifths of all clothing items are incinerated or thrown away within a year of being produced (https://modaloop.co/surdurulebilir-moda/).

Social Foresights

This challenge brings us to the second issue, which is the heightened interest of consumers in sustainability practices. Not only in the fashion industry, but in several other industries customers acknowledged the inevitable truth of scarce resources. Accelerating interest of governments, companies, and non-governmental organizations on sustainability is increasing the awareness and interest levels of consumers each day. Sensitivity toward, especially environmental sustainability escalated, hence, rather than purchasing new products, emerging business models try to encourage consumers to reconsider their approach to purchasing. Instead of leaning for brand new items, renting, swapping, or sharing practices are visible in the transportation and accommodation sectors. So, in that manner, the fashion industry needs to serve to meet the new demands of these fashion and environmental-conscious consumers. However, second-hand markets come with an inevitable problem of hygiene. Especially in the luxury fashion rental business, consumers will have substantial concerns about the hygiene of the items they purchase.

A novel niche segment in the market is named "frugalista" or "frugalist", which is defined as "people who live a frugal lifestyle but stay fashionable and healthy by swapping clothes, buying second-hand, growing their produce, etc." (Safire, 2008, https://www.nytimes.com/2008/11/23/magazine/23wwln-safire-t.html). When we check some important facts about the fashion industry, the emergence of such a segment is no surprise. The value of unused clothes in wardrobes is thought to be around $40 billion (https://modaloop.co/surdurulebilir-moda/). In other words, most optimistically, if the industry can find a way to decrease the negative impact on nature, without consumers' full devotion to sustainability practices, the big picture will be incomplete.

Needs and Challenges

The upcoming concerns in the environmental and social arena gave birth to new needs and challenges. The new circular fashion tries to pave a novel way to contribute to sustainable fashion by giving life to overconsumption, products that are waiting with tags in our closets or that have only been worn a few times and thrown away. The market needs to come up with sustainable but fashionable solutions, not forcing people to give up a particular lifestyle. It is evident that whole platforms emphasize how customers might contribute to the system by renting the items, not buying, but also looking good and stylish in these items. Also, a rising trend in the market is the consumers embracing collaborative consumption practices. The new "collaborative consumption" idea introduces the consumer that it is not mandatory to permanently own the item, but favors temporary access to products and not abandoning the hedonic experience of using high-end fashion products.

Customer Segment

The target consumer, for this business model, is no longer favoring trendy and fast fashion, which fosters over-consumption. The rising customer segment for this sustainability fashion practice is already aware of sustainability and has environmental consciousness and is willing to integrate these favorable attitudes into consumption habits. Yet, one important characteristic of the target segment is the fashion consciousness. That's why it is crucial to stress that the target consumer is composed of people who favor sustainable fashion practices, but not giving up their passion for luxury fashion as well. Second-hand luxury fashion consumers are a bit complicated to be profiled. Though gender (female intensive) and income level (middle-high and high-income level intensive) are useful to define the segment, age seems to vary. In that manner psychographic characteristics serve as unique characteristics of these platforms: high-end fashion involvement, innovativeness, value consciousness, and sustainability awareness. One platform defined its customer segment as individuals who are passionate about fashion and follow the latest trends without compromising environmental and economic concerns.

Key Resources

Key resources are identified as the combination of tangible and intangible resources the company owns, starting from the raw material to the disposal of the finished items to deliver value to the target segment (Garcia et al., 2012; Osterwalder & Pigneur, 2013). In that manner, acquisition of high-end and authentic fashion items, preparing an easy-to-use online platform to meet providers and beneficiaries, order-taking and payment processing technological infrastructure, encouraging and convincing people to involve in these collaborative consumption practices in multiple media, and establishing and maintaining communication & coordination with ecosystem collaborators can be counted as key resources of these rental platforms.

Circular Value Chain

It is vital to delineate the full set of stakeholders that are affected and can influence the whole business, besides clarifying the key resources (Daou et al., 2020). In that manner, in these platforms, the consumers are either acting as a user/beneficiaries or a provider of luxury fashion items. The platforms need to be in contact with several collaborators, such as carriers & delivery companies to transmit the items to beneficiaries, dry cleaning services to ensure the hygiene of the items, tailors to offer customized temporary solutions for the items, and professional photographers to present high-quality images of the items.

Cost Structure

Forecasting the costs of the related activities is needed for the sustainability of the operations. Hence, in the basic sense costs can be divided as fixed and variable. Fixed costs represent the rent of the headquarters, salaries of the key personnel, administrative costs like maintaining the website, and communication expenditures. On the other hand, variable costs include collaborator-associated costs like delivery, dry cleaning, and tailoring operations.

Stakeholders Relationship

The longevity of the business success is heavily dependent on the healthy relationships the company forms, with the diverse stakeholders. The recent paradigm enforces any entity to develop a trust-based and close relationship, namely with the consumers. Hereby it is interesting to underline that consumers also serve as a supplier of items and users of the items. In that sense, retaining customers to ensure satisfaction is a vital issue. In addition, coordination among the various stakeholders, such as carriers & delivery companies, dry cleaning services, and tailors are prioritized to convey the smooth flow of operations to the end user.

Communication and Sales

This part identifies different ways adopted to engage and attract all the stakeholders to fulfill the promised value (Daou et al., 2020). In that manner, these companies adopt three media channels: social media, press releases, and website-integrated blogs. Instagram, Facebook, and LinkedIn posts are the most frequent message delivery channels. Also, press coverage indicates that co-founders are willing to share their stories, motives, and enthusiasm about recent sustainable fashion practices via interviews. The website is not only a sales channel but also a communication channel, providing blogs on diverse topics of sustainable fashion, user experiences, and compelling news.

Unique Circular Value Proposition

A unique circular value proposition clarifies what a consumer acquires by choosing the company's offering (Osterwalder & Pigneur, 2013). Reflecting the desire for innovation and variety in consumers' wardrobes with a proactive and sustainable philosophy without compromising the joy of luxury fashion is the core value proposed to the target segment. It has two major parts. The first one is the extended use of these expensive fashion items, by giving the consumers a chance to refrain from purchasing novel premium fashion items, which are blending economic and environmental benefits. The second one is by this indirect way contributing to environmental sustainability, decreasing textile and accessories waste.

Revenue Streams

This part defines the revenue streams created for the unique value proposed to the market (Daou et al., 2020). This flow includes one main stream: commissions coming from the beneficiaries of the items. The companies are working on an average of 40–50% of the item's price as "commission". Also, subscription-based platforms exist, whereby the platforms are requesting a fixed monthly fee from the users and rent a specified number of (4–5 pieces) items from the platform.

Circular Business Model and Innovation

The key feature of this business model is that the company is not holding any inventory of the items, which means a substantial cost reduction. Instead, consumers share their wardrobes and enjoy high-end fashion items by not paying the full price and extending the life cycle of the items by creating less textile waste, which represents a pure sharing economy practice.

5 Conclusion

Circular economy attracts attention from various stakeholders across diverse industries. It not only directs an alternative to linear business practices, which insensibly damage scarce resources but also paves a way to comprehend the whole marketing world from a new angle, as inspiring sharing, renting, and swapping of the items instead of purchasing. In that manner, this study is designed to track the circular economy's approach to second-hand luxury fashion, as a novel business model of rental platforms. To realize that aim, first, the whole second-hand luxury fashion ecosystem is examined. Then the study focused on second-hand luxury fashion rental platforms, in terms of analyzing the overall process and applying Ecocanvas to these initiatives. The chapter emphasizes three main issues. First, these platforms serve to "reuse" these idle fashion items for other beneficiaries, which creates both economic and environmental value. In their study, Freudenreich and Schaltegger (2020) were referring to circular economy practice's major aims as "extended use", "reuse", and "partial use", whereby reuse means access to, either buying or renting clothing, previously owned by another individual, hence reducing the number of new productions and using the idle products as of extending their life cycle. Second, the revenue streams are interesting, whereby a subscription-based system encourages the users to have an ongoing relationship with other users and the platform. A commission-based system is beneficial for users who are more hesitant about this idea, by cutting a portion of the fee from the total price. In that manner, we believe like in other industries (scooters, cars, games, tv series, tv shows) this subscription-based service is promising. Likewise, one platform founder referred to that system as the "Netflix of fashion". Last, but not least, these platforms are proposing an emotional value attached to sharing of the items besides economic and environmental value. The platforms serve as a liaison for like-minded people having a passion for both fashion and the environment. In that manner, in the platforms, this feeling of "sharing your wardrobe among the sisters" is vastly underlined and prioritized. We believe the future of fashion is in a transition both in the second-hand and new product approach. Producers need to adapt to the changing needs and expectations of fashion consumers, and maybe even fast-fashion producers will be ensuring subscription-based services to the customers to enhance the full utilization of the product and minimize environmental harm. As for second-hand products, especially in luxury fashion, there is a substantial need to encourage the users to share, rent, or swap the items, which would enable economic, emotional, and environmental value.

Competing Interests The authors have no conflicts of interest to declare that are relevant to the content of this chapter.

References

Bick, R., Halsey, E., & Ekenga, C. C. (2018). The global environmental injustice of fast fashion. *Environmental Health, 17*(1). https://doi.org/10.1186/s12940-018-0433-7

Birtwistle, G., & Moore, C. M. (2007). Fashion clothing – Where does it all end up? *International Journal of Retail & Distribution Management, 35*(3), 210–216. https://doi.org/10.1108/09590550710735068

Bocken, N. M. P., & Short, S. W. (2021). Unsustainable business models – Recognising and resolving institutionalised social and environmental harm. *Journal of Cleaner Production, 312*, 127828. https://doi.org/10.1016/j.jclepro.2021.127828

Braun, A.-T., Schöllhammer, O., & Rosenkranz, B. (2021). Adaptation of the business model canvas template to develop business models for the circular economy. *Procedia CIRP, 99*, 698–702. https://doi.org/10.1016/j.procir.2021.03.093

Campos Franco, J., Hussain, D., & McColl, R. (2019). Luxury fashion and sustainability: Looking good together. *Journal of Business Strategy, 41*(4), 55–61. https://doi.org/10.1108/jbs-05-2019-0089

Charnley, F., Knecht, F., Muenkel, H., Pletosu, D., Rickard, V., Sambonet, C., Schneider, M., & Zhang, C. (2022). Can digital technologies increase consumer acceptance of circular business models? The case of second-hand fashion. *Sustainability, 14*(8), 4589. https://doi.org/10.3390/su14084589

Chesbrough, H. W. (2004). Open innovation: The new imperative for creating and profiting from technology. *European Journal of Innovation Management, 7*(4), 325–326. https://doi.org/10.1108/14601060410565074

Daou, A., Mallat, C., Chammas, G., Cerantola, N., Kayed, S., & Saliba, N. A. (2020). The Ecocanvas as a business model canvas for a circular economy. *Journal of Cleaner Production, 258*, 120938. https://doi.org/10.1016/j.jclepro.2020.120938

Dominguez, M. F., & Bhatti, Y. A. (2022). From waste to luxury fashion at Elvis & Kresse: A business model for sustainable and social innovation in the circular economy. *Sustainability, 14*(19), 11805. https://doi.org/10.3390/su141911805

Dissanayake, D., Tilt, C., & Qian, W. (2019). Factors influencing sustainability reporting by Sri Lankan companies. Pacific Accounting Review, 31(1), 84–109.

Ellen MacArthur Foundation. (2015). Circular economy introduction. https://www.ellenmacarthurfoundation.org/topics/circular-economy-introduction/overview

Eisenhardt, K. M., & Martin, J. A. (2000). Dynamic capabilities: what are they?. Strategic management journal, 21(10-11), 1105–1121.

Eisenhardt, K. M. (1989). Building theories from case study research. Academy of management review, 14(4), 532–550.

Faria, R., Lopes, I., Pires, I. M., Marques, G., Fernandes, S., Garcia, N. M., Lucas, J., Jevremović, A., Zdravevski, E., & Trajkovik, V. (2020). Circular economy for clothes using web and mobile technologies – A systematic review and a taxonomy proposal. *Information, 11*(3), 161. https://doi.org/10.3390/info11030161

Farrant, L., Olsen, S. I., & Wangel, A. (2010). Environmental benefits from reusing clothes. *The International Journal of Life Cycle Assessment, 15*(7), 726–736. https://doi.org/10.1007/s11367-010-0197-y

Fernandes, S., Lucas, J., Madeira, M. J., Cruchinho, A., & Honório, I. D. (2018). Circular and collaborative economies as a propulsion of environmental sustainability in the new fashion business models. *Innovation, Engineering and Entrepreneurship*, 925–932. https://doi.org/10.1007/978-3-319-91334-6_127

Freudenreich, B., & Schaltegger, S. (2020). Developing sufficiency-oriented offerings for clothing users: Business approaches to support consumption reduction. *Journal of Cleaner Production, 247*, 119589. https://doi.org/10.1016/j.jclepro.2019.119589

Goworek, H. (2011). Social and environmental sustainability in the clothing industry: a case study of a fair trade retailer. Social Responsibility Journal, 7(1), 74–86.

Garcia, F. A., Marchetta, M. G., Camargo, M., Morel, L., & Forradellas, R. Q. (2012). A framework for measuring logistics performance in the wine industry. *International Journal of Production Economics, 135*(1), 284–298.

Geissdoerfer, M., Savaget, P., Bocken, N. M. P., & Hultink, E. J. (2017). The circular economy – A new sustainability paradigm? *Journal of Cleaner Production, 143*, 757–768. https://doi.org/10.1016/j.jclepro.2016.12.048

Jia, F., Yin, S., Chen, L., & Chen, X. (2020). The circular economy in the textile and apparel industry: A systematic literature review. *Journal of Cleaner Production, 259*, 120728. https://doi.org/10.1016/j.jclepro.2020.120728

Joy, A., Sherry, J. F., Venkatesh, A., Wang, J., & Chan, R. (2012). Fast fashion, sustainability, and the ethical appeal of luxury brands. *Fashion Theory, 16*(3), 273–295. https://doi.org/10.2752/175174112x13340749707123

Kant, R. (2012). Textile dyeing industry an environmental hazard. Natural Science, 04(01), 22–26. https://doi.org/10.4236/ns.2012.41004.

Kerr, J., & Landry, J. (2017). Pulse of the fashion industry. In *Global fashion agenda*. The Boston Consulting.

Kessous, A., & Valette-Florence, P. (2019). "From Prada to Nada": Consumers and their luxury products: A contrast between second-hand and first-hand luxury products. *Journal of Business Research, 102*, 313–327. https://doi.org/10.1016/j.jbusres.2019.02.033

Kirchherr, J., Reike, D., & Hekkert, M. (2017). Conceptualizing the circular economy: An analysis of 114 definitions. *Resources, Conservation and Recycling, 127*, 221–232. https://doi.org/10.1016/j.resconrec.2017.09.005

Lewandowski, M. (2016). Designing the business models for circular economy – Towards the conceptual framework. *Sustainability, 8*(1), 43. https://doi.org/10.3390/su8010043

Liu, L., Liang, Y., Song, Q., & Li, J. (2017). A review of waste prevention through 3R under the concept of circular economy in China. *Journal of Material Cycles and Waste Management, 19*(4), 1314–1323. https://doi.org/10.1007/s10163-017-0606-4

Magretta, J. (n.d.). Why business models matter. *Harvard Business Review*. Retrieved March 20, 2023.

Manninen, K., Koskela, S., Antikainen, R., Bocken, N., Dahlbo, H., & Aminoff, A. (2018). Do circular economy business models capture intended environmental value propositions? *Journal of Cleaner Production, 171*, 413–422. https://doi.org/10.1016/j.jclepro.2017.10.003

Murray, A., & Scuotto, V. (2016). The business model canvas. *Symphonya. Emerging Issues in Management*, 94–109. https://doi.org/10.4468/2015.3.13murray.scuotto

Murray, A., Skene, K., & Haynes, K. (2015). The circular economy: An interdisciplinary exploration of the concept and application in a global context. *Journal of Business Ethics, 140*(3), 369–380. https://doi.org/10.1007/s10551-015-2693-2

Niinimäki, K., Peters, G., Dahlbo, H., Perry, P., Rissanen, T., & Gwilt, A. (2020). The environmental price of fast fashion. *Nature Reviews Earth & Environment, 1*(4), 189–200. https://doi.org/10.1038/s43017-020-0039-9

Nußholz, J. L. K. (2018). A circular business model mapping tool for creating value from prolonged product lifetime and closed material loops. *Journal of Cleaner Production, 197*, 185–194. https://doi.org/10.1016/j.jclepro.2018.06.112

Osterwalder, A., & Pigneur, Y. (2013). *Business model generation a handbook for visionaries, game changers, and challengers*. Wiley.

Pal, R., & Gander, J. (2018). Modelling environmental value: An examination of sustainable business models within the fashion industry. *Journal of Cleaner Production, 184*, 251–263. https://doi.org/10.1016/j.jclepro.2018.02.001

Persson, O., & Hinton, J. B. (2023). Second-hand clothing markets and a just circular economy? Exploring the role of business forms and profit. *Journal of Cleaner Production, 390*, 136139. https://doi.org/10.1016/j.jclepro.2023.136139

Pieroni, M. P. P., McAloone, T. C., & Pigosso, D. C. A. (2019). Business model innovation for circular economy and sustainability: A review of approaches. *Journal of Cleaner Production, 215*, 198–216. https://doi.org/10.1016/j.jclepro.2019.01.036

Pollard, J., Osmani, M., Grubnic, S., Díaz, A. I., Grobe, K., Kaba, A., Ünlüer, Ö., & Panchal, R. (2023). Implementing a circular economy business model canvas in the electrical and electronic manufacturing sector: A case study approach. *Sustainable Production and Consumption, 36*, 17–31. https://doi.org/10.1016/j.spc.2022.12.009

Purvis, B., Mao, Y., & Robinson, D. (2018). Three pillars of sustainability: In search of conceptual origins. *Sustainability Science, 14*(3), 681–695. https://doi.org/10.1007/s11625-018-0627-5

Quantis (2018). Measuring fashion: insights from the environmental impact of the global apparel and footwear industries. Full report and methodological considerations. quantis-intl.com https://quantis-intl.com/measuring-fashionreport.

Richardson, J. (2008). The business model: An integrative framework for strategy execution. Strategic Change, 17(5-6), 133–144.

Safire, W. (2008, November 21). Frugalista. *The New York Times*. https://www.nytimes.com/2008/11/23/magazine/23wwln-safire-t.html

Schaltegger, S., Hansen, E. G., & Lüdeke-Freund, F. (2015). Business models for sustainability. *Organization & Environment, 29*(1), 3–10. https://doi.org/10.1177/1086026615599806

Sürdürülebilir Moda. Modaloop. (n.d.). https://modaloop.co/surdurulebilir-moda/

Teece, D. J. (2010). Business models, business strategy and innovation. *Long Range Planning, 43*(2–3), 172–194. https://doi.org/10.1016/j.lrp.2009.07.003

Uçar, E., Dain, M.-A. L., & Joly, I. (2020). Digital technologies in circular economy transition: Evidence from case studies. *Procedia CIRP, 90*, 133–136. https://doi.org/10.1016/j.procir.2020.01.058

United Nations. (n.d.). *Sustainability*. United Nations. Retrieved March 21, 2023, from https://www.un.org/en/academic-impact/sustainability

Urbinati, A., Chiaroni, D., & Chiesa, V. (2017). Towards a new taxonomy of circular economy business models. *Journal of Cleaner Production, 168*, 487–498. https://doi.org/10.1016/j.jclepro.2017.09.047

Weber, S. (2018). A circular economy approach in the luxury fashion industry: A case study of Eileen fisher. *Sustainable Luxury*, 127–160. https://doi.org/10.1007/978-981-13-0623-5_7

Yawar, S. A., & Kuula, M. (2021). Circular economy and second-hand firms: Integrating ownership structures. *Cleaner Logistics and Supply Chain, 2*, 100015. https://doi.org/10.1016/j.clscn.2021.100015

Yorulmaz Özsümer, S. (2021, December 11). *İkinci El Moda akımı neden yükselişte?: Vogue Türkiye*. Vogue. https://vogue.com.tr/moda/ikinci-el-moda-akimi-neden-yukseliste

Yin, R. K. (2018). Case study research and applications (Vol. 6). Thousand Oaks, CA: Sage.

Zamani, B., Sandin, G., & Peters, G. M. (2017). Life cycle assessment of clothing libraries: Can collaborative consumption reduce the environmental impact of fast fashion? *Journal of Cleaner Production, 162*, 1368–1375. https://doi.org/10.1016/j.jclepro.2017.06.128

Zott, C., & Amit, R. (2010). Business model design: An activity system perspective. *Long Range Planning, 43*(2–3), 216–226. https://doi.org/10.1016/j.lrp.2009.07.004

Can Luxury Be Sustainable and Still Create Value for a Sustainable Future?

Aslı Tolunay and Fulya Midilli Muskara

1 Introduction

While our planet's scarce resources are gradually eroding and consumers are becoming more concerned about their spending's detrimental impacts (Sun et al. 2021), especially on the environment, the number of global brands that are becoming conscious of their corporate obligations and are introducing new strategies for a sustainable and better world are increasing (Cuomo et al., 2019).

In a similar fashion, luxury industry, which is growing steadily, is facing its own paradigm shift (Henninger et al., 2017). Bain & Company Report on luxury consumer trends (Bain & Company, 2024) shows that after consumers limited their social spending as a reaction of the Covid-19 pandemic, luxury market is booming and it is expected to grow 4% to 8% annually to to €2.5 trillion by 2030. A record high of €283billion in personal luxury goods was achieved in 2022. The market for luxury goods is substantial and has a role in shaping and adjusting to society trends (Pai et al., 2022). In particular, the market for luxury goods has raised its awareness toward social and environmental sustainability (Pai et al., 2022). Some prominent luxury brands are at the forefront of sustainable change (Joy et al., 2012), despite their products' exclusive attributes (Henninger et al., 2017) and sustainability and luxury being perceived as a contradiction by some consumers (Kapferer & Michaut, 2015). Large luxury companies, particularly those focused on fashion industry, have adopted sustainability as a core aspect of their operations and are moving beyond the chance to distinguish themselves apart from competitors (Lopez et al., 2023). As such, sustainability practices such as transparency in the supply chain (Han et al., 2017) involving labor and animal cruelty are adopted by a growing number of

A. Tolunay (✉) · F. M. Muskara
Yeditepe University, Istanbul, Turkey
e-mail: asli.tolunay@yeditepe.edu.tr

N. Ketenci (ed.), *Transition to the Circular Economy Model*, CSR, Sustainability, Ethics & Governance, https://doi.org/10.1007/978-3-031-52700-5_7

luxury brands. Luxury companies such as LVMH, Kering, and Chanel published their sustainable reports and strategies (Lopez et al., 2023). Also, many luxury brands such as Cartier, Gucci, Sergio Rossi, Yves Saint Laurent, Stella McCartney, and Porsche introduce sustainable products to the market (Sun et al., 2021), and have embodied green attributes into their product developments in order to reduce the unfavorable effects of value-creation process (Pai et al., 2022). More than 260 luxury jewelry brands have Responsible Jewelry Council certificate, which states that the brands follow the environmental, ethical, and social criteria (Athwal et al., 2019), while still concentrating on uniqueness, craftsmanship, and superior quality (Cuomo et al., 2019). These sustainable actions confirm the growing attention and devotion of luxury firms to environment and verify luxury and sustainability to be no longer mutually exclusive (Henninger et al., 2017).

Against this background, scholars have concentrated on the factors such as communication, innovation, and supply chain to explore how the consumers are influenced by these factors within sustainable luxury (Amatulli et al., 2021; Lopez et al., 2023). In line with that, limited research on sustainable luxury find that sustainability and luxury are mutually beneficial (Cervellon, 2013; Henninger et al., 2017) and exclusivity and longevity create a link between these two notions (Carcano, 2013). Studies identify that sustainable practices strengthen the values of consumers significantly (Cervellon & Shammas, 2013; Shukla, 2011) and influence conscious consumers' purchase intentions (Amatulli et al., 2018; De Angelis et al., 2017) as they can express themselves socially through sustainable luxury consumption (Sexton & Sexton, 2014; Osburg et al., 2019; Janssen et al., 2017). Therefore, luxury advertisers aim to address the sustainability trend as it gained momentum in the society (Pai et al., 2022). Nonetheless, this limited work falls short of clarifying how sustainable luxury is understood and valued by the luxury consumers (Athwal et al., 2019). Consequently, changing the mindset of the consumers about the hedonic value of sustainable luxury is a challenge for luxury brands.

Turkey, as a growing market with a growing number of luxury consumers, is a major market for most luxury brands. While there is a growing interest on sustainability and constant messaging from mass brands on sustainability (https://www.pazarlamasyon.com/tuketiciler-360-derece-surdurulebilirlik-bekliyor-arastirma), there is no evidence on the attitude of Turkish luxury consumers on sustainable luxury practices.

This exploratory study aims to fill this gap in identifying Turkish luxury consumers' perceptions and attitudes toward luxury brands with sustainable practices. With this aim, scripts from 12 in-depth interviews with luxury consumers have been analyzed; emergent patterns have been identified and discussed. The body of this study is structured as follows. First, a literature review on sustainability and luxury products and the perception and attitudes of consumers have been undertaken. Second, the methodology is discussed, and the data used for the study is described. Third, the results obtained from luxury respondents are examined. Finally, the manuscript ends with a conclusion and discussion along with the limitations of the study and future research directions.

2 Literature Review

Luxury does not have a universally recognized meaning, but the term “luxus” is taken from Latin and it denotes excellence, exclusivity, extravagance, conspicuous consumption, excess spending, superior craftsmanship, and pleasure (Wells et al., 2021, Kuşçu, 2020). Scholars categorize luxury in words as heritage, high-priced, hedonic experience, and tailored customized service (Cuomo et al., 2019; Kapferer & Michaut, 2015) and it is mostly identified with self-enhancement values (Amatulli et al., 2018).

Luxury brands provide not only functional benefits but also experiential benefits through uniqueness and distinctiveness as well as symbolic benefits through conspicuousness and extravagance (Radon, 2012; Wiedmann et al., 2009; Sexton & Sexton 2014). The concept of limited availability and rarity is the most lasting and distinguishing aspects of luxury (Beckham & Voyer, 2014). The underlying premise of luxury goods is that the less of the population afford the product makes the product rare and that elevates the worth and prestige of the consumers (Lynch et al., 2022). Due to limited availability, luxury is available to selective minority, and this takes luxury to the highly desired status, rather than ordinary (Wong & Dhanesh, 2017). Premium price, high quality, and heritage of passing valuables through generations are the other unique features of luxury (Kapferer & Michaut, 2015), which express wealth for conspicuous and materialist consumers (Veblen, 1889).

While the luxury market resides on these pillars, consumer awareness of present ecological problems is growing. As a result, consumers think that they can alter the status quo of the environment by shaping their attitudes and beliefs (Carranza et al., 2022). Despite numerous justifications for the attitude-behavior gap, a compelling theoretical framework of luxury fashion consumption patterns remains to be unclear (Carranza et al., 2022). Luxury may seem to be not connected with sustainability, civil rights, or environmental issues (Winston, 2016); however, media and activist groups spotlight luxury brands that are documented with animal abuse, environmental damage, and poor labor conditions (Caixiong, 2011) which harms the reputation of some luxury brands (Bendell & Kleanthous, 2007).

Even through the contradiction between luxury and sustainability, there are overlapping points particularly the durability features which distinguish luxury brands (Carranza et al., 2022). Slow fashion movement has gained acceptance lately as it encourages buying less, but in a good quality so that allows the consumer to keep it for a longer period. Furthermore, circular economy is gaining popularity as it fosters donation, recycling, and giving the clothes a second life by selling (Lopez et al., 2023). Luxury brand may strengthen the company’s image and reputation by adopting sustainability (Carranza et al., 2022). Heider’s balance theory (1958) is used by scholars to grasp the oxymoron of sustainability and luxury. Based on this view, people generally strive for internal harmony and order across their attitudes, behaviors, and values. Hence consumers are likely to alter their attitudes or behavior for maintaining the balance (Carranza et al., 2022).

Previous literature on sustainable luxury finds that sustainable products signal prosperity and strengthen the values of consumers significantly (Cervellon & Shammas, 2013; Shukla, 2011) as they are more expensive than mainstream products (Griskevicus et al., 2010) and consumers perceive sustainable luxury made from rare materials more valuable than other luxury goods (Davies et al., 2012). For instance, buying a Gucci Rainforest Bag may indicate that the consumer is environmentally conscious in addition to signaling status and money (Griskevicius et al., 2010). Therefore, conspicuous consumption has been shifted to green conspicuous consumption (Griskevicius et al., 2010) with luxury consumers expressing their actual and social selves (Osburg et al., 2019; Janssen et al., 2017) while engaging in responsibility in environmental issues (Cvijanovich, 2011) and considering ethical brands (Wang et al., 2021). Consumers' sense of identification and self-expression may be associated with sustainable luxury brands, while self-evaluations can be associated with craftsmanship that utilizes verifiable sources and adheres to sustainability standards (Pai et al., 2022).

Yet, research studies on why consumers consider or do not consider sustainability while purchasing luxury products provide mixed findings on how consumers view sustainability and luxury. Consumers seek to maximize the pleasure from the purchase of the luxury product. While Chernev and Blair (2015) show that consumers' quality perceptions can be increased by sustainable features, the perceived quality of luxury is low (Achabou & Dekhili, 2013) when recycled materials like vegetable leather or sustainable labeling are used (Beckham & Voyer, 2014) as these conflict with individuals' beliefs on luxury. Similarly, using organic raw sources is viewed as unfavorable as consumers perceive them as dirty (Streit & Davies, 2013). On the contrary, luxury goods are perceived to be timeless, long-lasting, and durable (Athwal et al., 2019), which is congruent with sustainability (Kessous et al., 2016) as preservation defines sustainability and sustainable products are manufactured with high-quality raw materials (Kapferer, 2010). Also, scarcity is a critical feature of luxury (Janssen et al., 2014); however, consumers do not prioritize scarcity in sustainable luxury (Wang et al., 2021). And finally, sustainable luxury products are limited, genuine, and unique (Moscardo & Benckendorff, 2010) and consumers prefer sustainable luxury when rarity, trend, and guilt-free enjoyment are linked to sustainable aspects (Amatulli et al., 2021; Wang et al., 2021).

All these inconsistencies in sustainable luxury consumption raise fruitful research questions such as how luxury shoppers link sustainability and luxury and perceive sustainable luxury.

3 Methodology

Structured online interviews lasting approximately 30 minutes were undertaken with a total of 12 interviewees (see Table 1) that were selected purposefully based on the research questions of the study. The questions were designed to elicit subjective perspectives of interviewees' attitudes and perceptions of luxury and then that

Table 1 Demographic profile ($n = 12$)

Respondent	Age	Occupation	Respondent	Age	Occupation
F 01	34	Academician	F 05	65	Lawyer
M 01	25	Marketing Manager	F 06	42	Merchandiser
F 02	38	Lawyer	M 03	45	Sales Manager
F 03	35	Export Manager	M 04	45	Vice President
F 04	38	Academician	M 05	34	Purchasing Manager
M 02	38	Marketing Manager	F 07	45	Country Manager

Source: The table is prepared by the authors

of sustainable luxury and their link with each other. The interviews were all performed in Turkish, and the transcriptions were then translated into English. Overall 10,056 words of data were recorded, transcribed, and analyzed using QDA Minor Software. To eliminate any potential bias, all transcriptions were systematically explored and methodically categorized in order to find significant emerging patterns. This approach entailed identifying key concepts in line with the research questions as initial codes and thereafter individual codes in accordance with the literature. The key concepts are luxury perception, sustainable luxury perception, current state of sustainable luxury, and link between luxury and sustainable luxury labeled as four main categories. The final code frame consisted of 26 individual codes located across the four main categories that were then interpreted inductively and conclusions drawn. The codes were interpreted on a manifest level (meaning visible in the text) followed by a latent level (considering the deeper meaning of the text) (Bengtsson, 2016). Table 2 along with Fig. 1 displays the four main categories, 11 sub-categories, and 26 codes along with their frequency, the number of cases, and word count.

4 Findings and Discussion

Each category is explained in more detail below.

Category 1: What Is Luxury?
This category entails respondents' perception of luxury. The results of the scripts reveal that having high functional value (price, product, and life quality), high symbolic value (actual and ideal self-image), high hedonic value (better self and personal history (family and social)), as well as country of origin (COO) and high awareness were the main elements of luxury identified by the respondents. As can be seen from Fig. 2, making users feel better about themselves is the most frequently mentioned characteristics, followed by having high product quality and high price.

In line with previous literature stating that brands enable individuals' hedonic benefits (Lageat et al., 2003) by making them feel special (Holmqvist et al., 2020), better and proud about themselves (Keller, 2017), feeling better emerged as the

Table 2 Categories and codes identified in the analysis

Category	Code	Count	Count %	Cases	Cases %
What defines luxury	Coo	1	0.40	1	8.3
What defines luxury	High awareness	6	2.50	5	41.7
What defines luxury\high hedonic values	Feeling better	22	9.30	9	75
What defines luxury\high hedonic values\personal history	Self-inclusion – family	9	3.80	5	41.7
What defines luxury\high hedonic values\personal history	Self-inclusion – social	8	3.40	6	50
What defines luxury\high in functional value	High price	11	4.60	8	66.7
What defines luxury\high in functional value\quality	Life quality	10	4.20	4	33.3
What defines luxury\high in functional value\quality	Product quality	20	8.40	8	66.7
What defines luxury\high in symbolic values	Actual self-image	4	1.70	3	25
What defines luxury\high in symbolic values	Ideal self-image	10	4.20	5	41.7
What is sustainable luxury	Company strategy	15	6.30	8	66.7
What is sustainable luxury\hedonic value	Joy in heritage	4	1.70	3	25
What is sustainable luxury\hedonic value	Joy in using	6	2.50	4	33.3
What is sustainable luxury\symbolic value	Self-verification	4	1.70	3	25
What is sustainable luxury\symbolic value	Social image	13	5.50	6	50
What is sustainable luxury\utilitarian value	Functional	8	3.40	5	41.7
What is sustainable luxury\utilitarian value	Recyclable	7	3.00	4	33.3
What is sustainable luxury\utilitarian value	Social impact	20	8.40	10	83.3
Current state of sustainable luxury	Not ready	3	1.30	2	16.7
Current state of sustainable luxury\ diverse awareness	High	9	3.80	7	58.3
Current state of sustainable luxury\ diverse awareness	Low	19	8.00	8	66.7
Current state of sustainable luxury\ diverse interest	High int	3	1.30	3	25
Current state of sustainable luxury\ diverse interest	Low int	6	2.50	5	41.7
Link to luxury	Lower quality	7	3.00	4	33.3
Link to luxury	No difference – not aware	4	1.70	3	25
Link to luxury	No link	8	3.40	4	33.3

Source: The table is prepared by the authors

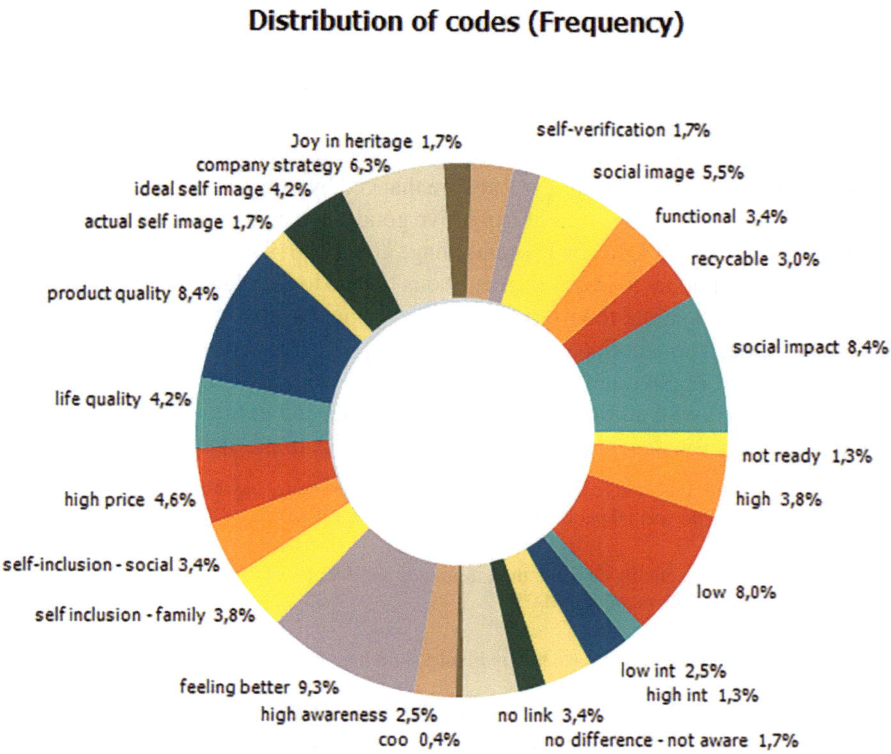

Fig. 1 Distribution of codes. (Source: The figure is prepared by the authors)

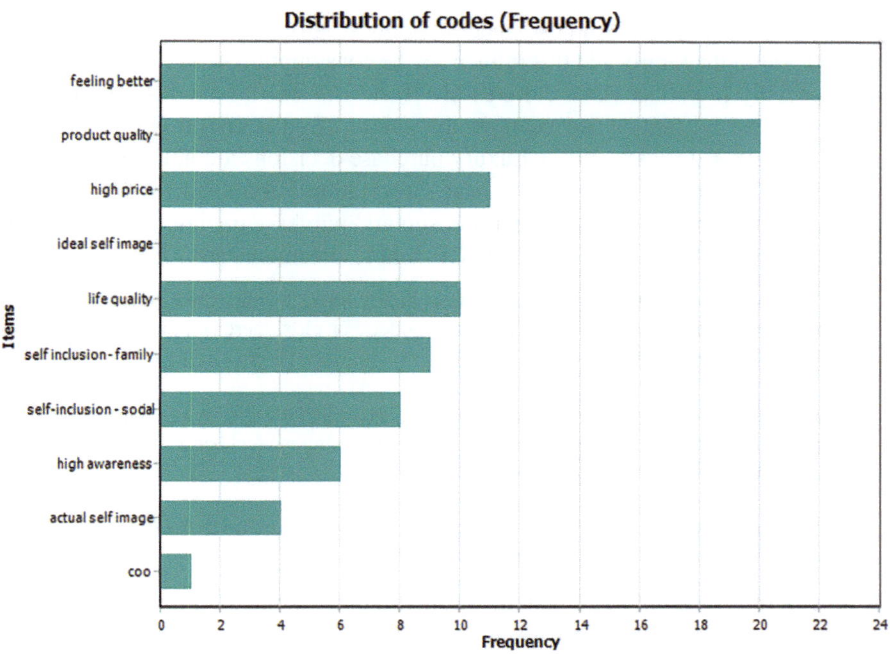

Fig. 2 Distribution of codes in luxury perception. (Source: The figure is prepared by the authors)

most frequently mentioned aspect of luxury by the respondents. Using luxury and being able to feel special is the number one benefit that luxury users get. Several studies indicate that being unique is one of the main features of luxury brands (Jain, 2019). Consumer preference for brands is enhanced by rarity, and the desire of owning is even stronger in the event of expensive goods, and a product's uniqueness may enhance one's "self-image" and "social image" (Jain, 2019). Furthermore, the motivation of an individual to invest in prestigious brands to be related to a desired reference group and separate themselves from less appealing groups can be referred to as social value. The emotional benefits of luxury spending are referred to as hedonism (Kumagai & Nagasawa, 2021). In addition, uniqueness is found to be positively associated with attitudes toward luxury brands and in turn, improve purchase intention (Vigneron & Johnson, 2004; Jain, 2019). Example statements include:

> Maybe it's all to make me feel special, I don't know. I can prefer anything that I will use in special places with special people to be more luxurious. (M 01)

> For me, luxury is a quality concept and I think it is a concept that makes people's life easier and makes them feel valuable. (M 05)

> Even though I know I don't have to buy luxury, I am happy when I use it. (F 06)

In addition, respondents also mentioned that using luxury makes them feel better as they perceive it as part of themselves since they inherited luxury usage either from their families or from their social circle. The influence of families and peers on individuals' brand-related decisions has been widely documented in literature (Childers & Rao, 1992). The focus on ancestral heritage on luxury consumption has gained attention by few studies, since the values, attitudes, and lifestyles can be formed within the family and this influences the consumption habits of the individuals especially in collectivistic cultures like Turkey as one's attitudes and behavior are influenced by family and peers in the nature of collectivism (Kessous et al., 2016; Lacroix & Jolibert, 2017). Luxury purchase decisions are not preferred to be taken in isolation, consumers like to have information from all accessible channels and social influence positively effects consumers' purchase intentions (Vigneron & Johnson, 2004; Shukla & Purani, 2012). Example statements are:

> In fact, you do not see that you use products as luxury because you started using them at a young age, as you have your family as a role model. For girls, there is a mother as a role mode front of you. (F 04)

> I started because the people around me were using luxury and it was seen as a status symbol in my working environment. So, I started to use it for making me feel better there and to get a place for myself in the company I work for. (F 07)

> Since I entered the business life, as the positions have changed, my understanding of luxury has increased gradually, and it still continues. (M 04)

As one of the emergent functional themes with respect to luxury, luxury consumerism is related to being high-priced and high quality. In addition to being desired for the functionality and superior quality, luxury products influence the consumers' perception about the price (Shukla & Purani, 2012). Consumers' views of quality are positively influenced by price, where a higher price typically indicates higher quality. In many collectivist societies, prestige-seeking by purchasing expensive products is accepted (Shukla, 2011). Greater economic expense correlates positively with the total value of the brand when it comes to luxury. Therefore, price plays a significant role in luxury. In other words, a greater cost of purchase strengthens the attractiveness and uniqueness of a luxury brand (Shukla & Purani, 2012).

> Luxury is money, things that can be bought and obtained with a lot of money. (F 03)

> The price of something is high and the quality is also high. I find these two facts in the right ratio in terms of quality and price. (F 06)

Next, respondents mentioned improved life quality due to usage of luxury. Consumers have higher purchase intentions toward luxury goods since they think that these types of goods have better functional value as the nature of these products is perceived to be durable and having high quality (Wiedmann et al., 2007; Islam et al., 2021) in addition to a longer lifespan (Wiedmann et al., 2007). The terms of luxury and quality are synonymous within the minds of the consumer (Dubois et al., 2001) and the quality and performance of a luxury product is the major distinction from non-luxury products (Vigneron & Johnson, 2004), leading to better performance and easier task accomplishments.

> It is a lifestyle with good quality. (F 02)

> It is a concept that makes people's life easier and valuable. (M 05)

> Since I entered the business life, as the positions in the company have changed, my understanding of luxury has gradually increased. A Mercedes car is a luxury for me, both in terms of safety and comfort. Recently I bought a watch (Rolex), it is this luxury for me and I wear it with pleasure. These are the prestige side of the business. (M 04)

While product quality as a functional value is in general strongly associated with luxury by both men and women, when gender disparities were examined, they displayed differences in terms of life quality and high price (see Table 3). Women associate luxury more with higher prices and men more with increased life quality.

Table 3 Distribution of functional value between men and women

	F (%)	M (%)
Product quality	46.2	50
Life quality	15.4	28.6
High price	38.5	21.4

Source: The table is prepared by the authors

Individuals achieve their social status through the extrinsic cues of the luxury brands and their socio-psychological needs are satisfied by impressing the society (Amatulli & Guido, 2011; Shukla, 2011). As an inborn human drive, gaining social status is associated with higher resource of privilege and hierarchy-level excellence (Ali et al., 2019). The significant factor for purchasing luxury brands happens to be materialism (Islam et al., 2021). Materialistic consumers are prone to seek products which strengthen their social status and reflect their achievements (Ali et al., 2019) and materialistic people place material gain at the heart of their life and consider them as a guide to happiness (Richins & Fournier, 1991). According to the social identity theory, materialist consumers consider the luxury good ownership as a sign of prestige or status indicator and therefore, they are inclined to purchase conspicuous luxury products (Christopher & Schlenker, 2004; Sexton & Sexton 2014). Additionally, the purchases can increase positive word-of-mouth and in turn, create brand ambassadors (Amatulli et al., 2018; De Angelis et al., 2017).

> We can say that the effect of word-of-mouth communication and social norm is very high. I think it is related to the collectivist culture, seeing your friend in your own home environment, and getting information about it first. While it will benefit you in terms of time, my friend says it is also in her own house. This is completely a status indicator; it is used because of symbolic meanings. Both the functional and hedonic benefit are very important to me, and this leads me to luxury products. (F 04)

Besides signaling and social factors, self-identity influences the consumer's motivation toward luxury consumption (Wiedmann et al., 2007). Therefore, luxury brands are purchased for self-expression and self-presentation (Janssen et al., 2017; Tsai, 2005).

> I use luxury products in the field of clothing because I see that it can represent a style that belongs to me. Secondly, since I use it frequently in daily life, quality is important. Quality and style are top priority for me. (M 05)

Category 2: What Is Sustainable Luxury?

This category entails respondents' perception of sustainable luxury. The results of the scripts reveal that sustainable luxury is perceived as a company strategy providing functional benefits such as recyclability and sustainable quality, symbolic benefits such as social image and self-verification as well as hedonic benefits such as joy in using, being able to inherit something valuable to off-springs and supporting social well-being. As can be seen from Fig. 3, social impact of using sustainable luxury and hence supporting social well-being is the most frequently mentioned benefit provided by sustainable luxury, followed by being just a company strategy.

While majority of the respondents view sustainable luxury as just a company strategy to attract either a younger or a more conscious audience, they also mention that sustainable luxury products can provide stability and durability as they are mostly recyclable. Sustainability issues are turned to be prevalent in the luxury industry as a result of broad interest in promoting sustainable consumption, and more luxury brands have embraced environmental concerns to promote sustainability (Athwal et al., 2019). Due to the current industry dynamics toward ethical and sustainable consumption, marketers want to draw attention to the shopping behavior

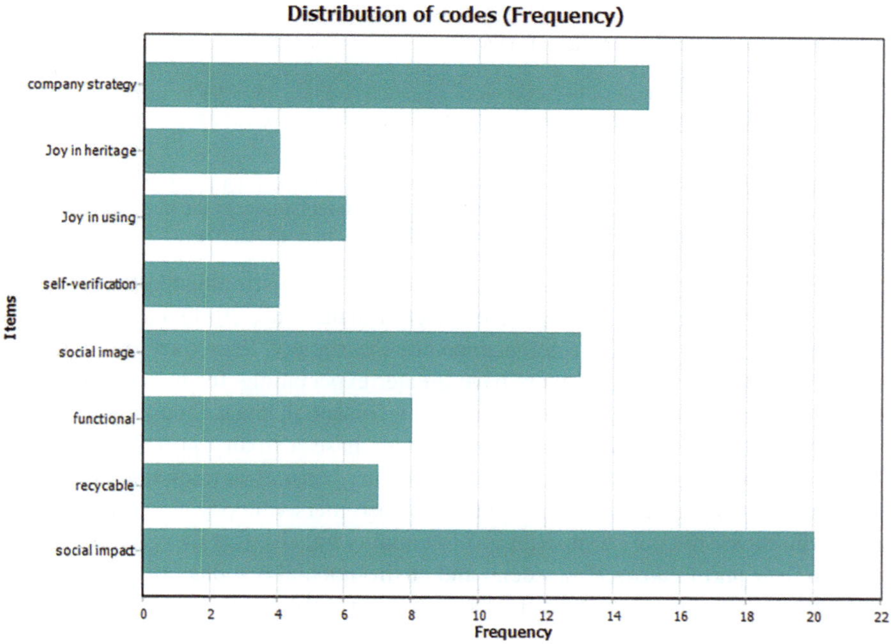

Fig. 3 Distribution of codes in sustainable luxury perception. (Source: The figure is prepared by the authors

of purchasing sustainable products by promoting an image that the use of sustainable product contributes to a greener society (Kim et al., 2019). Companies' sustainable and ethical activities are frequently reflected through their green advertising statements, which have a favorable influence on customers' perceptions and attitudes (Kim et al., 2019). Perceived brand activities toward green initiatives improve consumers' attitudes about the brand along with increasing positive E-WOM in addition to purchase intention (Carranza et al., 2022). Statements that can be categorized under this heading are:

> It's just that brands have turned to advertising and make propaganda about sustainability so much that every product we buy is built on sustainability. I'm talking about textiles again. (F 06)

> It seems to me that brands that want to look more innovative and younger somehow can promote sustainable luxury. Sustainable products are trying to appeal to the younger generation, maybe to a higher segment, by emphasizing their innovative aspects. (M 01)

> I do not think that the target audience of companies is acting very sustainable in such products. they are producing a product and at that moment they are actually combining the brand with veganism, which is one of the important issues of that day, and I think that's how they want to attract the attention of target audience. Otherwise, I don't think they have an ideology of selling vegan leather jackets 24/7. (M 02)

> In order to be a sustainable product, the source of that product must be upcycled into production. Because the best resource is the product you produce, and the product's efficiency would be very high when you recycle the same product. The concept of reuse – repair already comes to the fore in the concept of sustainability, and in order to understand the sustainability terminology, it is necessary to know these concepts. (M 05)

> I can say that sustainable luxury brands have more forward-looking plans and would be more permanent in the future. We can think of the past and the future in the same way, coming from not just 10 years like 50 years, but much longer periods. (F 07)

Sustainable consumption practices intend to benefit the environment, save resources in the long term, and contribute to the society (Islam et al., 2021) and respondents mention the joy they find in doing good for the society, their own children, and themselves. Given that consumers have greater expectations for luxury goods and how they are manufactured, sustainability is essential, even though it does not directly affect the individuals' decision to purchase a luxury good (Kapferer & Michaut-Denizeau, 2015). In a similar vein, luxury consumers think that luxury and sustainability engaged and reciprocal terms. Customers who pay a premium luxury goods anticipate not only a superior level of quality but also that these luxury brands will do their part in advocating social and environmental responsibility. Customers think that any luxury brands must adhere to the principles of "doing good with no harm" and therefore consumers think luxury reflects sustainability as a key component (Henninger et al., 2017).

> But when the luxury product is sustainable, the idea that it is a contribution to the world or society will make people more comfortable to use it a little more, and I will feel more comfortable as well. (F 01)

> When we say sustainable, we know that it has a benefit in this world. both in production and in terms of reusability. (M 05)

> One thinks that people with high awareness who make conscious choices about their own future will prefer these types of products. (M 03)

> Likewise, if we want to be permanent, or if we want something to belong to a certain generation, you know, I don't have any children, but I would love to give my own belongings to my child and use the same things as I do. (F 07)

When sustainability statements are linked to status-related advantages, positive attitudes are formed within the minds of the consumers (Steinhart et al., 2013). As in traditional luxury consumption, respondents stated that they use sustainable luxury either to reflect themselves or to comply with the norms and values of their social circle.

> On the other hand, people will still be able to see that I pay so much money." (F 01)

> And now, the importance of this sustainability is emphasized very intensely in schools. In fact, I can say that the children are also conscious for the last two years, I have been on this subject both in terms of being an example for my child, and in terms of the fact that this subject is mentioned in many of his school projects, like separating the garbage bins. (F 04)

> Because I think A/B and higher groups give more importance to this type of communication and give higher value to using this type of products. Not only within the scope of sustainable luxury, but people in general use these products to feel different from other people, and somehow, they actually prefer to select companies that are more socially aware. (M 01)

Category 3: Current State in Sustainable Luxury?
The interviews provided opposite insights on the status of sustainable luxury and as Table 2 reveals, luxury consumers are either unaware of sustainable luxury, have never purchased one sustainable luxury item or unaware that they have purchased one. Purchasing sustainable luxury is not a priority for the majority; therefore, luxury consumers are not the primary driving factor of the development of luxury industry (Rolling & Sadachar, 2018; Dekhili & Achabou, 2016; Beckham & Voyer, 2014; Achabou & Dekhili, 2013; Cervellon & Shammas, 2013) and due to lack of prestige and appeal, brand awareness is still low for sustainable brands (Dekhili et al., 2019).

> The concept of sustainability is everywhere, but I never thought of sustainable luxury. (F 07)

> Sustainable luxury is something I've never heard of, so I can't think of anything. (F 01)

> I don't have such perception of sustainable luxury, so it didn't exist for me until I heard this word. (M 03)

> I think there is a gap in the market in this regard. The products of the brands I bought did not have a marketing strategy that would create such awareness in me. If I own a few luxury items, I haven't heard anything about it from the salesperson or the manager. This is because the seller does not bring this issue to the fore, rather than why the consumer does not choose the sustainable product. Even when buying the watch, if the seller says that we benefit our planet with sustainability in the production of this watch, saying that we benefit our planet as follows, he can convince me to pay 500 Euros more. More specific and beautiful marketing strategies can create awareness in the customer. Maybe that's why there are no people around me who buy sustainable luxury products. (M 04)

In addition, while majority reflect negativity, the respondents still have diverse opinions on the public interest on sustainable luxury with some stating that the public is even not ready.

> But as I said, unfortunately Turkey is not ready for this. I wish we had this opportunity in this country, there are conversations like that, but unfortunately, as far as I see, it does not exist in terms of consumption. (F 01)

Category 4: Link Between Luxury and Sustainability?
The sustainable luxury brand is defined as green, ecologically friendly, and cost-effective in the long term (Septianto et al., 2021) which makes some luxury consumers consider the attributes of sustainable luxury unappealing while for others pleasure gained from luxury is decreased by sustainable luxury (Cervellon & Shammas, 2013) since luxury has long been associated with excessive consumption

Table 4 Current state of sustainable luxury

Category	Code	Count	% Codes	Cases	% Cases
Current state of sustainable luxury\diverse awareness	Low	19	8.30	8	66.7
Current state of sustainable luxury\diverse awareness	High	9	3.90	7	58.3
Current state of sustainable luxury\diverse interest	Low int	6	2.60	5	41.7
Current state of sustainable luxury\diverse interest	High int	3	1.30	3	25
Current state of sustainable luxury	Not ready	3	1.30	2	16.7

Source: The table is prepared by the authors

and extravagance, which are the contradicting points against sustainability (Yang et al., 2017; Veblen, 1889), (see the details in Table 4).

> Luxury is consumed fast, and it is unsustainable. Sustainability cannot be luxury. The two terms conflict with each other. Recycled product cannot be a luxury. Luxury cannot be a synthetic product. I think it's on the market because it's cheap. It cannot be healthy and comfortable; it makes you sweat. Therefore, it does not carry the characteristics of luxury. Clothing can be recycled, but it is not luxury. (F 05)

> It's just wrong for a sustainable product to look luxurious. I don't see luxury in sustainability (M 05)

Nonetheless, some respondents have negative thoughts on sustainable luxury goods as they consider the sustainable aspects may decrease their perceived quality (Achabou & Dekhili, 2013). Using recycled sources in luxury garment is perceived as a contradiction with prestige (Achabou & Dekhili, 2013) and sustainable labeling on a luxury product is found to be less appealing (Beckham & Voyer, 2014). As such the consumers' perception toward luxury weakens when sustainable materials are used (Dekhili et al., 2019) and sustainable luxury is perceived to be poor quality. High status, prestige, and social power are not well symbolized by sustainable luxury (Beckham & Voyer, 2014).

> The quality of a sustainable luxury product is different because of the used materials as it was made from something recyclable. (F 02)

> Can't expect it to be that high quality. It doesn't give that feeling even when you touch the product. I don't look at the content because fashion and trend are more important to me. (F 06)

Furthermore, we found that the majority of the respondents consider sustainable luxury in a negative way in terms of status indication. In addition, materialistic consumers are taking less ethical/sustainable decisions in collectivist cultures like Turkey (Wang et al., 2021).

> I do not find sustainable luxury very realistic in Turkish conditions, but in general, what I have observed in Turkey is the products they buy and try to use as a status indicator, feeling that they belong to that brand. For sustainable luxury, people need to be above a certain income level so that they can keep their relationship with the brand. However, this is difficult in Turkey…These products may appeal to a narrower market. I do not think that the target audience of the companies are focusing on sustainability at that moment. (M 02)

5 Conclusion

Through the investigation of in-depth interviews conducted with luxury consumers, this paper identifies some novel insights into luxury brands. The findings, which are categorized into four topics to analyze the consumers, do not only shed light on the perception and current situation of sustainable luxury but also provide insight into the condition and definition of luxury. Luxury being perceived very relatively (Mortelmans, 2005) and perceptions of what makes up "luxury" have changed with time (Cristini et al., 2017), an updated understanding of luxury is valuable in addition to the understanding of sustainable luxury.

Luxury consumption is defined as a pause of enjoyment where problems in the outside world are temporarily disregarded (Kapferer, 2010). Besides the functional value, luxury goods portray a particular brand image that enables a particular status to the consumer (Boardman et al., 2022). In addition, the majority of consumers purchase luxury products as a symbolic value to express their personality (Shukla, 2011). One of the reasons individuals purchase luxury products is to satisfy a personal need and indulge in luxury spending, which is associated with hedonism (Henninger et al., 2017). Self-value arises from the emotional value from luxury brands and is usually referred to as hedonic need, which refers to the desire to experience positive feelings from consumption (Vigneron & Johnson, 2004). In addition, hedonic experiences, which result in personal motivations for luxury consumption, are motivated by positive feelings such as feeling happy or satisfied (Cuomo et al., 2019; Wiedmann et al. (2007). On the contrary, the conceptual environment associated with sustainability which includes phrases like reduce, protect, respect, give back, and cause no damage, is substantially distinct from luxury (Kapferer & Michaut, 2015). Luxury goods are associated with personal pleasure, superficiality, and ostentation, whereas sustainable development evokes ethics, altruism, sobriety, and balance (Wang et al., 2021).

Initially, despite the perceived contradiction that consumers see between the notions of sustainability and luxury, this paper initially finds that the concepts of luxury and sustainability overlap as they both focus on quality, permeance, and durability. However, the results also reveal that perception of luxury is subjective and is heavily influenced by perceived quality, while sustainability particularly using recyclable sources in luxury is perceived to reflect lower quality. Therefore, luxury brands need to be cautious about the detrimental impact of sustainability on luxury products. Additionally, similar to the confusion in luxury, some respondents are unsure what sustainable luxury entails. They have not purchased sustainable luxury and have no idea where to purchase these products. However, driven by the desire to distinguish themselves from the others, the shift from "owning" to "sharing and experiencing" and from "seeking prestige" to "self-actualization and personal growth", luxury consumers' concerns about environment and social problems may result in higher purchase intention toward sustainable luxury goods. As a result, luxury brands need to concentrate on symbolic gains and build cultural capital to nurture their brand identity that is valued by today's luxury consumers and prioritize communication strategies accordingly. Appropriate product positioning and message framing intermediates the behavioral change significantly (Amatulli et al., 2021; Klotz et al., 2018). Loss-framed message with facts can be very influential for altering attitudes, since consumers are more concerned about losses than gains (Kahneman & Tversky, 2013). Furthermore, educating the consumers about the durability and high quality is critical for luxury brands. Government and effective opinion leaders can play an essential part in consumer trainings. Fair and transparent treatment in environment and supply chain needs to be promoted in campaigns, because they create positive and strong attitudes in consumers. Marketing campaigns may play a greater role in influencing individuals for the durability of sustainable luxury goods, which will enable consumers to gain more information about the sustainability practices of luxury brands and change their attitudes. Luxury brands are based on appearance and perceptions; therefore, celebrity endorsement can promote the sustainable luxury brands effectively (Radon, 2012), celebrity endorsements can have a significant influence on consumer awareness and positive attitude toward sustainable luxury and in turn, it may enhance the brand equity (Keller, 2017). Since consumer perceptions toward sustainable luxury have a significant and direct influence on consumers' willingness to purchase sustainable luxury product, luxury brands should concentrate their efforts on altering negative attitudes toward sustainable luxury, one should stress on concepts that promote self-transcendence and self-enhancement (Carranza et al., 2022).

6 Limitation and Future Research

This study offers insights for luxury brands in their sustainability journey. However, it should be noted that this is just an exploratory study conducted with purposively selected respondents reflecting a certain segment of the society. Enlarging the focus of the study to diverse segments and to other stakeholders might provide a deeper understanding. Even though the limited number of participants in the research could be seen as a limitation since the study is concentrated on Turkish consumers who buy luxury goods in Turkey, it offers an understanding of a target audience that will continuously have a significant influence on the economic contribution of the luxury industry (Hancock, 2017). This study does not intend to generalize its outcomes: instead, the aim is to shed light on a fast-growing audience, emphasizing which drives individuals to purchase luxury goods and to reveal whether sustainability plays a significant role in the decision-making process. The findings illustrate that while sustainability does not directly influence consumer behavior, it remains crucial for brands to effectively identify themselves with CSR initiatives, because these are the fundamental requirements expected by consumers. Nevertheless, luxury companies should avoid making this broadly apparent through their means of communication which might make customers skeptical. The results of this study should be expanded by conducting a questionnaire and executing a cluster analysis, which would enable generalizing these results.

Competing Interests The authors have no conflicts of interest to declare that are relevant to the content of this chapter.

References

Achabou, M. A., & Dekhili, S. (2013). Luxury and sustainable development: Is there a match? *Journal of Business Research, 66*(10), 1896–1903.

Ali, A., Xiaoling, G., Ali, A., Sherwani, M., & Muneeb, F. M. (2019). Customer motivations for sustainable consumption: Investigating the drivers of purchase behavior for a green-luxury car. *Business Strategy and the Environment, 28*(5), 833–846.

Amatulli, C., & Guido, G. (2011). Determinants of purchasing intention for fashion luxury goods in the Italian market: A laddering approach. *Journal of Fashion Marketing and Management, 15*, 123–136.

Amatulli, C., De Angelis, M., Korschun, D., & Romani, S. (2018). Consumers' perceptions of luxury brands' CSR initiatives: An investigation of the role of status and conspicuous consumption. *Journal of Cleaner Production, 194*, 277–287.

Amatulli, C., De Angelis, M., & Donato, C. (2021). The atypicality of sustainable luxury products. *Psychology & Marketing, 38(11), 1990–2005.*

Athwal, N., Wells, V. K., Carrigan, M., & Henninger, C. E. (2019). Sustainable luxury marketing: A synthesis and research agenda. *International Journal of Management Reviews, 21*(4), 405–426.

Bain & Company. (2024). *Long Live Luxury: Converge to Expand through Turbulence*. Fall–Winter 2024.

Beckham, D., & Voyer, B. G. (2014). *Can sustainability be luxurious? A mixed-method investigation of implicit and explicit attitudes towards sustainable luxury consumption*. ACR North.

Bendell, J., & Kleanthous, A. (2007). Deeper luxury. *WWF-UK, Godalming*.

Bengtsson, M. (2016). How to plan and perform a qualitative study using content analysis. *NursingPlus Open, 2*, 8–14.

Boardman, R., Zhou, Y., & Guo, Y. (2022). Chinese consumer attitudes towards second-hand luxury fashion and how social media eWoM affects decision-making. In *Sustainable luxury: An international perspective* (pp. 241–269). Springer.

Caixiong, Z. (2011). Letter calls Gucci stores sweatshops. *The China Daily News*, 2011–10.

Carcano, L. (2013). Strategic management and sustainability in luxury companies: The IWC case. *Journal of Corporate Citizenship, (52), 36–54.*

Carranza, R., Zollo, L., Díaz, E., & Faraoni, M. (2022). Solving the luxury fashion and sustainable development "oxymoron": A cross-cultural analysis of green luxury consumption enablers and disablers. *Business Strategy and the Environment, 32*(3).

Cervellon, M. C. (2013). Conspicuous conservation: Using semiotics to understand sustainable luxury. *International Journal of Market Research, 55*(5), 695–717.

Cervellon, M. C., & Shammas, L. (2013). The value of sustainable luxury in mature markets: A customer-based approach. *Journal of Corporate Citizenship, 52*, 90–101.

Chernev, A., & Blair, S. (2015). Doing well by doing good: The benevolent halo of corporate social responsibility. *Journal of Consumer Research, 41*(6), 1412–1425.
Childers, T. L., & Rao, A. R. (1992). The influence of familial and peer-based reference groups on consumer decisions. *Journal of Consumer Research, 19*(2), 198–211.
Christopher, A. N., & Schlenker, B. R. (2004). Materialism and affect: The role of self-presentational concerns. *Journal of Social and Clinical Psychology, 23*(2), 260–272.
Cristini, H., Kauppinen-Räisänen, H., Barthod-Prothade, M., & Woodside, A. (2017). Toward a general theory of luxury: Advancing from workbench definitions and theoretical transformations. *Journal of Business Research, 70*, 101–107.
Cuomo, M. T., Foroudi, P., Tortora, D., Hussain, S., & Melewar, T. C. (2019). Celebrity endorsement and the attitude towards luxury brands for sustainable consumption. *Sustainability, 11*(23), 6791.
Cvijanovich, M. (2011). Sustainable luxury: Oxymoron. *Lecture in Luxury and Sustainability. Lausanne, July*.
Davies, I. A., Lee, Z., & Ahonkhai, I. (2012). Do consumers care about ethical-luxury? *Journal of Business Ethics, 106*, 37–51.
De Angelis, M., Adıgüzel, F., & Amatulli, C. (2017). The role of design similarity in consumers' evaluation of new green products: An investigation of luxury fashion brands. *Journal of Cleaner Production, 141*, 1515–1527.
Dekhili, S., & Achabou, M. A. (2016). Is it beneficial for luxury brands to embrace CSR practices? In *Celebrating America's pastimes: Baseball, hot dogs, apple pie and marketing?* (pp. 3–18). Springer.
Dekhili, S., Achabou, M. A., & Alharbi, F. (2019). Could sustainability improve the promotion of luxury products? *European Business Review, 31*, 488–511.
Dubois, B., Laurent, G., & Czellar, S. (2001). *Consumer rapport to luxury: Analyzing complex and ambivalent attitudes* (No. 736). HEC Paris.
Griskevicius, V., Tybur, J. M., & Van den Bergh, B. (2010). Going green to be seen: Status, reputation, and conspicuous conservation. *Journal of Personality and Social Psychology, 98*(3), 392.
Han, J., Seo, Y., & Ko, E. (2017). Staging luxury experiences for understanding sustainable fashion consumption: A balance theory application. *Journal of Business Research, 74*, 162–167.
Hancock, R. (2017). Islamic Environmentalism: Activism in the United States and Great Britain. Routledge.
Henninger, C. E., Alevizou, P. J., Tan, J., Huang, Q., & Ryding, D. (2017). Consumption strategies and motivations of Chinese consumers: The case of UK sustainable luxury fashion. *Journal of Fashion Marketing and Management, 21*(3), 419–434.
Holmqvist, J., Visconti, L. M., Grönroos, C., Guais, B., & Kessous, A. (2020). Understanding the value process: Value creation in a luxury service context. *Journal of Business Research, 120*, 114–126.
Islam, T., Wang, Y., Ali, A., & Akhtar, N. (2021). Path to sustainable luxury brand consumption: Face consciousness, materialism, pride and risk of embarrassment. *Journal of Consumer Marketing, 39*(1).
Jain, S. (2019). Factors affecting sustainable luxury purchase behavior: A conceptual framework. *Journal of International Consumer Marketing, 31(2), 130–146.*
Janssen, C., Vanhamme, J., Lindgreen, A., & Lefebvre, C. (2014). The Catch-22 of responsible luxury: Effects of luxury product characteristics on consumers' perception of fit with corporate social responsibility. *Journal of Business Ethics, 119*(1), 45–57.
Janssen, C., Vanhamme, J., & Leblanc, S. (2017). Should luxury brands say it out loud? Brand conspicuousness and consumer perceptions of responsible luxury. *Journal of Business Research, 77*, 167–174.
Joy, A., Sherry, J. F., Jr., Venkatesh, A., Wang, J., & Chan, R. (2012). Fast fashion, sustainability, and the ethical appeal of luxury brands. *Fashion Theory, 16*(3), 273–295.

Kahneman, D., & Tversky, A. (2013). Prospect theory: An analysis of decision under risk. In *Handbook of the fundamentals of financial decision making: Part I* (pp. 99–127). World Scientific.

Kapferer, J. N. (2010). All that glitters is not green: The challenge of sustainable luxury. *European Business Review, 2*, 40–45.

Kapferer, J. N., & Michaut, A. (2015). Luxury and sustainability: A common future? The match depends on how consumers define luxury. *Luxury Research Journal, 1*(1), 3–17.

Keller, K. L. (2017). Managing the growth tradeoff: Challenges and opportunities in luxury branding. In *Advances in luxury brand management* (pp. 179–198). Palgrave Macmillan.

Kessous, A., Boncori, A. L., & Paché, G. (2016). Are consumers sensitive to large retailers' sustainable practices? A semiotic analysis in the French context. *Journal of Retailing and Consumer Services, 32*, 117–130.

Kim, J. E., Lloyd, S., Adebeshin, K., & Kang, J. Y. M. (2019). Decoding fashion advertising symbolism in masstige and luxury brands. *Journal of Fashion Marketing and Management, 23*(2), 277–295.

Klotz, L., Weber, E., Johnson, E., Shealy, T., Hernandez, M., & Gordon, B. (2018). Beyond rationality in engineering design for sustainability. *Nature Sustainability, 1*(5), 225–233.

Kumagai, K., & Nagasawa, S. Y. (2021). Moderating effect of brand commitment on apparel brand prestige in upward comparisons. *Journal of Global Fashion Marketing, 12*(3), 195–213.

Kuşçu, A. T. (2020). Inconspicuous luxury consumption: Another form of new luxury? In *Building consumer-brand relationship in luxury brand management* (pp. 65–85). IGI Global.

Lacroix, C., & Jolibert, A. (2017). Mediational role of perceived personal legacy value between consumer agentic generativity and attitudes/buying intentions toward luxury brands. *Journal of Business Research, 77*, 203–211.

Lageat, T., Czellar, S., & Laurent, G. (2003). Engineering hedonic attributes to generate perceptions of luxury: Consumer perception of an everyday sound. *Marketing Letters, 14*, 97–109.

López, B., Rangel-Pérez, C., & Fernández, M. (2023). Sustainable strategies in the luxury business to increase efficiency in reducing carbon footprint. *Journal of Business Research, 157*, 113607.

Lynch, M. J., Long, M. A., & Stretesky, P. B. (2022). Averting your gaze with sustainable, green marketing claims: A critique of luxury commodity production sustainability claims, with evidence from the diamond industry. *Sociological Spectrum, 42*(4–6), 278–293.

Mortelmans, D. (2005). Sign values in processes of distinction: The concept of luxury. *Semiotica, 157*, 497–520.

Moscardo, G., & Benckendorff, P. (2010, November). *Sustainable luxury: Oxymoron or comfortable bedfellows*. In Proceedings of the 2010 international tourism conference on global sustainable tourism, Mbombela, Nelspruit, South Africa (pp. 15–19).

Osburg, V. S., Akhtar, P., Yoganathan, V., & McLeay, F. (2019). The influence of contrasting values on consumer receptiveness to ethical information and ethical choices. *Journal of Business Research, 104*, 366–379.

Pai, C. Y., Laverie, D., & Hass, A. (2022). Love luxury, love the earth: An empirical investigation on how sustainable luxury consumption contributes to social-environmental well-being. *Journal of Macromarketing, 42*(4), 640–654.

Radon, A. (2012). Luxury brand exclusivity strategies-An illustration of a cultural collaboration. *Journal of Business Administration Research, 1*(1), 106.

Richins, M., & Fournier, S. (1991). Some theoretical and popular notions concerning materialism. *Journal of Social Behavior and Personality, 6*(6), 403–414.

Rolling, V., & Sadachar, A. (2018). Are sustainable luxury goods a paradox for millennials? *Social Responsibility Journal.*

Septianto, F., Seo, Y., & Errmann, A. C. (2021). Distinct effects of pride and gratitude appeals on sustainable luxury brands. *Journal of Business Ethics, 169*(2), 211–224.

Sexton, S. E., & Sexton, A. L. (2014). Conspicuous conservation: The Prius halo and willingness to pay for environmental bona fides. *Journal of Environmental Economics and Management, 67*(3), 303–317.

Shukla, P. (2011). Impact of interpersonal influences, brand origin and brand image on luxury purchase intentions: Measuring interfunctional interactions and a cross-national comparison. *Journal of World Business, 46*(2), 242–252.

Shukla, P., & Purani, K. (2012). Comparing the importance of luxury value perceptions in cross-national contexts. *Journal of Business Research, 65*(10), 1417–1424.

Streit, C. M., & Davies, I. A. (2013). Sustainability isn't sexy. In *Sustainability in fashion and textiles: Values, design, production and consumption* (p. 207). Routledge.

Steinhart, Y., Ayalon, O., & Puterman, H. (2013). The effect of an environmental claim on consumers' perceptions about luxury and utilitarian products. *Journal of Cleaner Production, 53, 277–286.*

Sun, Y., Luo, B., Wang, S., & Fang, W. (2021). What you see is meaningful: Does green advertising change the intentions of consumers to purchase eco-labeled products?. *Business Strategy and the Environment, 30(1), 694–704.*

Tsai, S. P. (2005). Impact of personal orientation on luxury-brand purchase value: An international investigation. *International Journal of Market Research, 47*(4), 427–452.

Veblen, T. (1889). *The theory of the leisure class*. Macmillian.

Vigneron, F., & Johnson, L. W. (2004). Measuring perceptions of brand luxury. *Journal of Brand Management, 11*(6), 484–506.

Wang, P., Kuah, A. T., Lu, Q., Wong, C., Thirumaran, K., Adegbite, E., & Kendall, W. (2021). The impact of value perceptions on purchase intention of sustainable luxury brands in China and the UK. *Journal of Brand Management, 28*(3), 325–346.

Wells, V., Athwal, N., Nervino, E., & Carrigan, M. (2021). How legitimate are the environmental sustainability claims of luxury conglomerates? *Journal of Fashion Marketing and Management.*

Wiedmann, K. P., Hennigs, N., & Siebels, A. (2007). Measuring consumers' luxury value perception: A cross-cultural framework. *Academy of Marketing Science Review, 2007*, 1.

Wiedmann, K. P., Hennigs, N., & Siebels, A. (2009). Value-based segmentation of luxury consumption behavior. *Psychology & Marketing, 26*(7), 625–651.

Winston, A. (2016). Luxury brands can no longer ignore sustainability. *Harvard Business Review*, 1–3.

Wong, J. Y., & Dhanesh, G. S. (2017). Communicating corporate social responsibility (CSR) in the luxury industry: Managing CSR–luxury paradox online through acceptance strategies of coexistence and convergence. *Management Communication Quarterly, 31*(1), 88–112.

Yang, Y., Han, H., & Lee, P. K. (2017). An exploratory study of the mechanism of sustainable value creation in the luxury fashion industry. *Sustainability, 9*(4), 483.

The More Supportive, the Better, the More Adaptive, the Best: Leadership Support, Strategic Flexibility and Green Management Practice Adoption in SMEs

Rifat Kamasak and Deniz Palalar Alkan

1 Introduction

Growing global concerns associated with the natural environment, such as alarming ozone depletion, air and water pollution, soil erosion and declining biodiversity, compelled firms to engage in sustainable, eco-friendly business practices (Yao et al., 2023; Shoaib et al., 2022). One of the biggest challenges to integrating eco-friendly business practices into business plans is the perception that environmental concerns will impede the economic growth of firms (Kamasak et al., 2019: Leonidou et al., 2016) or will be too costly for consumers (Lavuri, 2022). Therefore, this perception has resulted in the absence of green management practices (GMPs), which are essential for the sustainable development of firms and countries.

Sustainable, eco-friendly business practices are gaining traction but are still new for many businesses, especially in developing countries (Bhattacharjee et al., 2023). Some scholars (Nguyen & Adomako, 2022; Freeman, 2010) suggest that firms in developing countries are less likely to adopt GMPs due to weak stakeholder pressures and institutional mechanisms. The Green Industrial Policy Report by Altenburg and Assmann (2017) states that green management in developing economies should be the focal concern of research since "the need to accelerate wealth creation [in these countries] is greatest, and many stakeholders perceive this as incompatible with environmental conservation" (p. 2). Indeed, many developing countries, i.e. China, India and Turkey, where firms may voluntarily engage in eco-friendly

R. Kamasak
University of Reading, Henley Business School, Reading, UK
e-mail: r.kamasak@henley.ac.uk

D. P. Alkan (✉)
University of Reading, Henley Business School, Reading, UK

Yeditepe University, Istanbul, Turkey
e-mail: deniz.alkan@yeditepe.edu.tr

N. Ketenci (ed.), *Transition to the Circular Economy Model*, CSR, Sustainability, Ethics & Governance, https://doi.org/10.1007/978-3-031-52700-5_8

practices, suffer from an economic development model that remains detrimental to natural resources and disregard habitats (Kamasak et al., 2023; Wang et al., 2023: Kiefer et al., 2019).

However, integrating GMPs into firms' vision and strategies is pivotal in addressing developing countries' geographic, climatic and socioeconomic vulnerabilities. Among the largest developing countries, Turkey faces significant challenges to climate change impacts, high carbon footprint and emission, and macro-financial volatility (World Bank Group, 2022; Kamasak & Yavuz, 2015). Against these potential threats, there need to be more satisfactory efforts from Turkish companies. Sustainable Economy and Finance Research Association (SEFIA) and 350 Association for Climate (2022) report that only 6 out of the top 25 companies listed on the Istanbul Stock Exchange Index (BIST-100) aim for net zero emissions.

The unconcerned endeavour and weak performance of Turkish firms on environmental issues throughout the years become evident when comparing the results of the Carbon Disclosure Project (CDP) conducted by PwC in 2013 (CDP, 2013). The 2013 CDP results, which revealed that only 39 out of the 410 companies listed on BIST-100 disclosed their carbon emission strategies for global climate change, present the limited progress achieved over a decade. Therefore, the approach of Turkish firms to "climate change, fossil fuel assets and investments, clean energy investments, net zero, carbon footprint and carbon neutral target setting, environmental, social and governance (ESG) practices" (SEFIA and 350 for Climate, 2022, p. 3) appeared unfavourable.

Most empirical environmental sustainability and green management research (i.e. Novitasari et al., 2023; Huo et al., 2021; Zhang et al., 2019) concentrates on the corporate environmental performance of large firms. However, the collective impact of small and medium-sized enterprises (SMEs) on harming the environment is undeniable (Yu et al., 2023; Leonidou et al., 2016). Xing et al. (2016) highlight that "being smaller does not make companies immune from being equally heavy polluters" (p. 192). Therefore, reducing the environmental harm of SMEs is a critical success factor in greening the economy and addressing this challenge is a priority for managers and other decision-makers.

Despite a common cliché stating that environmental concerns frequently hinder firms' growth, many studies (Yue et al., 2023; Zu & Cong, 2021; Shah & Soomro, 2020) suggest that GMPs can improve organisational performance while concurrently safeguarding the natural environment. GMPs can improve organisational processes eco-friendly, facilitate product design and raw material use, and enable firms to differentiate themselves from their competitors, thereby enhancing reputation and boosting market performance (Yue et al., 2023; Menguc et al., 2010). Ioannou and Serafeim (2015) consider GMPs a firm-level organisational capability that can sustain the competitive advantage of firms. Therefore, eco-friendly business practices like GMPs evolve into a strategic imperative beyond a discretionary corporate social responsibility component. Given the strategic nature of eco-friendly business practices, supportive leadership that initiates and motivates the related interventions (Biswas et al., 2022; Kamasak et al., 2016a) and the mechanisms that help firms to reconfigure and deploy their resource base, i.e. strategic flexibility (Kamasak et al.,

2017a, 2019) play critical roles in GMP implementation. Hence, adopting green management principles in a firm may depend on the support from the leadership team and the capabilities to create new resource combinations for the proper environmental procedures, namely strategic flexibility.

This study explores the impact of supportive (or ecocentric) leadership and the combined effects of supportive leadership and strategic flexibility on Turkish SMEs' GMP implementation.

2 Theory and Hypotheses

Many factors affect firms' eco-friendly strategy adoption. The importance of institutional factors such as "government quality, the extent of state ownership, policies, regulations, norms, and the degree of financial development" (Kearney 2012, p. 161) is mainly mentioned in the literature. The reason behind the influential role of institutional factors is their ability to compel organisations to adopt environmentally sound strategies, including GMPs. Institutional encouragements and impositions consist of policies, laws and regulations in favour of eco-friendly practices. However, in developing countries where business, bureaucracy and government are closely linked, and corruption and rent shifting are widespread, institutional pressures might not always work satisfactorily (Cavusgil et al., 2021; Kamasak & Yavuz, 2015). Within this context, where weak institutional infrastructure and jurisdictional inefficiency exist, firms in developing countries may find alternative ways to bypass legal obligations concerning GMPs. Corruption and other unethical courses of action can play pivotal roles in this situation. In such a scenario, firms should embrace an internal perspective as their strategic outlook to adhere to GMPs and enhance their competitiveness. Therefore, instead of relying on compelling laws and rules, a supportive leadership style with an ecocentric approach could be more beneficial for implementing GMPs.

Strategic choices of organisations are predicted by leadership styles (Kumar & Paraskevas, 2018). Leadership is crucial "to study in organisational contexts since successful leadership can make a contribution towards survival of the firm, poor leadership may lead to organisational failure" (Lin & Ho, 2011, p. 69). Numerous studies (i.e., Li et al., 2020; Nicolaides, 2017) show that integrating environmentally sustainable practices into a firm's corporate strategy aligns with the leader's vision, beliefs and attitudes, which are "characterised by the valuing of nature for its own sake, as well as the belief that humans do not exist apart from nature and are thus inextricably linked to its survival" (Biswas et al., 2022, p. 1707). A firm's sustainable development and going-green decisions may require strategic and organisational changes that leaders determine. Supportive leaders with ecocentric nature facilitate the workflows, processes and implementation of GMPs. Furthermore, ecocentric and supportive leaders provide employees with a sense of vision, motivation and inspiration to implement GMPs. Therefore, we hypothesise that:

H_1: Supportive (ecocentric) leadership is positively related to firms' GMPs.

Firms operate in dynamic environments where sudden shifts regarding consumer preferences, market expectations, government regulations and other external conditions occur. Business environments have even more volatility, particularly in developing countries (Cataltepe et al., 2023). To reconfigure and deploy their resources and unlock their capabilities in line with the requirements of high-velocity environments, firms need to dynamically manage their resource base through effective mechanisms such as strategic flexibility (Kamasak et al., 2017b). Strategic flexibility refers to "the capability of rapidly recombining and reconfiguring the firms' resource stocks and executing the actions undertaken by teams, units or the entire firm in real time" (Kamasak et al., 2017a, p. 358). The types of resources and capabilities that firms need to use are related to their environmentally conscious initiatives integrated into their corporate strategies. Strategic flexibility enables firms to allocate their resources to achieve optimum utilisation and shift their limited resources towards the needs of these environmentally conscious initiatives comprising GMPs. Thus, it is hypothesised:

H_2: Strategic flexibility is positively related to firms' GMPs.

Supportive leadership is vital in effectively executing firms' GMPs that necessitate shifts in firms' resource base. The relationship between GMP implementation, ecocentric leadership and strategic flexibility is more intricate than a direct cause-and-effect suggestion. When a firm with an ecocentric leader or management team can utilise a high strategic flexibility mechanism that helps it deploy its resources following eco-friendly practices timely and effectively, its GMP adoption can be enhanced. We suggest that GMP implementation can be facilitated by combining supportive leadership with strategic flexibility, and it is imperative to test their interactive effect in influencing the adoption of GMPs. Accordingly, we hypothesise that:

H_3: The combined effect of ecocentric leadership and strategic flexibility will be most significant in adopting GMPs.

3 Methods

Sample and Data Collection

The sample was selected from the records of the associations that serve in the chemical and petrochemical industries. These industries consist of firms that manufacture paint and coatings, fertiliser, detergent, cosmetics and personal care, plastics, rubber and inorganic chemicals. The toxic effects of chemical products on human health and the environment are evident, so it is essential to foster the adoption of GMPs in these hazardous industries. Furthermore, the report by the Investment Office of the Presidency of the Turkish Republic states that the country "has ambitious 2023 targets for the chemical industry, which include reaching USD 50 billion in chemical exports, thus capturing 0.79% share of the global chemicals market" (Investment Office, 2021). The sample comprised micro, small and medium-sized firms with equal or less than 250 employees and USD 50 million in annual turnover, according to the SME definition by the European Union (European Commission, 2021). We obtained the database of SMEs from the Turkish Chemical Society (TKD), the Turkish Plastics Industrialists' Federation (PLASFED), The Association of Cosmetics and Cleaning Products Industrialists (KTSD) and The Association of Paint Industry (BOSAD). The databases of the associations included a total number of 3847 registered firms that can be classified as SMEs in 2022. A self-administered online questionnaire was sent to only one executive from each firm, and 358 usable questionnaires were obtained. Therefore, the response rate was 9.3%.

Measurement Instrument

As the measurement instrument, we used a questionnaire with three construct categories: ecocentric leadership, strategic flexibility and green management practices. While six items measure ecocentric leadership (Uddin et al., 2020), nine measure strategic flexibility (Zhou & Wu, 2010; Wei et al., 2014). Six questions assess firms' GMP adoption (Lin & Ho, 2011), and two items categorise the demographics (age and size). Age and size were controlled in the analyses (Kamasak et al., 2016b). All responses to the construct items were recorded on a 5-point Likert scale.

Reliability and Validity

The reliability and validity issues were assessed by the factor loadings of the items, Cronbach's alpha values of the constructs, and correlations between the variables (inter-item correlations). The unidimensionality of all constructs was ensured by exploratory factor analysis (EFA) with Varimax rotation. The analysis yielded three constructs. All items were loaded into their expected constructs with factor loadings equal to or greater than 0.50 (Hair et al., 1998). Thus, the constructs seemed appropriate to measure structural variables. These three factors explained 81.739% of the total variance. The constructs with alpha values equal to or greater than 0.70 were accepted as reliable (Saunders et al., 2007). Cronbach's alpha values of the constructs are ecocentric leadership ($\alpha = 0.897$), strategic flexibility ($\alpha = 0.902$) and GMP adoption ($\alpha = 0.841$). Correlations between variables were investigated to assess multicollinearity, where highly correlated independent variables can predict each other and result in misleading findings in regression analysis (Saunders et al., 2007). The correlations between all variables were below 0.80, which did not indicate a multicollinearity problem.

Analyses and Findings

The data were analysed by a four-step hierarchical regression analysis, where we entered each set of independent variables into the model and calculated the incremental changes of the R^2 statistic and the β coefficients. We first entered age and size as the control variables. In the second step, we entered ecocentric leadership (EL) and strategic flexibility (SF) in the third step. Finally, we entered the interaction term of EL and SF (EL × SF) in the fourth step to predict the implementation of GMPs (Table 1). Table 1 presents the processes and results of the regression analyses.

In Model 1, the control variables, firm age and size, explained no significant variance in GMP adoption. In Model 2, EL was entered into the model, and a positive significant relationship between EL and GMP adoption was found (β = 0.364**, $p < 0.05$). Therefore, H_1 is supported. The EL variable added a further 13.8% [(ΔR^2 = 0.138); (F = 2.412, $p < 0.05$)] significant variation to the model. The entrance of SF in Model 3 significantly affected GMP adoption (β = 0.208**, $p < 0.05$), thus, H_2 is also supported. The addition of SF increased variation to 24.3% with an additional 7.6% [(ΔR^2 = 0.076); (F = 2.536, $p < 0.05$)]. In Model 4, the interaction of EL and SF was significant on GMP adoption with the greatest β value (β = 0.479**, $p < 0.05$). R^2 change was also significant, and the addition of the interactive effect of EL and SF provided the highest variation in the model with 21.9% [(ΔR^2 = 0.219); (F = 2.884, $p < 0.05$)].

Given the greatest β value achieved and the highest contribution to the explanation in variance provided on GMP adoption by the interaction of EL and SF, H_3 is confirmed.

Table 1 The results of regression analyses

DV: GMP adoption predictors	Model 1	Model 2	Model 3	Model 4
Firm size	0.019	0.017	0.018	0.013
Firm age	0.011	0.008	−0.006	0.021
EL		0.364**		
SF			0.208**	
EL × SF				0.479**
R^2	0.029	0.167	0.243	0.462
ΔR^2	–	0.138	0.076	0.219
F	1.163	2.412**	2.536**	2.884**

**$p < 0.05$ (two-tailed)
Notes: *DV* Dependent Variable; $N = 358$
Source: The table is prepared by the authors

4 Discussion

Drawing on an empirical study in the chemical and petrochemical industries in Turkey, we presented the impact of ecocentric leadership, strategic flexibility and their combined effects on GMP implementations of SMEs. The considerable synergistic impact arising from the interplay of ecocentric leadership and firms' strategic flexibility was particularly evident. Leaders' (or owners') significant influence on environmental sustainability in SMEs should be considered a key outcome. Ecocentric leaders can significantly impact employees, and a leader's strong commitment to environmentally sustainable practices inspires employees to develop an attitude towards GMP implementation throughout the organisation. Therefore, leaders at any level should embody a role model for eco-friendly practices to ensure a cleaner and less polluted environment for current and future generations. Given the predominant hierarchical culture where employees prioritise leader influence in Turkey (Kabasakal & Bodur, 2008), an adequate and timely display of leadership that supports eco-friendly practices can encourage employees to engage in GMPs proactively.

The significant association between strategic flexibility and GMPs might be related to the high environmental turbulence and uncertainty in markets in Turkey. A green business strategy crafted by senior management and integrated into corporate principles requires optimum resource allocation and capability development (Leonidou et al., 2017). Strategic flexibility empowers firms to allocate their resources per the demands of green business strategy and enhances their operational efficiency in volatile environments.

High unpredictability and fierce competition may compel especially SMEs with financial limitations to focus on their manufacturing and market operations with no concern for the environment. Thus, challenging business conditions and cost concerns may discourage especially SMEs from adopting GMPs that SMEs may deem as part of their corporate social responsibility. Moreover, in contrast to developed countries, where firms emphasise sustainability and environmentalism, firms in developing countries prioritise rapid growth and profitability. These circumstances can create barriers for SMEs to adopt GMPs. Strong leadership endorsing eco-friendly practices and strategic flexibility for optimal resource allocation can facilitate the adoption of GMPs by SMEs. This might be an explanation for the emergence of the most significant impact created by the leadership and strategic flexibility synergy that the study found.

Competing Interests The authors have no conflicts of interest to declare that are relevant to the content of this chapter.

References

Altenburg, T., & Assmann, C. (Eds.). (2017). *Green industrial policy. Concept, policies, country experiences*. UN Environment; German Development Institute/Deutsches Institut für Entwicklungspolitk (DIE).

Bhattacharjee, P., Howlader, I. I., Rahman, M. A., Taqi, M. M. M., Hasan, M. T., Ali, S. M., & Alghababsheh, M. (2023). Critical success factors for circular economy in the waste electrical and electronic equipment sector in an emerging economy: Implications for stakeholders. *Journal of Cleaner Production, 401*, 136767.

Biswas, S. R., Uddin, M. A., Bhattacharjee, S., Dey, M., & Rana, T. (2022). Ecocentric leadership and voluntary environmental behavior for promoting sustainability strategy: The role of psychological green climate. *Business Strategy and the Environment, 31*(4), 1705–1718.

Cataltepe, V., Kamasak, R., Palalar, A. D., & Bulutlar, F. (2023). Dynamic and marketing capabilities as determinants of firm performance: Evidence from the automotive industry. *Journal of Asia Business Studies, 17*(3), 617–638.

Cavusgil, T., Ghauri, P. N., & Liu, L. A. (2021). *Doing business in emerging markets* (3rd ed.). Sage.

European Commission. (2021). *The definition of micro, small and medium-sized enterprises*. Retrieved from https://ec.europa.eu/transparency/documents-register/detail?ref=SWD(2021)279&lang=en

Freeman, R. E. (2010). *Strategic management: A stakeholder approach*. Cambridge University Press.

Hair, J. F., Anderson, R. E., Tatham, R. L., & Black, W. C. (1998). *Multivariate data analysis*. Prentice Hall.

Huo, B., Wang, K., & Zhang, Y. (2021). The impact of leadership on supply chain green strategy alignment and operational performance. *Operations Management Research, 14*(1–2), 152–165.

Investment Office. (2021). *Bright spot for chemical investments in Türkiye*. https://www.invest.gov.tr/en/library/publications/lists/investpublications/chemicals-industry.pdf

Ioannou, I., & Serafeim, G. (2015). The impact of corporate social responsibility on investment recommendations: Analysts' perceptions and shifting institutional logics. *Strategic Management Journal, 36*(7), 1053–1081.

Kabasakal, H., & Bodur, M. (2008). In S. Chhokar, F. C. Brodback, & R. J. House (Eds.), *Culture and leadership across the world: The globe book of in-depth studies of 25 societies*. Taylor and Francis.

Kamasak, R., & Yavuz, M. (2015). Economic development, market characteristics and current business conditions in Turkey: A guide for successful operations. In B. Christiansen & M. M. Erdogdu (Eds.), *Comparative economics and regional development in Turkey* (pp. 336–354). IGI Global.

Kamasak, R., Yozgat, U., & Yavuz, M. (2016a). Government policies, implementation leadership and green management practices in an emerging economy. *International Journal of Trade, Economics and Finance, 7*(4), 97–101.

Kamasak, R., Yozgat, U., & Yavuz, M. (2016b). *Importance of strategic flexibility on the knowledge and innovation relationship: An emerging market study*. In International Conference on Management and Information Technology, 11 December, Istanbul, Turkey, (Elsevier Procedia – Social and Behavioral Sciences, Vol. 229C, pp. 126–132).

Kamasak, R., Yozgat, U., & Yavuz, M. (2017a). Knowledge process capabilities and innovation: Testing the moderating effects of environmental dynamism and strategic flexibility. *Knowledge Management Research & Practice, 15*(3), 356–368.

Kamasak, R., Yavuz, M., & Özturk, T. Y. (2017b). Reducing risk through strategic flexibility and implementation leadership in high-velocity markets. In U. Hacioglu, H. Dincer, & N. Alayoglu (Eds.), *Global business strategies in crisis: Strategic thinking and development* (pp. 273–286). Springer.

Kamasak, R., James, S. R., & Yavuz, M. (2019). The interplay of corporate social responsibility and corporate political activity in emerging markets: The role of strategic flexibility in nonmarket strategies. *Business Ethics: A European Review, 28*(3), 305–320.

Kamasak, R., Ozbilgin, M. F., Yavuz, M., April, K., & Vassilopoulou, J. (2023). 'We can't go back to normal': Diversity management in global organisations: Introducing the global value chain (GVC) approach. In C. Maheshkar & V. Sharma (Eds.), *Handbook of research on cross-cultural business and management* (pp. 229–263). Vernon Press.

Kearney, C. (2012). Emerging markets research: Trends, issues and future directions. *Emerging Markets Review, 13*(2), 159–183.

Kiefer, C. P., Gonzalez, P. D. R., & Carrillo-Hermosilla, J. (2019). Drivers and barriers of eco-innovation types for sustainable transitions: A quantitative perspective. *Business Strategy and the Environment, 28*(1), 155–172.

Kumar, A., & Paraskevas, J. P. (2018). A proactive environmental strategy: Analyzing the effect of SCM experience, age, and female representation in TMTs. *Journal of Supply Chain Management, 54*(1), 20–41.

Lavuri, R. (2022). Organic green purchasing: Moderation of environmental protection emotion and price sensitivity. *Journal of Cleaner Production, 368*, 133113.

Leonidou, L. C., Christodoulides, P., & Thwaites, D. (2016). External determinants and financial outcomes of an eco-friendly orientation in smaller manufacturing firms. *Journal of Small Business Management, 54*(1), 5–25. https://doi.org/10.1111/jsbm.12121

Leonidou, L. C., Christodoulides, P., Kyrgidou, L. P., & Palihawadana, D. (2017). Internal drivers and performance consequences of small firm green business strategy: The moderating role of external forces. *Journal of Business Ethics, 140*(3), 585–606.

Li, Z., Xue, J., Li, R., Chen, H., & Wang, T. (2020). Environmentally specific transformational leadership and employee's pro-environmental behavior: The mediating roles of environmental passion and autonomous motivation. *Frontiers in Psychology, 11*, 1–13.

Lin, C. Y., & Ho, Y. H. (2011). Determinants of green practice adoption for logistics companies in China. *Journal of Business Ethics, 98*(1), 67–83.

Menguc, B., Auh, S., & Ozanne, L. (2010). The interactive effect of internal and external factors on a proactive environmental strategy and its influence on a firm's performance. *Journal of Business Ethics, 94*(2), 279–298.

Nguyen, N. P., & Adomako, S. (2022). Stakeholder pressure for eco-friendly practices, international orientation, and eco-innovation: A study of small and medium-sized enterprises in Vietnam. *Corporate Social Responsibility and Environmental Management, 29*(1), 79–88.

Nicolaides, A. (2017). Ethical practices, eco-centric business and environmental sustainability. *Journal of Human Ecology, 57*(1–2), 1–10.

Novitasari, M., Wijaya, A. L., Agustin, N. M., Gunardi, A., & Dana, P. (2023). Corporate social responsibility and firm performance: Green supply chain management as a mediating variable. *Corporate Social Responsibility and Environmental Management, 30*(1), 267–276. https://doi.org/10.1002/csr.2353

Saunders, M., Lewis, P., & Thornhill, A. (2007). *Research methods for business students* (4th ed.). Pearson Education.

SEFIA and 350 for Climate. (2022). *Climate change and sustainability research: Outlook on BIST 30 companies*. Retrieved from https://sefia.org/en/publications/climate-change-and-sustainability-research-outlook-on-bist-30-companies/

Shah, N., & Soomro, B. A. (2020). Internal green integration and environmental performance: The predictive power of proactive environmental strategy, greening the supplier, and environmental collaboration with the supplier. *Business Strategy and the Environment, 30*(2).

Shoaib, M., Nawal, A., Zámečník, R., Korsakienė, R., & Rehman, A. U. (2022). Go green! Measuring the factors that influence sustainable performance. *Journal of Cleaner Production, 366*, 132959.

The CDP Report. (2013). *Sector insights: What is driving climate change action in the world's largest companies?* [Online]. https://www.cdp.net/cdpresults/cdp-global-500-climate-change-report-2013.pdf

Uddin, M. A., Akter, R., Al-Amin, M., Rahman, M. S., & Ferdausy, S. (2020). How do socially responsible human resource management and voluntary green behavior influence organizational competitiveness? *Studies in Business and Economics, 15*(2), 243–255.

Wang, C., Wei, Y., & Wu, L. (2023). Global eco-innovation and its local impact in emerging economies: Boundary conditions of environmental regulations and pollution intensity. *Journal of Product Innovation Management*, 1–33. https://doi.org/10.1111/jpim.12675

Wei, Z., Yi, Y., & Guo H. (2014). Organisational learning, ambidexterity, strategic flexibility, and new product development. *Journal of Product Innovation Management, 31*, 832–847.

World Bank Group. (2022). *Türkiye country climate and development report* (CCDR series). World Bank.

Xing, K., Qian, W., & Zaman, A. U. (2016). Development of a cloud-based platform for footprint assessment in green supply chain management. *Journal of Cleaner Production, 139*, 191–203.

Yao, S., Pan, Y., Wang, L., Sensoy, A., & Cheng, F. (2023). Building eco-friendly corporations: The role of minority shareholders. *Journal of Business Ethics, 182*, 933–966. https://doi.org/10.1007/s10551-022-05291-y

Yu, F., Cao, J. Y., & Shi, Y. (2023). Double-threshold effect of technological innovation on environmental-responsibility fulfilment: Evidence from high-polluting SMEs in China. *Journal of Small Business Management, 61*(4), 1871–1895. https://doi.org/10.1080/00472778.2020.1867736

Yue, X., Huo, B., & Ye, Y. (2023). The impact of coercive pressure and ethical responsibility on cross-functional green management and firm performance. *Journal of Business & Industrial Marketing, 38*(5), 1015–1028.

Zhang, D., Rong, Z., & Ji, Q. (2019). Green innovation and firm performance: Evidence from listed companies in China. *Resources, Conservation and Recycling, 144*, 48–55.

Zhou, K. Z., & Wu, F. (2010). Technological capability, strategic flexibility, and product innovation. *Strategic Management Journal, 31*(5), 547–561.

Zu, X., & Cong, Y. (2021). Green at source: An empirical examination of the effectiveness and sustainability of operational-level environmental management practices in US industry. *Total Quality Management & Business Excellence*, 1–20.

Time-Scale Behaviour of Co-movements Between Renewable Energy Stocks and Other Financial Assets

Sercan Demiralay, Hatice Gaye Gencer, and Selçuk Bayraci

1 Introduction

Industrialization in the late nineteenth century has transformed societies and economies by mass production and technological developments that heavily relied on fossil fuel consumption. However, starting by the 1980s, the rapidly diminishing finite sources of fossil energy, and climate change have begun to threaten the global economy. The nuclear energy production invented in 1948,[1] as an alternative source to fossil fuel, lost significant grounds after the accidents and natural disasters occurring in the plants, such as the Three Mile Island (TMI) accident in March 1979, the Chernobyl disaster in April 1986 and tsunami in the Japanese Fukushima-Daiichi plant on March 11, 2011.[2] Ferstl et al. (2012) document a 7.71% decline in the S&P Global Nuclear Energy Index on the first trading day after the Japanese disaster,

[1] In 1954, the Obninsk Nuclear Power Plant was established as the world's first nuclear power station in the then Soviet Union and currently there are about 450 plants operating in the World (see www.iaea.org).

[2] The Fukushima nuclear accident prompted German government to enact the permanent shutdown of its nuclear power stations until 2022 (see Bohl et al., 2013).

S. Demiralay
Nottingham Trent University, Nottingham, UK
e-mail: sercan.demiralay@ntu.ac.uk

H. G. Gencer (✉)
Yeditepe University, Istanbul, Turkey
e-mail: gaye.gencer@yeditepe.edu.tr

S. Bayraci
Borusan Otomotiv, Istanbul, Turkey
e-mail: selcuk.bayraci@borusanotomotiv.com

N. Ketenci (ed.), *Transition to the Circular Economy Model*, CSR, Sustainability, Ethics & Governance, https://doi.org/10.1007/978-3-031-52700-5_9

while the S&P Global Clean Energy Index rose by 4.55%.[3] As stated by Wen et al. (2014) slowing the pace of economic growth in favour of reducing carbon emissions and fossil fuel consumption cannot be an option, thereby, renewable energy[4] sources are explored to alternate fossil fuel for maintaining a sustainable economic growth with environmentally friendly practices.

By the turn of the twenty-first century, the world has staged the advancements in artificial intelligence and robotics which ushered the rise of the fourth Industrial Revolution. Hence, energy security, climate change and peak oil concerns along with technological innovations and social responsibility issues have forced the renewable energy sector to rapid growth (Ayres et al., 2007; Shackley & Green, 2007; Buonocore et al., 2012; Ortas & Moneva, 2013). Different scenarios of the International Energy Agency (IEA) predict an average annual growth rate between 7.3% and 10.4% in the global clean energy demand for the years from 2007 to 2030.[5] Currently, more than 130 countries promote green energy investments and, globally, the investments in renewable energy sector amounted almost USD 2.5 trillion between 2011 and 2020, with about USD 300 billion per year in recent years.[6] Furthermore, recent events and heightened geopolitical risk appear to transform the energy sector. More specifically, the Russian military invasion of Ukraine started on February 24, 2022 was responded by the Western countries through imposing sanctions on the Russian economy including import controls that ban oil and natural gas imports from Russia to the Eurozone and the USA. As a result, many Western countries including Germany plans to increase their green energy investments in the years ahead to ease Russian energy reliance.

On top of these, widespread usage of internet technologies and spur of social media in every aspect of life from politics to economics have changed the manners in both business and financial practices. Consequently, moral concerns have started to become of focus in investments. Lately, a wide variety of organizations including universities, communities, pension funds, and charitable foundations are divesting from fossil fuel investments to perform their moral obligations in addressing climate change[7] as a result of the pressure exerted on these organizations by their stakeholders.[8] Therefore, the social demand for clean sources of energy places fossil

---

[3] The S&P Global Nuclear Energy Index is a worldwide index consisting 24 companies in nuclear businesses and the S&P Global Clean Energy Index is comprised of 30 companies that are in clean energy-related businesses (see Ferstl et al., 2012).

[4] In this paper, renewable energy, clean energy, new energy and alternative energy are all used interchangeably.

[5] See International Energy Agency Reports for 2009 at https://www.iea.org/reports/world-energy-outlook-2009 and also Sadorsky (2012) for a brief summary of the report.

[6] Global Landscape of Renewable Energy Finance 2021, International Renewable Energy Agency Report, https://irena.org/-/media/Files/IRENA/Agency/Publication/2021/Nov/IRENA_Global_Landscape_Renewable_Energy_Finance_2021.pdf.

[7] See Henriques and Sadorsky (2018) for a detailed discussion of divestments.

[8] See http://gofossilfree.org and Arabella Advisors (2018) among others for a detailed list of divestments.

fuels as stranded assets,[9] initiating an eminent risk factor for investors. Since divestments from fossil fuels would reduce portfolio diversification, investors may enhance portfolio efficiency by substituting fossil fuel stocks with those of clean energy shares (Henriques & Sadorsky, 2018). Henceforth, alternative energy stocks are substantial investment options in portfolio construction in the new era amidst the socially responsible investing motives and technological innovations.

On these grounds, scholars have diverted their efforts to study the dynamics of renewable energy equity returns to infer first-hand evidence of portfolio construction and risk management. Although there is a consensus in academia on the fact that there is no theoretical foundation for the relationship between clean energy investments and various economic, financial and socio-political issues, a mushrooming empirical work emerged in the field of new energy economics. The literature on clean energy investments widely investigates the linkages between the prices of oil and alternative energy stocks (Wen et al., 2014; Dutta, 2017; Ferrer et al., 2018; Elie et al., 2019; Zhang et al., 2020; Kanamura, 2020; Corbet et al., 2020), while another strand of research focuses on the interdependence between clean energy and technology stocks (Henriques & Sadorsky, 2008; Sadorsky, 2012; Kumar et al., 2012; Inchauspe et al., 2015; Ahmad, 2017; Ahmad & Rais, 2018; Maghyereh et al., 2019; Baur & Smales, 2019). Yet another branch of financial research examines portfolio diversification with alternative energy investments (Ortas & Moneva, 2013; Ahmad et al., 2018; Henriques & Sadorsky, 2018). Some scholars highlight the hedging potential of commodities, particularly gold and the energy commodities against renewable energy equities (Wen & Nguyen, 2017; Elie et al., 2019; Dutta et al., 2020; Nguyen et al., 2020). The relevant studies in the existing literature utilize various statistical methods including Vector Autoregressive Models (Henriques & Sadorsky, 2008; Kumar et al., 2012), Multivariate GARCH applications (Sadorsky, 2012; Wen et al., 2014; Ahmad, 2017; Ahmad & Rais, 2018; Ahmad et al., 2018; Kanamura, 2020; Dutta et al., 2020), Copulas (Reboredo, 2015; Wen & Nguyen, 2017; Reboredo & Ugolini, 2018; Elie et al., 2019) and Wavelet methods (Reboredo et al., 2017; Maghyereh et al., 2019; Zhang et al., 2020).

In this study, we analyse the linkages between renewable energy equities and various investment assets, employing the wavelet coherence analysis as a novel and auspicious technique that enables us to examine dynamic co-movements across time and frequency domains. Identifying the dynamics across frequencies is of utmost importance to investors, as they constitute a heterogenous group with "*very different beliefs, objectives, preferences, and institutional constraints as well as distinct levels of information assimilation and risk tolerance* (Ferrer et al., 2018, *p.2)*". Utilizing the phase differences, we further investigate the lead-lag relationships in the time-scale space, providing additional insights in terms of forecasting ability. Moreover, we use rolling window analysis to quantify the time-varying frequency-dependent correlations. We analyse the changes in the dynamic correlations during

[9] Bos and Gupta suggest that stranded assets are assets that lose their economic value before the end of their useful life as the result of changes in market forces, technological innovations, societal norms, legislation and environmental conditions.

the most recent Coronavirus crash, which constitutes a remarkable systematic risk factor as it is totally unprecedented in this new era of extensive globalization. Accordingly, our main contributions are two-fold: First, this paper extends the existing literature, as it is, to the best of our knowledge, the first study that analyses time-frequency co-dependency between four different clean energy stock indices and various other asset classes; second, our study is different from the existing literature as our findings incorporate the impact of the COVID-19 era on the interferences between clean energy stocks and various investment vehicles. Therefore, we provide fresh evidence regarding how renewable energy equities co-move with different asset classes during the COVID-19 pandemic. Our empirical findings offer significant insights and implications for financial market participants in terms of efficient risk diversification and portfolio construction, as they can make use of the relevant information.

On these grounds, our aim is to present a comprehensive analysis on the dynamic relation between various clean energy indices, namely, the Wilder Hill Clean Energy Price Index, the NASDAQ Clean Edge Green Energy Price Index, the First Trust Global Wind Energy ETF and the Ardour Solar Energy Price Index, and different investment alternatives, which are two strategic commodities (gold and oil), two strategic sectors (technology and oil and gas), the implied volatility index (VIX) as a proxy of the investor sentiment and bonds as quality assets. Gold and oil are widely traded strategic commodities, affecting extensively the prices in the equity and commodity markets, and hence having significant impacts on the global economic activity (Baruník et al., 2016). The bulk of prior studies find VIX to be an efficient hedge for stocks (Hood & Malik, 2013; Basher & Sadorsky, 2016) as there exists a negative relationship between the VIX and the stock returns (Whaley, 2009). In previous empirical studies, a negative link between stock prices and interest rates is documented as high-interest rates lead to higher discount rates in equity pricing (Shiller & Beltratti, 1992; Connolly et al., 2005). Consequently, bonds are deemed as quality assets; particularly, at times of higher market volatility, investors shift their stock holdings towards bonds which is described as the "flight-to-quality" phenomenon in finance literature (Hartmann et al., 2004; Baur & Lucey, 2009; Dajcman, 2015; Ferrer et al., 2016; Bayraci et al., 2018).

In line with the above discussions, our analysis reveals significant empirical findings for investors, traders and portfolio managers in terms of portfolio construction, risk management and hedging, which can be briefly summarized as follows: First, wavelet coherences provide evidence of low (high) co-movements at high (low) frequencies, suggesting that potential investment benefits of alternative energy stocks significantly depend on the investment horizon. Second, renewable energy indices exhibit strong and positive inter-linkages with oil and gas companies and technology stocks across all scales, while they display significant positive dependence on crude oil only at low frequencies. Third, frequency-dependent correlations between alternative energy equities and the VIX are negative which implies the potential hedging benefits of the so-called "fear gauge" index. Fourth, we find weak co-dependence of renewable energy stocks with gold and bond investments, substantiating the diversification properties of these assets in a mixed portfolio. Lastly, the results provide evidence of frequency-dependent lead-lag relationships between clean energy equities and other investment assets.

As stated earlier, the results of this study provide beneficial implications for portfolio investors who seek for precise horizon and causality-specific information to construct efficient hedging and diversification strategies. Likewise, authorities can establish policy-based incentives to promote the alternative energy sector to warranty a sustainable economic growth. Our study differs from similar efforts in the sense that, we include four alternative energy indices in our analyses, while previous literature has mostly studied a single clean energy index. Additionally, the preceding empirical work heavily focuses on the dependence of renewable energy returns on oil and technology stocks, spending relatively negligible efforts in exploring the relationship dynamics of alternative energy equities with other financial assets. For this reason, by examining the dynamic interactions between clean energy indices and a number of different assets, we capture a superior and a thorough understanding of the aspects in alternative energy investments. This understanding is crucial in conferring information on how to efficiently hedge clean energy investments which represent relatively a new asset class that embodies significant uncertainties (Ahmad et al., 2018).

2 Literature Review

As briefly mentioned before, there has been a growing endeavour in the existing literature to analyse the investment characteristics of alternative energy equities. More particularly, the connectedness of new energy stocks with traditional and alternative investments has attracted significant interest from scholars. They have shown the greatest interest in studying the linkages between oil, as one of the strategic commodities, and renewable energy investments. The negative effects of rising oil prices on the economic activity, along with its exerted pressure on inflation rates, are investigated widely (Fama, 1981; Darby, 1982; Hamilton, 1983; Cunado & Perez, 2005; Kilian, 2008; Kumar & Managi, 2009). Managi and Okimoto (2013) discuss that most of the recessions in the USA are anteceded by large oil shocks to exemplify the eminence of oil prices on the real economy. Henceforth, there are many studies evincing a negative linkage between oil price escalations and equity prices (Hamilton, 1983; Huang & Masulis, 1996; Jones & Gautam, 1996; Sadorsky, 1999, 2001; Park & Ratti, 2008; Henriques & Sadorsky, 2008; Driesprong et al., 2008; Kilian & Park, 2009; Salisu et al., 2020; Akhtaruzzaman et al., 2020). As oil is a factor of production, oil price shocks negatively affect the earnings of businesses in general, which resultantly lead to a fall in stock prices.[10] Furthermore, surges in oil prices cause a

[10] See Narayan and Sharma (2011) among others.

rise in the inflation rates forcing Central Banks to increase the interest rates which consequently raises the discount rate in the equity pricing.[11] However, as suggested by several scholars, the oil price increases may work to the advantage of some industries, in particular the renewable energy sector (Kumar et al., 2012; Madaleno & Pinho, 2014). The rise in oil prices diverts companies to alternative energy sources to minimize production costs and avoid from excessive fluctuations in manufacturing costs that cause undesirable oscillation in company profits and firm value.

The abundant literature on the relation between oil prices and renewable energy stocks confers various results. Reboredo (2015) suggests positive time-varying dependence between oil and renewable energy returns with symmetric tail dependence implying that the two markets boom and crash together. He reports that extreme oil price movements increase the Value-at-Risk (VaR) of renewable energy portfolios by 30% posing symmetric impact on both short and long positions except for solar energy stocks which retain upper tail independence. Dutta (2017) documents that the implied volatility of crude oil has positive and significant predictive power on the realized variance of the clean energy equity returns. Reboredo et al. (2017) evince a weak co-movement between oil prices and renewable energy stock returns in the short-run, while in the long-run the relation is stronger mainly for the period 2008–2013. Assessing the impact of the energy prices (oil, gas, electricity and coal) on clean energy stock returns, Reboredo and Ugolini (2018) document that oil prices contribute most to the renewable energy equity returns in the USA, and electricity prices determine the clean energy stock yields in the EU. Maghyereh et al. (2019) validate significant return spillovers between oil prices and clean energy stock yields only at long horizons while volatility spillovers are significant both at short and long horizons, where in the latter they are punctuated. In a more recent study, Zhang et al. (2020) distinguish the effects of oil supply, oil aggregate demand and oil-specific demand shocks on clean energy stocks, signifying the asymmetric impact of oil-specific demand shocks on clean energy stocks in the long run. Analysing the co-movements and spillovers between the prices of oil and renewable energy stocks during the COVID-19 pandemic, Corbet et al. (2020) vindicate economically meaningful positive spillovers from declining oil prices to renewable energy equities, specifically for the incidence of negative WTI oil prices on April 20, 2020. They suggest that in the COVID-19 period, the global supply chain system was disrupted in an unprecedented way, forcing countries to convert to domestic economic resources and production, which soared the interest in the renewable energy sector as a convenient local source.

In a similar vein, relevant empirical studies concentrate on the interactions between conventional and renewable energy companies. Wen et al. (2014) suggest that new energy stock investments are riskier and more speculative than those of the traditional energy companies, providing evidence of significant asymmetric return spillovers between Chinese fossil fuel and new energy stocks for the period between 2006 and 2012. Their results also show that positive news related to new energy

[11] See Henriques and Sadorsky (2008) among others.

stocks lead to a fall in fossil fuel equity prices on the following day, while good news about traditional energy stocks causes price increases in new energy shares with a lag of a trading day. In a similar study, Henriques and Sadorsky (2018) document that highest risk-adjusted returns are encountered for the portfolio that consists of clean energy stocks with no fossil fuel shares in it, giving evidence for enhanced portfolio performance in case of divestment from fossil fuel to clean energy investments.

As indicated earlier, renewable energy sector is highly dependent on technological innovations and developments, specifically in the field of energy transfers and storage. For this reason, technology and alternative energy sectors are seen as highly related. Henriques and Sadorsky (2008) suggest that lagged oil prices, technology stock returns and interest rates Granger cause the stock prices of alternative energy companies; however, their study substantiates that technology stocks have a larger impact on the returns of alternative energy equities. Kumar et al. (2012) conclude that returns of three different alternative energy indices are explained by the lagged oil prices, high technology equity returns and interest rates, applying a VAR framework. In a similar domain, Sadorsky (2012) applies multivariate GARCH models to investigate the volatility spillovers between oil prices and clean energy and technology equities. He documents that clean energy and technology stocks' returns are intricately connected with significantly strong dynamic conditional correlations. Managi and Okimoto (2013) apply a Markov-switching vector autoregressive model to analyse the interactions among the prices of oil, clean energy and technology stocks between 2001 and 2010. Their findings corroborate that clean energy stocks are riskier than technology stocks and that oil prices positively affect the prices of alternative energy shares after the structural change in the oil market which corresponds to late 2007. In a different study, Ahmad (2017) examines the return and volatility spillovers among the prices of oil, clean energy and technology stocks between 2005 and 2015. He reckons the vital role of technology stocks in the return and volatility spillovers of renewable energy equities.

More recently, scholars have also started investigating the relationships between renewable energy stock prices and various other investment assets, such as commodities, bonds and the volatility indices. Ahmad and Rais (2018) investigate the time-varying return and volatility spillovers between clean energy and aggregate and technology equity returns along with four energy commodity prices. Their results reveal that energy commodities share limited dependence with the alternative energy assets offering superior hedging and risk reduction, whereas technology stocks dominate the return dynamics of new energy companies. Ahmad et al. (2018) examine the inter-dependence among alternative energy equity returns and the prices of gold and oil along with the VIX and the volatility index of crude oil. They acknowledge the VIX, retaining the highest hedging effectiveness for clean energy stocks followed by oil investments. In the same strain, Ferrer et al. (2018) investigate the time and frequency dynamics of connectedness among stock returns of clean energy, technology and oil and gas companies along with oil prices, the VIX and the bond yields. They confirm significant return and volatility spillovers in the short run and a strong connectedness between clean energy and technology stocks.

Dutta et al. (2020) extend Ahmad et al.'s (2018) work, incorporating three alternative clean energy indices along with the volatility indices of oil, gold and silver in their analyses, whereby their findings point out that the oil volatility index appears to be the most applicable hedge for alternative energy assets.

A new branch of literature has emerged investigating the hedging potential and safe-haven quality of gold against renewable energy equities. The hedging and safe-haven properties of gold against traditional assets are studied vastly in the literature (Hillier et al., 2006; Baur & Lucey, 2010; Baur & McDermott, 2010; Mensi et al., 2015; Arouri et al., 2015). Gold is suggested as a hedge against inflation caused by the rising oil prices (Reboredo, 2013; Beckmann & Czudaj, 2013). Wen and Nguyen (2017) examine the diversification potential of commodities for Chinese energy stocks and substantiate the hedging and safe haven qualities of gold against energy equities, while these properties of gold are found to be the most stable for renewable energy assets. Elie et al. (2019) examine the safe-haven property of gold against clean energy stocks along with crude oil for the period between 2003 and 2018, and provide evidence that gold acts as a weak safe-haven against clean energy stocks. Additionally, Uddin et al. (2019) advocate that gold can offer diversification benefits in portfolios with alternative energy equities in normal or bullish markets, however, not in bearish markets, as gold and renewable stock returns are positively correlated in bearish market conditions.

3 Methodology

In this study, we firstly rely on the continuous wavelet transform (CWT)-based techniques of cross wavelet power, phase difference and cross wavelet coherency proposed by Torrence and Compo (1998) to examine the interactions between two-time series at various frequencies and how they advance over periods with the functionality of cross wavelet techniques (for technical details see Aguiar-Conraria et al., 2008; Kuşkaya & Bilgili, 2020; Vacha & Barunik, 2012; Torrence & Webster, 1999; Mallat, 1989; Rhif et al., 2019; Gallegati, 2008).

4 Data

Our data set consists of four alternative energy indices, namely the Wilder Hill Clean Energy Price Index (ECO), the NASDAQ Clean Edge Green Energy Price Index (CELS), the First Trust Global Wind Energy ETF (FAN) and the Ardour Solar Energy Price Index (SOLRX). Along with the alternative energy indices, following Ferrer et al. (2018), we include the S&P 500 Oil, Gas and Consumable Fuels Price Index, the S&P GSCI Crude Oil Index, the CBOE Volatility Index (VIX), the ARCA Tech 100 Price Index and the 10-year US Government bond yields. Additionally, we incorporate the S&P GSCI Gold Index to our data set pursuing Uddin et al. (2019). Table 1 lists the details of the indices used in the study. As each index is founded on

Table 1 Description of the indices

Segment	Index	Coverage
Clean Energy	Wilder Hill Clean Energy Index (ECO)	The index is designed to measure the performance of companies engaged in the clean energy sector. It comprises of alternative energy companies including solar, geothermal, wind, hydrogen and wave that create a societal transformation towards cleaner energy and decarbonization. However, investors can invest in the Invesco WilderHill Clean Energy (ETF) symbolized as PBW which tracks this index.
Clean Energy	NASDAQ Clean Edge Green Energy Index (CELS)	The Nasdaq Clean Edge Green Energy Index (CELS) is a modified market capitalization-weighted index designed to track the performance of companies that are manufacturers, developers, distributors, and/or installers of clean-energy technologies.
Clean Energy	Ardour Solar Energy Index (SOLRX)	The Index provides exposure to publicly traded companies from around the world that derive at least 66% of their revenues from solar power and related products and services. On a weighted basis, the companies in the Index derive in excess of 90% of their revenues from the solar industry.
Clean Energy	First Trust Global Wind Energy ETF (FAN)	First Trust Global Wind Energy Fund is an exchange-traded fund incorporated in the USA. The Fund seeks investment results that correspond generally to the price and yield (before fees & expenses) of the ISE Global Wind Energy Index. The index is a modified market capitalization-weighted index of publicly traded companies throughout the world that are active in the wind energy industry.

(continued)

Table 1 (contiuned)

Segment	Index	Coverage
Commodity	S&P GSCI Crude Oil Index	The S&P GSCI Crude Oil index provides a publicly available benchmark for investment performance in the crude oil market.
Commodity	S&P GSCI Gold Index	The S&P GSCI Gold Index, a sub-index of the S&P GSCI, provides a publicly available benchmark tracking the COMEX gold future.
S&P 500	The CBOE Volatility Index (VIX)	The VIX reflects the market's expectation of 30-day volatility of the S&P 500 index.
Government Bonds	Standard and Poor's U.S. Government Bond Index	This index measures the performance of U.S. dollar-denominated U.S. Treasury and U.S. agency debt issued in the U.S. domestic market.
Technology	NYSE Arca Tech 100 Index (PSE)	The index is price-weighted, and consists of 100 stocks from a spectrum of different industries including data storage and processing, computer hardware and software, electronics, telecommunications, healthcare equipment and biotechnology.
Energy	S&P 500 Oil, Gas and Consumable Fuels Price Index (SP500.101020)	The index consists of all companies that play a part in the oil, gas and consumable fuels business. It is highly concentrated, and the two largest companies of the index are Exxon Mobil Corp. and Chevron Corp.

a different date, the data period is adjusted according to the date of establishment of the alternative energy series. Therefore, the starting date is 19th June 2008 for the First Trust Global Wind Energy ETF, 3rd January 2005 for the Ardour Solar Energy, 20th November 2006 for the NASDAQ Clean Edge Green Energy and lastly, 29th December 2000 for the Wilder Hill Clean Energy.[12] The end date is the same however for all the series which is 17th December 2020. We use daily data to exquisitely capture the dynamics of the linkages between the indices across time and frequency and all the data series are in US Dollars.

[12] Following Ortas and Moneva (2013), we prefer to use full sample for each energy index to provide a more comprehensive overview rather than loosing information.

The NASDAQ Clean Energy is the alternative energy index that generates the highest mean return (0.034), and the Ardour Solar Energy has the highest standard deviation (4.121) in terms of the idiosyncratic risk. With the exception of the Ardour Solar Energy, all the alternative energy indices are negatively skewed implying that negative returns are more probable throughout the sample period. Furthermore, the return series for alternative energy assets are leptokurtic with fatter tails suggesting a higher probability of extreme returns. In terms of risk and return trade-off, the NASDAQ Clean Energy, among the four new energy indices, appears to be the most efficient alternative energy index among the others.[13] In all cases, gold and the technology stocks always provide positive mean returns with negative skewness, while oil always has negative mean returns with distributions skewed to the left. The mean values of the VIX and the S&P 500 Oil, Gas and Consumable Fuels Index vary between positive and negative values as the skewness parameters. Moreover, we observe positive average yields for the bond investments with mixed skewness values. In terms of the idiosyncratic risk, the VIX retains the highest values, followed by oil prices in most of the cases as also documented by Inchauspe et al. (2015) and Ferrer et al. (2018). As is a general feature of financial data, for the other series (gold, oil, VIX, S&P OGCF, ARCA Tech and the bond yields) we also document excess kurtosis.

5 Empirical Results

Wavelet Coherence Analysis

We employ wavelet coherence analysis to examine the co-movements between the alternative energy stock returns and the other financial assets in different time and frequency scales.[14] As stated by Torrence and Compo (1998), the wavelet coherence between two time series is the ratio of the cross-spectrum to the product of the spectrum of each series and can be deemed as the local correlation between them, both in time and frequency. Coherency close to 1 shows a strong dependency, while coherency close to 0 indicates no relation between the series. In the plots, the colour codes ranging from blue to red represent the coherence from 0 to 1. The statistical significance level of the wavelet coherency is derived from Monte Carlo simulations by generating large sets of surrogate pairs of the series. The wavelet phase differences reveal information related to both the direction and the causality of the relationship between the time series.

As the alternative energy indices are founded at different dates, the data starts from the date of establishment of each index, therefore the sample period changes for each time series. Based on estimations, we mostly document weak coherence

[13] The descriptive statistics of variables is available upon request.

[14] The wavelet coherency plots, together with the phase differences are available upon request.

between alternative energy stocks and gold across all the frequency bands. Interestingly, alternative energy stocks and gold exhibit an in-phase high coherency during the COVID-19 pandemic, where gold is leading, at investment horizons between 8 and 64 days. First Trust Energy ETF and gold returns display a strong positive co-movement for the period between 2014 and 2018, where gold prices lead the First Trust ETF at the 256 days frequency band. Wilder Hill energy index and gold returns demonstrate a strong and cyclical co-movement, where gold is lagging, at the 512 days frequency between 2007 and 2010, which coincides with the Global Financial Crisis (GFC). In two other incidents, the plots reveal gold's lagging position behind alternative energy stocks; when First Trust led gold returns at 64 days frequency band in 2013 and when Ardour Energy ETF led gold prices at 128 days frequency band during 2011 and 2012. Overall, the wavelet coherency plots provide evidence of a weak relation between alternative energy equities and gold returns, which implies that gold can provide strong diversification benefits. This is consistent with the findings of Wen and Nguyen (2017) who corroborate that gold offers the largest risk reduction and more stable diversification in portfolios with renewable energy shares.

Considering the wavelet coherency between the alternative energy stocks and oil, we can say that at higher frequencies oil prices and alternative energy indices do not co-move, confirming the empirics of Reboredo et al. (2017) and Ferrer et al. (2018). Across the 16–64 days band, there are some pockets of high positive coherence which are short-lived and dispersed over the entire sample period. However, in longer investment horizons (128 days and above), almost at all times, we observe persistent in-phase relation between the series, which is in line with the findings of Reboredo et al. (2017). The long-run persistent co-movements suggest that the relation is shaped by the evolution of long-term dynamics affecting both oil and alternative energy markets, whereas weak linkages in the short-run entail the independence of the price movements from short-lived shocks. Nonetheless, the long-run dependence between oil prices and renewable energy stocks lost momentum between 2013 and 2014 which is also mentioned by Ferrer et al. (2018), Uddin et al. (2019) and Maghyereh et al. (2019), before turning back to the prior state thereafter. Considering the causality, the phase difference yields mixed results, but predominantly, alternative energy indices lead oil prices specifically after 2015 at long-term investment horizons, substantiating the findings of Reboredo et al. (2017) and Ferrer et al. (2018), but contradicting those of Maghyereh et al. (2019) who advocate oil as the lead. Our results are consistent with previous literature (Reboredo et al., 2017; Ahmad, 2017; Reboredo & Ugolini, 2018; Ferrer et al., 2018) and can be explained by the substitution effect (Kumar et al., 2012; Ferrer et al., 2018; Uddin et al., 2019). Since oil and alternative energy sources are substitutes of each other, an increase (decrease) in oil prices results in a relative rise (fall) in the prices of the alternating sources, hence, oil price increases (decreases) provide an incentive (disincentive) for investments in clean energy projects as their expected profitability escalates (reduces). Thus, market conditions shaping the oil price movements also create an asymmetric effect on the market-based incentives for the investments in the renewable energy sector (Reboredo, 2015). Consequently, policy makers should implement policies to support the clean energy sector when oil prices are low to promote greener economies. Oil can provide limited hedging potential for alternative energy stocks for relatively short-term investments. However, for longer horizons adding oil to alternative energy equity portfolios may not offer any diversification benefits which is in line with the findings of Reboredo et al. (2017) and Maghyereh et al. (2019) who suggest that oil, as a commodity, is a weak diversifier for renewable energy stocks. Therefore, in the short run oil prices cannot offer a clue for forecasting alternative energy prices; however, in the long run, they can be used in projecting the renewable energy equity returns.

Our results indicate significant anti-cyclical coherence between alternative energy stocks and VIX at varying frequency bands. At lower frequencies (around 256 days), all the alternative energy indices display strong co-movements with the VIX, where the phase difference arrows point to the left, suggesting an anti-phase relationship. Furthermore, the VIX leads the other series indicating that a rise in the so-called fear gauge index causes a decline in the returns of the alternative energy stocks in long-term investment horizons. This result is in congruence with those of Ferrer et al. (2018) who state that the VIX acts as a net generator of spillovers. More specifically, significant out-of-phase coherency is the most persistent between NASDAQ Green Energy and the VIX, which exists at scales above 4 days throughout the entire data period. Likewise, we observe persistent strong coherence regions between First Trust Energy ETF and the VIX at higher frequencies (4–32 days) over the study period. Ardour Solar Energy ETF demonstrates the least persistent coherency with the VIX, particularly in higher frequencies. Alternative energy stock returns and the VIX record a negative strong co-movement during the COVID-19 pandemic across 25–256 days investment horizon, whereby, alternative energy equities lag behind the VIX. Therefore, it can be suggested that the VIX returns have a predictive power on the renewable energy stock prices in the long-term. Hence, the VIX can be regarded as an efficient hedge for the clean energy equities substantiating the results of Hood and Malik (2013) citing the VIX as a better hedge for US equities.

As for the pairs of alternative energy indices and oil and gas companies, we observe strong positive correlations between the series, particularly at lower frequencies around 256 days. At higher frequencies (between 4 and 64 days), the plots reveal the existence of frequent but relatively short-lived significant high coherency pockets where the arrows signal a cyclical relation. When it comes to the causality between the pairs, we observe mixed results in terms of the lead-lag relationships. First Trust ETF, NASDAQ Green Energy and Wilder Hill Clean Energy returns exhibit more persistent co-movements with the oil and gas companies at varying frequency bands throughout the data period; however, Ardour Solar Energy ETF shows less persistent coherency at higher frequencies. From the mid of 2019 onwards, alternative energy stocks record high positive correlations with the returns of the oil and gas equities across 16 to 128 days frequency which may imply that the fossil energy and renewable energy markets have become more integrated recently. Empirical evidence suggests a significant relation between the prices of oil and fossil fuel energy stocks with strong return spillovers from the stock prices of fossil fuel energy companies to the oil prices (Ferrer et al., 2018). Hence, the linkages between renewable energy indices and oil and gas equities are stronger than the relation between oil and alternative energy investments, with the exception of Ardour Solar Energy ETF.

Regarding wavelet coherency between alternative energy indices and technology stocks, our results manifest strong persistent co-movements which are in-phase across varying frequency bands for the entire study period. The plots divulge that NASDAQ Green and Wilder Hill Clean Energy returns display stronger persistence, where the significant positive correlations between the pairs exist at all frequencies even for very short-term investment horizons. Our findings are in line with those of Henriques and Sadorsky (2008), Sadorsky (2012), Managi and Okimoto (2013) and Ahmad (2017) who document a statistically significant positive impact of technology stock returns on alternative energy equity returns. Although the phase difference gives mixed results, we can conclude that mostly technology stocks are leading the alternative energy indices across different frequencies, which is consistent with Ahmad (2017) and Ahmad and Rais (2018). Again, Ardour Solar Energy ETF seems to be detached in that it exhibits less persistent high coherency with technology stocks overall. In consistence with the wavelet coherence results for the other investments, it is also apparent that technology stocks and alternative energy indices are strongly linked across all the scales during the COVID-19 pandemic.

For the coherency between alternative energy indices and the bond yields, our findings evince an overall weak co-movement. In the medium-term investment horizons, we can see rare short-lived pockets of high coherency between the pairs, and for longer investment horizons (around 256 days), the alternative energy indices and bond yields display infrequent incidences of significant negative correlations between 2010 and 2013, where bond yields are leading. Remarkably, Ardour Solar Energy ETF and bond yields record a significant negative interference for a longer period between 2006 and 2013 across 256 days with the bond yields' lead. Hence, our findings convey information about the hedging property of bond investments against the alternative energy stocks particularly at longer maturities. Similarly, Henriques and Sadorsky (2008) show a significant negative relationship between bond yields and alternative energy stock returns at long-term horizons. Unlike the other alternative assets in the study, the plots notably denote no significant linkages between alternative energy stocks and bond investments during the COVID-19 pandemic. Thus, the hedging potential of bonds is also marked for the recent Coronavirus crash.

To sum up, wavelet coherence analysis reveals that the co-movements between the pairs of alternative energy indices and other investments vary across calendar time and holding periods. Therefore, our results provide important aspects in portfolio construction and hedging strategies, as investors have heterogeneous expectations and preferences in financial markets. Overall, our wavelet coherence analyses yield results in line with the findings of Madaleno and Pinho (2014) who attest that highest coherences occur in crisis periods and in the 256–512 days investment horizon.

Rolling Wavelet Correlations

We continue our study with the rolling window analysis in an attempt to quantify the wavelet correlations across the frequencies. The rolling window is established at 1024 days, and the rolling window starts at 18th June 2013 for First Trust ETF, at 4th January 2010 for Ardour ETF, at 18th November 2011 for NASDAQ Green and at 4th January 2006 for Wilder Hill. The wavelet scales range from 1 to 8: d1 (2–4 days), d2 (4–8 days), d3 (8–16 days), d4 (16–32 days), d5 (32–64 days), d6 (64–128 days), d7 (128–256 days) and d8 (256–512 days).[15]

The rolling wavelet correlations vary significantly across time and scale between the alternative energy stocks and the other assets. In order to efficiently hedge their portfolio risk, investors seek precise information, henceforth, the correlations at different investment horizons provide eminent evidence in portfolio construction and risk management. As one of our emphasis is on the market interferences during the Coronavirus crash, additionally we conduct t-test analysis to analyse if there are any significant changes in the rolling window correlations before and after the COVID-19 outbreak. We take 11th March 2020 as the date of the Coronavirus epidemic, which is the day the WHO announced COVID-19 as a global pandemic. Table 2 presents the t-test results.

The rolling window correlations between alternative energy indices and gold returns signify an investment horizon between 128 and 512 days, and show the most variation in correlations across time in all cases. At low scales, where short-term investments (below 8 days) are undertaken, the fluctuations in the correlations are milder between alternative energy equities and gold. Notably, the sign of the linkages is predominantly negative at lower scales for the period from 2016 to the beginning of 2020, implying that gold acts as a hedge against alternative energy equities for the last few years in short maturities. Except for the First Trust ETF, the alternative energy indices exhibit negative correlations with gold between 2013 and 2018 across 512 days band, where the correlations fall about −0.8 in 2014. Our finding provides evidence of the potential hedging property of gold against the alternative energy stocks at long-term investments within that period. Our results contradict those of Elie et al. (2019) who suggest that gold is a weak safe-haven asset for Wilder Hill Clean Energy ETF. The rolling window correlations shift between negative and positive values over the sample period, which is in congruence with Ahmad et al. (2018) and Uddin et al. (2019) who also substantiate similar findings. Furthermore, after 2018 onwards, the correlations increase and reach approximately 0.7 at the beginning of 2020 across 512 days band. However, with the Corona outbreak, there is a sudden dive in the level of the inter-linkages and the correlations become negative again between gold and both NASDAQ Green and Wilder Hill, verifying the safe haven quality of gold investments during the most recent

[15] The rolling wavelet correlations plots are available upon request.

Table 2 T-tests between the means of rolling correlations before and after the COVID-19 pandemic

	Ardour Solar			First Trust Wind			Wilder Hill			Nasdaq Green		
Scales	$\mu_{Pre\text{-}Covid19}$	$\mu_{Post\text{-}Covid19}$	p value	$\mu_{Pre\text{-}Covid19}$	$\mu_{Post\text{-}Covid19}$	p value	$\mu_{Pre\text{-}Covid19}$	$\mu_{Post\text{-}Covid19}$	p value	$\mu_{Pre\text{-}Covid19}$	$\mu_{Post\text{-}Covid19}$	p value
With gold												
1	−0.058	0.003	0.000	−0.055	0.019	0.000	−0.068	0.016	0.000	−0.090	0.005	0.000
2	−0.140	−0.087	0.000	−0.053	0.004	0.000	−0.138	−0.105	0.000	−0.152	−0.119	0.000
3	0.022	0.269	0.000	−0.031	0.204	0.000	−0.023	0.311	0.000	−0.068	0.282	0.000
4	−0.034	0.163	0.000	0.096	0.303	0.000	−0.065	0.165	0.000	−0.065	0.169	0.000
5	−0.068	0.230	0.000	−0.027	0.248	0.000	−0.076	0.253	0.000	−0.101	0.230	0.000
6	−0.042	0.158	0.000	0.031	0.171	0.000	−0.121	0.079	0.000	−0.125	0.076	0.000
7	0.159	0.062	0.000	0.324	0.077	0.000	0.016	−0.111	0.000	−0.022	−0.143	0.000
8	0.549	0.392	0.000	0.596	0.589	0.602	0.499	0.281	0.000	0.455	0.251	0.000
With oil												
1	0.273	0.248	0.000	0.300	0.331	0.000	0.346	0.414	0.000	0.302	0.410	0.000
2	0.298	0.205	0.000	0.242	0.195	0.000	0.329	0.258	0.000	0.272	0.228	0.000
3	0.360	0.241	0.000	0.400	0.271	0.000	0.399	0.313	0.000	0.336	0.299	0.000
4	0.531	0.420	0.000	0.397	0.403	0.031	0.542	0.437	0.000	0.461	0.401	0.000
5	0.457	0.426	0.000	0.290	0.442	0.000	0.434	0.447	0.066	0.348	0.392	0.000
6	0.248	0.393	0.000	0.351	0.501	0.000	0.348	0.552	0.000	0.267	0.474	0.000
7	0.268	0.432	0.000	0.362	0.671	0.000	0.470	0.722	0.000	0.441	0.697	0.000
8	0.313	0.267	0.000	0.585	0.510	0.000	0.469	0.306	0.000	0.380	0.223	0.000
With oil & gas												
1	0.394	0.441	0.000	0.486	0.682	0.000	0.586	0.743	0.000	0.590	0.743	0.000
2	0.491	0.435	0.000	0.488	0.543	0.000	0.605	0.650	0.000	0.579	0.618	0.000
3	0.536	0.495	0.000	0.606	0.689	0.000	0.644	0.724	0.000	0.623	0.698	0.000
4	0.625	0.630	0.415	0.635	0.763	0.000	0.736	0.775	0.000	0.698	0.725	0.000
5	0.581	0.679	0.000	0.576	0.791	0.000	0.635	0.800	0.000	0.603	0.800	0.000
6	0.289	0.633	0.000	0.548	0.732	0.000	0.456	0.737	0.000	0.431	0.765	0.000
7	0.351	0.354	0.789	0.330	0.584	0.000	0.585	0.652	0.000	0.598	0.723	0.000
8	0.239	0.160	0.000	0.535	0.441	0.000	0.446	0.161	0.000	0.522	0.074	0.000
With technology												
1	0.481	0.482	0.974	0.587	0.767	0.000	0.723	0.820	0.000	0.813	0.862	0.000
2	0.560	0.494	0.000	0.639	0.698	0.000	0.741	0.771	0.000	0.805	0.818	0.000
3	0.614	0.585	0.002	0.675	0.770	0.000	0.761	0.819	0.000	0.824	0.858	0.000
4	0.625	0.631	0.486	0.698	0.743	0.000	0.777	0.814	0.000	0.844	0.864	0.000
5	0.647	0.690	0.000	0.704	0.820	0.000	0.729	0.817	0.000	0.856	0.896	0.000
6	0.527	0.730	0.000	0.670	0.791	0.000	0.716	0.827	0.000	0.793	0.885	0.000
7	0.354	0.552	0.000	0.532	0.772	0.000	0.617	0.809	0.000	0.628	0.850	0.000
8	0.367	0.533	0.000	0.606	0.733	0.000	0.603	0.701	0.000	0.708	0.652	0.000
With VIX												
1	−0.398	−0.336	0.000	−0.591	−0.582	0.000	−0.612	−0.586	0.000	−0.653	−0.612	0.000
2	−0.467	−0.356	0.000	−0.575	−0.499	0.000	−0.574	−0.532	0.000	−0.610	−0.559	0.000

(continued)

Table 2 (continued)

	Ardour Solar			First Trust Wind			Wilder Hill			Nasdaq Green		
Scales	$\mu_{\text{Pre-Covid19}}$	$\mu_{\text{Post-Covid19}}$	*p* value	$\mu_{\text{Pre-Covid19}}$	$\mu_{\text{Post-Covid19}}$	*p* value	$\mu_{\text{Pre-Covid19}}$	$\mu_{\text{Post-Covid19}}$	*p* value	$\mu_{\text{Pre-Covid19}}$	$\mu_{\text{Post-Covid19}}$	*p* value
3	−0.530	−0.449	0.000	−0.624	−0.537	0.000	−0.682	−0.605	0.000	−0.708	−0.604	0.000
4	−0.536	−0.460	0.000	−0.674	−0.547	0.000	−0.713	−0.639	0.000	−0.740	−0.640	0.000
5	−0.557	−0.536	0.000	−0.635	−0.658	0.000	−0.620	−0.626	0.000	−0.682	−0.671	0.000
6	−0.527	−0.645	0.000	−0.642	−0.688	0.000	−0.622	−0.676	0.000	−0.618	−0.723	0.000
7	−0.365	−0.378	0.155	−0.380	−0.576	0.000	−0.634	−0.647	0.066	−0.643	−0.717	0.000
8	−0.282	−0.316	0.007	−0.572	−0.523	0.000	−0.597	−0.389	0.000	−0.695	−0.317	0.000
With yields												
1	0.162	0.182	0.001	0.168	0.263	0.000	0.243	0.290	0.000	0.253	0.299	0.000
2	0.187	0.147	0.000	0.165	0.089	0.000	0.183	0.136	0.000	0.179	0.130	0.000
3	0.049	0.062	0.050	0.036	0.066	0.000	0.007	0.042	0.000	0.000	0.037	0.000
4	−0.018	0.060	0.000	0.048	0.076	0.000	−0.029	0.071	0.000	−0.026	0.044	0.000
5	−0.121	−0.001	0.000	−0.144	0.005	0.000	−0.187	−0.010	0.000	−0.132	0.006	0.000
6	−0.170	−0.024	0.000	−0.330	−0.052	0.000	−0.221	0.021	0.000	−0.153	0.000	0.000
7	−0.203	−0.032	0.000	−0.155	−0.021	0.000	−0.309	−0.055	0.000	−0.284	−0.145	0.000
8	−0.222	−0.247	0.081	−0.314	−0.299	0.066	−0.321	−0.460	0.000	−0.413	−0.572	0.000

Source: The table is prepared by the authors
Notes. $\mu_{\text{Pre-Covid19}}$ and $\mu_{\text{Post-Covid19}}$ denote the average value of the wavelet correlations before and after the COVID-19 pandemic, respectively

Coronavirus market crash across long-term maturities, which presents a consistent finding with the wavelet coherency analysis discussed above.

As can be seen from Table 2, the t-test results reveal that the correlations between the gold and alternative energy pairs significantly fall in the post-COVID period in longer maturities, at the d7 and d8 scales (between 128 and 512 days), with the exception of First Trust ETF at the d8 (512 days) scale where the decrease is found to be insignificant. For all the other scales, corresponding to an investment horizon up to 128 days, the correlations between the series record significant increases in the post-COVID phase where, predominantly, the mean of the correlation coefficients are positive. However, despite the significant increases in the linkages and positivity in parameters, still the coefficients remain negative for Ardour ETF-Gold, Wilder Hill-Gold and NASDAQ Green-Gold pairs across the d2 scale (4–8 days). Thus, we can suggest that gold investments can provide safe haven properties only at longer horizons (128–512 days) and at holding periods between 4 and 8 days against alternative energy stocks during the novel Corona market crash. Nevertheless, gold's hedging quality dissipates against the alternative energy stocks in times of the recent market downturn at some short and medium-term maturities. This result is somewhat parallel to Uddin et al. (2019) who attest significant positive correlations between gold and clean energy stocks in bearish market conditions.

Considering the dynamicity in the correlations between the alternative energy indices and oil returns, we observe greater variations across time at higher scales of d7 and d8 in particular. Overall, the rolling wavelet correlations are always positive between the pairs at short and intermediate terms in line with previous literature (e.g. Sadorsky, 2012; Managi & Okimoto, 2013; Ahmad, 2017; Reboredo & Ugolini, 2018). Our findings show predominantly positive linkages across the long term, with rare incidents of negative correlations. We can see that the rolling correlations between NASDAQ Green and oil returns decrease to about −0.2 at d8 scale for a short while by the end of the first quarter of 2020 which coincides with the Corona outbreak. Negative correlations are also reported for Ardour ETF and oil prices across 512 days horizon at the beginning of 2018. Notably, the direction of the relation between Wilder Hill ETF and oil stays negative in the period from 2006 to 2008 for long-term investors, but for the other frequencies the correlations are mainly positive substantiating previous literature. Our t-test results mainly display a significant increase in the rolling wavelet correlations between oil and clean energy indices at d1, d5, d6 and d7 scales for the post-COVID era similar to those of Corbet et al. (2020) who attest significant increases in the dynamic correlations between oil and renewable energy stock prices in the aftermath of the Corona outbreak. However, from the t-test analysis, a significant decrease in correlations at the d2, d3, d4 and d8 frequency bands is also professed. Hence, our results highlight the importance of investor preferences in portfolio construction and hedging during the Corona market crash. Investors investing for maturities between 4–32 days and 256–512 days could hedge their renewable energy stocks with oil investments in the aftermath of the COVID-19 outbreak.

Regarding the rolling wavelet correlations between the alternative energy stocks and the VIX, in line with the previous findings of this study, at a first glance we can see that the correlations fluctuate more at higher scales, mainly d6, d7 and d8, while variations are much less across lower scales. The correlations are predominantly negative for the period under investigation at all scales with a few exceptions at investment horizons of 512 days where positive correlations are observed mostly at the beginning of 2020. We can say that alternative energy and the volatility indices exhibit a strong and persistent negative correlation particularly at longer investment horizons (above 256 days), with the coefficients reaching values as low as −0.8. The negative relationship between alternative energy equities and the VIX implies that the risk of alternative energy stock investments can be diversified with holdings in the VIX at short, inter-mediate and long-term maturities supporting Ahmad et al. (2018) who suggest that the VIX is the most suitable asset to hedge the clean energy equities. Looking at the negative correlations that persist over the data period, we can suggest that the VIX acts as a safe haven in the case of the Ardour ETF and Wilder Hill Energy index at longer investment horizons during the Eurozone sovereign debt crisis of 2010–2011. More specifically, the VIX also performs as a safe haven for Wilder Hill Energy index across all scales except d8 at times of the US sub-prime mortgage crisis between 2007 and 2009. However, we observe that the correlations significantly rise and reach as high as 0.6 for 512 days investment horizon during the Great Recession, indicating a coupling effect for Wilder Hill Energy and the VIX. The t-test analyses denote an overall significant increase in the correlations between alternative energy stocks and the VIX in both short-term (below 32 days) and long-term (256–512 days) holding periods in the aftermath of the

COVID-19 pandemic. On the contrary, the correlations record significant decreases at d6 and d7 scales in all cases, implying a bolstered hedging effect of the VIX against alternative energy equities for relatively longer investment horizons in the post-COVID era.

As for the pairs of alternative energy indices and oil & gas stocks, our findings reveal persistent and strong positive correlations throughout the examined period, substantiating those of Kumar et al. (2012) who report significant and positive connectedness between clean energy and traditional energy company equities. Consistent with our previous analyses, it is evident that the rolling wavelet correlations vary across scales, and again, fluctuations in the co-movements are apparently higher for longer investment horizons (above 256 days). Overall, for investment horizons below 64 trading days, the strong positive correlation coefficients (mostly in the range of 0.5–0.9) between alternative energy and oil & gas indices indicate that investors cannot enjoy any diversification benefits when they include the fossil energy stocks in a portfolio with alternative energy equities. Our findings are contrary to those of Wen et al. (2014) who report a negative relation between the returns of new energy and fossil fuel shares. We can see that the rolling correlations decrease to negative levels at the beginning of 2020 across the d8 scale for the pairs, except for the one with the First Trust ETF. The t-test results concede significant rises in the correlations for the post-COVID period across all the scales except the d8 (with the exception of Ardour ETF at the d3 scale). However, at the d8, the rolling correlations record significant falls for all of the alternative energy indices. Hence, we can suggest a decoupling of fossil energy and alternative energy stocks during the Corona epidemic at long-term investment horizons.

For the correlations between the alternative energy and technology stocks, it is visible that the interdependencies are highly strong and always in the same direction with a single and very short-lived exception for the Ardour ETF-Technology Index pair at the end of 2018, where a negative relation is detected. In line with the previous literature, our findings substantiate varying correlations across time and scale and again we perceive larger fluctuations in linkages at longer maturities (above 256 days). Predominantly, the coefficients are about 0.90 during 2012 and 2013 across the d8 scale (512 days) for all the pairs of alternative energy and technology equities examined. As energy production from renewable sources requires new and innovative technologies, the developments in technology also improve the production potentials from the renewable sources. Thus, the clean energy sector is significantly dependent on innovative technologies. For this reason, the two sectors are seen as significantly inter-related and considered as similar asset classes (Kumar et al., 2012; Sadorsky, 2012; Inchauspe et al., 2015; Bondia et al., 2016; Ferrer et al., 2018). There is a strong positive co-movement between the two sectors, which is also reflected in our findings as is seen from the correlation coefficients that are mostly above 0.70. Our rolling window correlation results along with those of the wavelet coherence analysis discussed in the preceding section, are similar to the findings of Henriques and Sadorsky (2008), Sadorsky (2012) and Ahmad (2017) who report significant positive relation between the Wilder Hill Clean Energy (ECO) and the ARCA Technology (PSE) indices, suggesting that investors view alternative energy investments as being more closely related to the technology sector. Overall, in line with Ahmad (2017), we can suggest that technology stocks offer limited portfolio diversification and hedging potentials for new energy stocks. Preponderantly, the t-test results signify statistically significant increases in the correlations at all scales in the post-COVID phase, excluding the Ardour ETF at d2, d3 and NASDAQ Clean Energy at d8 scales. Hence, it is also confirmed that technology stocks do not retain any hedging potential for alternative energy indices in the wake of the COVID-19 pandemic.

Based on the rolling wavelet correlation graphs, we can suggest that bond investments can efficiently hedge the risk of alternative energy indices at inter-mediate and long-term maturities as the correlations between the pairs are negative across d5, d6, d7 and d8 scales (above 64 days). Our results support the findings of Ahmad et al. (2018) who present negative correlations between bond yields and clean energy equity prices. However, for higher frequency bands (d1, d2, d3 and d4), the rolling wavelet correlations are always positive, but relatively low ranging from 0 to 0.3. Similarly, Kumar et al. (2012) also corroborate a significant positive impact of interest rates on clean energy stock prices at the short run. Therefore, our results reveal the importance of investor preferences, as investors with longer investment horizons would relish the diversification benefits of bond investments, while short-term investors would not be able to enjoy any benefit from hedging alternative energy market risk with bond instruments. Consistent with the previous literature, we report larger fluctuations in the correlations at higher scales implying that the diversification benefits derived from bond investments would change across time in relation to the variations in the co-movements. Thus, portfolio weights should be adopted to the changing covariation between alternative energy indices and bonds' returns over time. The t-test results denote significant but mild increases in the rolling correlations across d1, d3, d4, d5, d6 and d7 scales in the aftermath of the Corona outbreak, however, for the 4–8- and 256–512 days cycle, we witness significant decreases in the coefficients at the post-COVID period. Thus, it can be suggested that long-term investors can exploit the diversification benefits of bond investments during the most recent market crash of March 2020.

Implications

The empirical analysis of the dependence between renewable energy markets and traditional assets provides significant implications for both practitioners and policy makers. Firstly, it should be acknowledged that the co-movements vary not only over time but also over frequency, which underscores the importance of analysing the inter-linkages between financial assets both across time and frequency domains. Investors constitute a heterogenous group with different risk and maturity preferences which requires portfolio managers to apply portfolio construction and management strategies in accord with investors' inclinations. Investors with short-term horizons are affected by ephemeral news and sporadic occurrences, while those with long-term horizons focus on the systematic and enduring shocks in the financial markets. Predominantly, our results demonstrate that the linkages between alternative energy indices and the other assets are strong in the long-term with very weak co-movements in the short-term. Upon this finding, it can be suggested that there are almost no return transmissions between clean energy stocks and the other assets in the short run, implying that the renewable energy markets are affected from occasional, transitory shocks that are not transmitted to the other assets in short-term horizons. On the other hand, our results denote a strong return interaction in the long run which suggests that alternative energy markets may be primarily driven by the general economic fundamentals that also affect the other assets in long-term horizons. Notably, the rolling correlations fluctuate more for longer maturities above 128 days, whereas they display lower variations for shorter maturities. This finding may indicate that shocks in the long run that originate from the economic fundamentals are more influential in determining the pattern of the relationship between the clean energy stock prices and the other investments.

Both wavelet coherency and rolling-window correlation analyses reveal that clean energy returns and oil prices have persistent positive relation in the long investment horizons, while the relation is weak for shorter maturities. Therefore, renewable energy investors with short-term maturities can reduce their risk when they invest in oil as a commodity, however, there are no diversification benefits for long-term investors. In terms of policy implementations, the long-run positive relation between oil prices and alternative energy equity returns generates an asymmetric market-based incentive to promote renewable energy investments, only when oil prices are low (Reboredo, 2015; Reboredo et al., 2017). Likewise, the co-movements between alternative energy indices and the VIX are mostly stronger for longer maturities, however, the sign of the relation is negative, placing the VIX as a potential hedge for renewable energy stocks. This suggests that higher implied volatility in the stock market leads to significant falls in the clean energy sector returns, confirming the findings of previous studies documenting renewable energy equities as highly risky assets (Henriques & Sadorsky, 2008; Kumar et al., 2012; Bohl et al., 2013; Ortas & Moneva, 2013; Rezec & Scholtens, 2017). When it comes to the linkages between technology stock and alternative energy equity returns, we observe strong persistent co-movements with a positive sign across all frequencies, substantiating the results of the previous literature deeming these two sectors as highly similar (Kumar et al., 2012; Sadorsky, 2012; Ferrer et al., 2018). Technological innovations foster clean energy production and since the 1990's investors perceive the two sectors as closely linked. Hence, alternative energy investors cannot obtain any diversification when they include technology stocks in their green energy portfolios. However, the financial performance of the renewable energy firms can be predicted from the returns of the technology companies. Additionally, policy makers need to promote the development of the technology sector, in order to warranty a sustainable economic growth with environmentally friendly energy production.

Remarkably, the co-movements between renewable energy stocks and bond yields are very weak for short-term maturities, however, we observe negative persistent coherence between the clean energy and bond yield pairs in the long run during the Global Recession of 2007–2009 and the Eurozone Sovereign Debt Crisis of 2010–2011. Thus, our results indicate the diversification and hedging ability of government bonds in portfolios with clean energy equities for relatively short-term investors during extremely volatile market conditions. Our findings demonstrate gold as a potential hedge and diversifier against alternative energy indices and there exists almost no co-movements between the pairs with a few exceptions; Wilder Hill ETF returns exhibit positive linkages with gold prices during the Global Crisis of 2007–2009 in long-term horizons, and likewise, First Trust ETF and gold returns display a positive relation for longer maturities between 2014 and 2018. The long-run positive relation between gold and both Wilder Hill and First Trust ETFs may imply investors' attitude placing these indices to a position of a hedge against the inflation caused by the rise in the oil prices, as gold is widely acknowledged as an investment commodity to hedge the inflation imposed by the increasing oil prices (Reboredo, 2013; Beckmann & Czudaj, 2013). The co-movements between the renewable energy indices and oil & gas stock returns are positive and display stronger persistency at longer investment horizons similar to the coherency of oil and clean energy equities. Hence, oil & gas stocks cannot be used to hedge for the investment risk of alternative energy firms, but their returns can be predicted from the prices of oil & gas companies in the long run.

Consequently, our findings reveal that overall, the coherence between Ardour Solar Energy ETF and most of the other financial assets, namely, oil, oil & gas, technology and the VIX returns exhibit less persistence relative to the other alternative energy indices. In a similar vein, Reboredo et al. (2017) document lower dependence between oil prices and the Solar energy index compared to other general and sectoral renewable energy indices. This suggests that solar energy is distinct from the other clean energy alternatives in that it appears to have a lower degree of interlinkages with the financial assets. A plausible explanation can be that solar energy dates back older than the other renewable energy investments and has grown receiving more government incentives, as it has been considered a source of green energy to reduce greenhouse gas emissions and tackle climate change long before the emergence of the other renewable energy sources. Therefore, it can be suggested that investors put solar energy in a relatively distinct position than the other alternative energy assets, which is also advocated by the findings of Reboredo et al. (2017) who find upper tail independence only for Solar energy investments in extreme oil price movements. Hence, renewable energy sector portfolios with Solar energy equities may provide better diversification against oil, oil & gas, technology and the VIX investments. Additionally, policy makers should reinforce solar energy investments independently from oil prices.

Lastly, we can suggest that in the aftermath of the COVID-19 pandemic, the correlations between clean energy equity returns and the other investments mostly increased across frequencies. This finding shows the existence of the contagious flows between alternative energy stocks and the other assets at times of a turmoil, thus providing evidence of financial contagion during the most recent Coronavirus crisis, whereby, a revaluation of risk is materialized in the financial markets which increases their co-integration. A well-established literature in financial economics demonstrates that increased risk aversion and herding behaviour in times of extreme distress can lead to strengthened cross-market linkages and contagion (Boldanov et al., 2016; Uddin et al., 2019). Similarly, recent studies provide evidence of high level of co-movements across financial markets in the wake of the COVID-19 pandemic (see among others, Akhtaruzzaman et al., 2021; Matos et al., 2021; Okorie & Lin, 2021), supporting the existence of potential contagion incidences.

6 Conclusion

In the last decades, growing concerns about climate change and energy security along with the concerns of peak oil and socially responsible investing prompted the rapid development of the clean energy sector. Indubitably, the advancements in technology assured this swift progress, whereby, investors funnelled money in renewable energy companies as potential investments. Therefore, the financial performance of these companies is of significant importance to investors who have alternative energy equities in their portfolios. From that stance, identifying the dynamics of the relationship between clean energy stock returns and traditional assets is of crucial importance to practitioners. Additionally, the dynamic linkages between the renewable energy and the traditional asset markets convey eminent information to policy makers. As the alternative energy investments are of paramount importance for achieving a sustainable economy, policy makers can implement the necessary policies to promote the clean energy sector upon these dynamics. In order to elucidate the dependence structure between renewable energy equities and traditional assets, we conducted wavelet coherence analysis and measured the rolling window correlations to obtain information both in time and frequency scales. Identifying the frequency-specific dependence and causality between clean energy stock returns and traditional assets has significant implications in portfolio construction and risk reduction. Most recently, we have witnessed an unprecedented event with the outbreak of the COVID-19 pandemic and the Coronavirus crisis created a systemic risk factor. Consequently, by conducting t-test analysis on the rolling window wavelet correlations, we investigated the effect of the Corona outbreak on the inter-linkages between the returns of the clean energy equities and the traditional assets.

In this paper, the analyses on the relations between alternative energy indices and the traditional assets bestow important results for investors and policy makers. Firstly, we observe that the returns of renewable energy stocks are strongly and positively connected to technology stock prices, substantiating previous literature, as these two sectors are seen as highly similar by investors. Additionally, our findings document that the linkages between the prices of oil and alternative energy equities are less persistent in comparison to the association between technology and clean energy indices in congruence with the extant literature. Furthermore, we evince that the interferences with oil are positive, but, weak in the short run, however, for long investment horizons the co-movements strengthen, implying that short-term shocks in the oil market do not exert a prevalent influence on the renewable energy sector. Therefore, policy makers should promote investments in the renewable energy sector in the short run and, in the long run policies should be implemented asymmetrically to promote the green energy sector when oil prices are low. Gold is a strategic commodity, and our results indicate the hedging potential of gold investments in portfolios with clean energy stocks since the relationship between the returns of gold and alternative energy stocks is extremely weak. Moreover, we substantiate evidence for the diversification benefits and safe haven properties of the VIX against the renewable energy equities particularly at longer maturities. In our study, bond investments are also found to provide efficient hedging and diversification against alternative energy stocks. Fossil fuel sector has a significant weight in global equity markets, and we find strong positive linkages between oil & gas companies and renewable energy sector. Remarkably, these linkages are more pronounced than the co-movements between oil prices and alternative energy indices. Besides, our findings display significantly higher rolling correlations between the pairs at the post-COVID era, implying increased return spillovers among the assets at times of a market crash. Financial markets have become more integrated recently and at times of distress, contagious flows between financial assets are more common; a phenomenon which accentuates the importance of efficient portfolio hedging and risk diversification techniques.

Consequently, we observe that the Solar energy sector differentiates from the other renewable energy indices, exhibiting weaker and less persistent co-movements with the prices of oil, technology, oil & gas and the VIX indices. Specifically, our empirical evidence signifies the importance of the choice of investment maturity as we document varying degrees of coherence across both frequency and time. Therefore, for decent risk management practices, the inter-linkages between new energy stocks and the other assets should be demystified both at time and frequency domains. We report higher fluctuations in the rolling correlations for longer investment horizons which may imply that the long-term shocks are more influential in the dynamic relationships. Notably, investors with long investment horizons should contemplate the fact that the long-run co-movements are more volatile over time.

Competing Interests The authors have no conflicts of interest to declare that are relevant to the content of this chapter.

References

Advisors, A. (2018). The Global Fossil Fuel Divestment and Clean Energy Investment Movement–2018 Report.

Aguiar-Conraria, L., Azevedo, N., & Soares, M. J. (2008). Using wavelets to decompose the time–frequency effects of monetary policy. *Physica A: Statistical Mechanics and its Applications, 387*, 2863–2878.

Ahmad, W. (2017). On the dynamic dependence and investment performance of crude oil and clean energy stocks. *Research in International Business and Finance, 42*, 376–389.

Ahmad, W., & Rais, S. (2018). Time-varying spillover and the portfolio diversification implications of clean energy equity with commodities and financial assets. *Emerging Markets Finance and Trade, 54*(8), 1837–1855.
Ahmad, W., Sadorsky, P., & Sharma, A. (2018). Optimal hedge ratios for clean energy equities. *Economic Modelling, 72*, 278–295.
Akhtaruzzaman, M., Boubaker, S., Chiah, M., & Zhong, A. (2020). COVID– 19 and oil price risk exposure. *Finance Research Letters, 42*, 101882.
Akhtaruzzaman, M., Boubaker, S., & Sensoy, A. (2021). Financial contagion during COVID–19 crisis. *Finance Research Letters, 38*, 101604.
Arouri, M. E. H., Lahiani, A., & Nguyen, D. K. (2015). World gold prices and stock returns in China: Insights for hedging and diversification strategies. *Economic Modelling, 44*, 273–282.
Ayres, R. U., Turton, H., & Casten, T. (2007). Energy efficiency, sustainability and economic growth. *Energy, 32*(5), 634–648.
Baruník, J., Kočenda, E., & Vácha, L. (2016). Gold, oil, and stocks: Dynamic correlations. *International Review of Economics & Finance, 42*, 186–201.
Basher, S. A., & Sadorsky, P. (2016). Hedging emerging market stock prices with oil, gold, VIX, and bonds: A comparison between DCC, ADCC and GO-GARCH. *Energy Economics, 54*, 235–247.
Baur, D. G., & Lucey, B. M. (2009). Flights and contagion – An empirical analysis of stock-bond correlations. *Journal of Financial Stability, 5*, 339–352.
Baur, D. G., & Lucey, B. M. (2010). Is gold a hedge or a safe haven? An analysis of stocks, bonds and gold. *Financial Review, 45*(2), 217–229.
Baur, D. G., & McDermott, T. K. (2010). Is gold a safe haven? International evidence. *Journal of Banking & Finance, 34*(8), 1886–1898.
Baur, D. G., & Smales, L. A. (2019). *Oil prices and clean energy stock prices revisited*. Available at SSRN 3471866.
Bayraci, S., Demiralay, S., & Gencer, H. G. (2018). Stock-bond co-movements and flight-to-quality in G7 countries: A time-frequency analysis. *Bulletin of Economic Research, 70*(1), E29–E49.
Beckmann, J., & Czudaj, R. (2013). Gold as an inflation hedge in a time-varying coefficient framework. *The North American Journal of Economics and Finance, 24*, 208–222.
Bohl, M. T., Kaufmann, P., & Stephan, P. M. (2013). From hero to zero: Evidence of performance reversal and speculative bubbles in German renewable energy stocks. *Energy Economics, 37*, 40–51.
Boldanov, R., Degiannakis, S., & Filis, G. (2016). Time-varying correlation between oil and stock market volatilities: Evidence from oil-importing and oil-exporting countries. *International Review of Financial Analysis, 48*, 209–220.
Bondia, R., Ghosh, S., & Kanjilal, K. (2016). International crude oil prices and the stock prices of clean energy and technology companies: Evidence from non-linear cointegration tests with unknown structural breaks. *Energy, 101*, 558–565.
Buonocore, E., Franzese, P. P., & Ulgiati, S. (2012). Assessing the environmental performance and sustainability of bioenergy production in Sweden: A life cycle assessment perspective. *Energy, 37*(1), 69–78.
Connolly, R., Stivers, C., & Sun, L. (2005). Stock market uncertainty and the stock-bond return relation. *Journal of Financial and Quantitative Analysis, 40*(1), 161–194.
Corbet, S., Goodell, J. W., & Günay, S. (2020). Co-movements and spillovers of oil and renewable firms under extreme conditions: New evidence from negative WTI prices during COVID-19. *Energy Economics, 92*, 104978.
Cunado, J., & Perez, D.-G. F. (2005). Oil prices, economic activity and inflation: Evidence for some Asian countries. *The Quarterly Review of Economics and Finance, 45*(1), 65–83.
Dajcman, S. (2015). An empirical investigation of the nexus between sovereign bond yields and stock market returns – A multiscale approach. *Engineering Economics, 26*, 108–117.
Darby, M. R. (1982). The price of oil and world inflation and recession. *American Economic Review, 72*, 738–751.

Driesprong, G., Jacobsen, B., & Maat, B. (2008). Striking oil: Another puzzle? *Journal of Financial Economics, 89*, 307–327.
Dutta, A. (2017). Oil price uncertainty and clean energy stock returns: New evidence from crude oil volatility index. *Journal of Cleaner Production, 164*, 1157–1166.
Dutta, A., Bouri, E., Das, D., & Roubaud, D. (2020). Assessment and optimization of clean energy equity risks and commodity price volatility indexes: Implications for sustainability. *Journal of Cleaner Production, 243*, 118669.
Elie, B., Naji, J., Dutta, A., & Uddin, G. S. (2019). Gold and crude oil as safe-haven assets for clean energy stock indices: Blended copulas approach. *Energy, 178*, 544–553.
Fama, E. F. (1981). Stock returns, real activity, inflation and money. *American Economic Review, 71*, 545–565.
Ferrer, R., Bolós, V. J., & Benítez, R. (2016). Interest rate changes and stock returns: A European multi-country study with wavelets. *International Review of Economics & Finance, 44*, 1–12.
Ferrer, R., Shahzad, S. J. H., López, R., & Jareño, F. (2018). Time and frequency dynamics of connectedness between renewable energy stocks and crude oil prices. *Energy Economics, 76*, 1–20.
Ferstl, R., Utz, S., & Wimmer, M. (2012). The effect of the Japan 2011 disaster on nuclear and alternative energy stocks worldwide: An event study. *Business Research, 5*(1), 25–41.
Gallegati, M. (2008). Wavelet analysis of stock returns and aggregate economic activity. *Computational Statistics & Data Analysis, 52*(6), 3061–3074.
Hamilton, J. D. (1983). Oil and macroeconomy since World War II. *Journal of Political Economy, 91*, 228–248.
Hartmann, P., Straetmans, S., & De Vries, C. G. (2004). Asset market linkages in crisis periods. *Review of Economics and Statistics, 86*, 313–326.
Henriques, I., & Sadorsky, P. (2008). Oil price and the stock prices of alternative energy companies. *Energy Economics, 30*, 998–1010.
Henriques, I., & Sadorsky, P. (2018). Investor implications of divesting from fossil fuels. *Global Finance Journal, 38*, 30–44.
Hillier, D., Draper, P., & Faff, R. (2006). Do precious metals shine? An investment perspective. *Financial Analysts Journal, 62*(2), 98–106.
Hood, M., & Malik, F. (2013). Is gold the best hedge and a safe haven under changing stock market volatility? *Review of Financial Economics, 22*(2), 47–52.
Huang, R. D., & Masulis, R. W. (1996). Energy shocks and financial markets. *Journal of Future Markets, 16*, 1–27.
Inchauspe, J., Ripple, R. D., & Trück, S. (2015). The dynamics of returns on renewable energy companies: A state-space approach. *Energy Economics, 48*, 325–335.
Jones, C. M., & Gautam, K. (1996). Oil and stock markets. *Journal of Finance, 51*, 463–491.
Kanamura, T. (2020). A model of price correlations between clean energy indices and energy commodities. *Journal of Sustainable Finance & Investment, 12*(2), 1–41.
Kilian, L. (2008). Exogenous oil supply shocks: How big are they and how much do they matter for the U.S. economy? *Review of Economics and Statistics, 90*, 216–240.
Kilian, L., & Park, C. (2009). The impact of oil price shocks on the U.S. stock market. *International Economic Review, 50*, 1267–1287.
Kumar, S., & Managi, S. (2009). Energy price-induced and exogenous technological change: Assessing the economic and environmental outcomes. *Resource and Energy Economics, 31*(4), 334–353.
Kumar, S., Managi, S., & Matsuda, A. (2012). Stock prices of clean energy firms, oil and carbon markets: A vector autoregressive analysis. *Energy Economics, 34*(1), 215–226.
Kuşkaya, S., & Bilgili, F. (2020). The wind energy-greenhouse gas nexus: The wavelet-partial wavelet coherence model approach. *Journal of Cleaner Production, 245*, 118872.
Madaleno, M., & Pinho, C. (2014). Wavelet dynamics for oil-stock world interactions. *Energy Economics, 45*, 120–133.
Maghyereh, A. I., Awartani, B., & Abdoh, H. (2019). The co-movement between oil and clean energy stocks: A wavelet-based analysis of horizon associations. *Energy, 169*, 895–913.

Mallat, S. G. (1989). A theory for multiresolution signal decomposition: The wavelet representation. *IEEE Transactions on Pattern Analysis and Machine Intelligence, 11*(7), 674–693.
Managi, S., & Okimoto, T. (2013). Does the price of oil interact with clean energy prices in the stock market? *Japan and the World Economy, 27*, 1–9.
Matos, P., Costa, A., & da Silva, C. (2021). COVID-19, stock market and sectoral contagion in US: A time-frequency analysis. *Research in International Business and Finance, 57*, 101400.
Mensi, W., Hammoudeh, S., & Kang, S. H. (2015). Precious metals, cereal, oil and stock market linkages and portfolio risk management: Evidence from Saudi Arabia. *Economic Modelling, 51*, 340–358.
Narayan, P. K., & Sharma, S. S. (2011). New evidence on oil price and firm returns. *Journal of Banking & Finance, 35*(12), 3253–3262.
Nguyen, T. T. H., Naeem, M. A., Balli, F., Balli, H. O., & Vo, X. V. (2020). Time-frequency comovement among green bonds, stocks, commodities, clean energy, and conventional bonds. *Finance Research Letters, 40*, 101739.
Okorie, D. I., & Lin, B. (2021). Stock markets and the COVID-19 fractal contagion effects. *Finance Research Letters, 38*, 101640.
Ortas, E., & Moneva, J. M. (2013). The Clean Techs equity indexes at stake: Risk and return dynamics analysis. *Energy, 57*, 259–269.
Park, J., & Ratti, R. A. (2008). Oil price shocks and stock markets in the US and 13 European countries. *Energy Economics, 30*(5), 2587–2608.
Reboredo, J. C. (2013). Is gold a hedge or safe haven against oil price movements? *Resources Policy, 38*(2), 130–137.
Reboredo, J. C. (2015). Is there dependence and systemic risk between oil and renewable energy stock prices? *Energy Economics, 48*, 32–45.
Reboredo, J. C., & Ugolini, A. (2018). The impact of energy prices on clean energy stock prices. A multivariate quantile dependence approach. *Energy Economics, 76*, 136–152.
Reboredo, J. C., Rivera-Castro, M. A., & Ugolini, A. (2017). Wavelet-based test of co-movement and causality between oil and renewable energy stock prices. *Energy Economics, 61*, 241–252.
Rezec, M., & Scholtens, B. (2017). Financing energy transformation: The role of renewable energy equity indices. *International Journal of Green Energy, 14*(4), 368–378.
Rhif, M., Ben Abbes, A., Farah, I. R., Martínez, B., & Sang, Y. (2019). Wavelet transform application for/in non-stationary time-series analysis: A review. *Applied Sciences, 9*(7), 1345.
Sadorsky, P. (1999). Oil price shocks and stock market activity. *Energy Economics, 21*, 449–469.
Sadorsky, P. (2001). Risk factors in stock returns of Canadian oil and gas companies. *Energy Economics, 23*, 17–28.
Sadorsky, P. (2012). Correlations and volatility spillovers between oil prices and the stock prices of clean energy and technology companies. *Energy Economics, 34*, 248–255.
Salisu, A. A., Ebuh, G. U., & Usman, N. (2020). Revisiting oil-stock nexus during COVID-19 pandemic: Some preliminary results. *International Review of Economics & Finance, 69*, 280–294.
Shackley, S., & Green, K. (2007). A conceptual framework for exploring transitions to decarbonised energy systems in the United Kingdom. *Energy, 32*(3), 221–236.
Shiller, R. J., & Beltratti, A. E. (1992). Stock prices and bond yields: Can their comovements be explained in terms of present value models? *Journal of Monetary Economics, 30*(1), 25–46.
Torrence, C., & Compo, G. P. (1998). A practical guide to wavelet analysis. *Bulletin of the American Meteorological Society, 79*(1), 61–78.
Torrence, C., & Webster, P. J. (1999). Interdecadal changes in the ENSO–monsoon system. *Journal of Climate, 12*(8), 2679–2690.
Uddin, G. S., Rahman, M. L., Hedström, A., & Ahmed, A. (2019). Cross-quantilogram-based correlation and dependence between renewable energy stock and other asset classes. *Energy Economics, 80*, 743–759.
Vacha, L., & Barunik, J. (2012). Co-movement of energy commodities revisited: Evidence from wavelet coherence analysis. *Energy Economics, 34*(1), 241–247.

Wen, X., & Nguyen, D. K. (2017). Can investors of Chinese energy stocks benefit from diversification into commodity futures? *Economic Modelling, 66*, 184–200.
Wen, X., Guo, Y., Wei, Y., & Huang, D. (2014). How do the stock prices of new energy and fossil fuel companies correlate? Evidence from China. *Energy Economics, 41*, 63–75.
Whaley, R. E. (2009). Understanding the VIX. *The Journal of Portfolio Management, 35*(3), 98–105.
Zhang, H., Cai, G., & Yang, D. (2020). The impact of oil price shocks on clean energy stocks: Fresh evidence from multi-scale perspective. *Energy, 196*, 117099.

The Impact of the Environmental Problems on the Protest Movement in Contemporary Society (Kyrgyzstan's Case)

Bauyrzhan Simagambetov and Yelnur Seitkozha

1 Introduction

Environmental problems are not new to the world. In recent times, however, the impact of these problems has become more apparent and has led to an increase in the protest movement. The protest movement is a collective expression of concern and dissatisfaction with various issues that affect the environment. The impact of environmental problems on the protest movement is a complex issue that requires a detailed examination.

The environment is facing various problems such as climate change, deforestation, pollution, and loss of biodiversity, to name a few. These problems have led to severe consequences such as rising sea levels, increased temperatures, erratic weather patterns, and the extinction of several species. These consequences have not only affected the environment but also the livelihoods of millions of people around the world. As a result, people have begun to protest against these issues.

The impact of environmental problems on the protest movement is multifaceted. Firstly, the severity of the environmental problems has led to an increase in the number of protests. People have become more aware of the impact of these problems and have realized that they need to take action to address them. This has led to the formation of various organizations and groups that focus on environmental issues. These groups have organized protests and rallies to bring attention to these issues and demand action from governments and corporations.

B. Simagambetov (✉)
Al-Farabi University, Almaty, Kazakhstan

Y. Seitkozha
Ablai Khan University, Almaty, Kazakhstan

N. Ketenci (ed.), *Transition to the Circular Economy Model*, CSR, Sustainability, Ethics & Governance, https://doi.org/10.1007/978-3-031-52700-5_10

Secondly, environmental problems have also impacted the nature of protests. In the past, protests were often focused on political or social issues. However, with the increasing severity of environmental problems, the focus of protests has shifted to environmental issues. This is evident in the large-scale climate strikes that have taken place in various parts of the world. These protests have been organized by young people who are concerned about the future of the planet and the impact of environmental problems on their lives.

Thirdly, environmental problems have also led to a change in the way protests are conducted. With the advent of social media, protests have become more organized and more visible. Activists are now able to use social media to organize and promote protests. They can also use social media to share information and raise awareness about environmental problems. This has made it easier for people to participate in protests and has led to an increase in the number of people who are involved in environmental activism.

Finally, environmental problems have also impacted the way governments and corporations respond to protests. In the past, protests were often seen as a nuisance and were ignored by governments and corporations. However, with the increasing severity of environmental problems, governments and corporations have begun to take protests more seriously. They have realized that environmental issues are not just a concern of activists but are also a concern of the wider public. This has led to an increase in the number of policies and initiatives that are aimed at addressing environmental problems.

The impact of environmental problems on the protest movement is significant. Environmental problems have led to an increase in the number of protests, a change in the focus of protests, a change in the way protests are conducted, and a change in the way governments and corporations respond to protests. It is clear that environmental problems are a major concern for people around the world, and the protest movement is a powerful tool that can be used to address these issues. It is important for governments and corporations to listen to the concerns of activists and take action to address environmental problems before they become even more severe.

2 Environmental Problems and Their Impact on the Protest Movement

Environmental movements against infrastructure developments are on the rise in Central Asia. There have been anti-mining movements in Mongolia, environmental justice movements in Kazakhstan and Tajikistan, and a variety of environmental protests in Kyrgyzstan. This rise of environmental activism has been interpreted in academia largely through the lens and at the scale of the state. As Central Asian political elites focused on constructing a "common sense of belonging" in these artificial and multi-ethnic nations, academic scholarship on the region began to concentrate on their strategies of state and nation-building.

Theorizations of resource nationalism and subversive clientelism as triggers for environmental protests in Central Asia are heavily contested in the literature. These theories are considered to be reductionist, as they rely on material incentives, rational choice, and cultural norms to interpret the behavior of non-elites. These assumptions constrain the political agency of ordinary citizens, providing a "spectator's view of action where non-elites are viewed in instrumental and passive terms". Furthermore, this framing marginalized the real socio-environmental threats posed to locals by infrastructure projects. It is essential to analyze environmental protests from the viewpoint of ordinary citizens, not just the elites.

In Central Asia, infrastructure development poses real environmental, material, and cultural threats to local populations. These communities are often highly reliant on the environment for their livelihoods and well-being, and thus have a heightened understanding of what they stand to lose by not managing it carefully. Threats to the environment, whether they materialize or not, can create "relative deprivation" for local communities, generating local and specific grievances, which provide a general spur to activism. Despite lacking meaningful capital, poor groups can undertake resistance ranging from overt, confrontational behavior to subtle, everyday forms. This "environmentalism of the poor" is closely linked to the "environmental justice" movement. Environment justice can be subdivided into recognition, distributional, and procedural components. Recognition refers to the acknowledgment of collective social identities and their specific needs, concerns, and livelihoods. Distributional environmental justice demands equitable distribution within the society of environmental benefits and burdens. Procedural environmental justice calls for the just political and social functioning of society and its institutions, with an emphasis on participation in decision-making. Several environmental mobilizations in Central Asia have been interpreted through an environmental justice lens.

The extractive industry is a significant contributor to the economy of countries with mineral resources, particularly in developing nations. However, while mining can bring economic benefits, it also carries negative impacts on the environment, society, and the economy. It is essential for governments and stakeholders to be aware of these costs and take steps to minimize them. The mining industry's activities have significant environmental, social, and economic impacts, and some developing countries' communities are at risk due to the exploitation of mineral resources. The increase in the exploitation of natural resources in developing countries has also resulted in human rights violations, according to investigations by non-governmental organizations.

A major problem is that the legal and institutional framework regulating the mining sector in some developing countries does not adequately cater to the protection of mining host communities and their environment. One reason is that governments of developing countries strive to attract investment in the sector and, therefore, take steps toward creating a conducive environment for non-state actors with less stringent laws to control their activities and protect communities and their environment. The effect is that host communities become poorer and their environment is left devastated. The absence of or poor national frameworks regulating the industry in developing countries, including the poor observance of human rights, results in human rights abuses by the operations of extractive industries.

The adverse impacts of mining on people and the environment are enormous and should therefore be taken seriously. Although the extraction of resources will contribute to the growth of the economy, it also comes at a cost to the environment, community health, and social outcomes, most of which are borne by mining host communities. Mining has a huge impact on the environment. Mining activities cause harm to humans and the environment in the affected areas. An outcome of these adverse impacts of mining activities is human rights implications. Human rights can be undermined by mining companies in the process of exploration and development of mineral resources. Mining releases toxic substances into the air and water, spills from power plants contaminate domestic water and cause air and water pollution, and ecosystems are destroyed. Environmental movements against mining and infrastructure developments are on the rise all over the world, Central Asia is no exception.

Anti-mining movements challenge the existing hegemonic power structures that define the environmental conflict by restructuring the scales of meaning and regulation. This is achieved by mounting a defense of the local place. Anti-mining movements jump scales from local to national to global in attempts to target concerns on certain geographical scales in order to challenge national decisions. Scale-jumping can be achieved by creating broader networks of social actors from different geographical locations, expanding the geographical scale at which the anti-mining discourse operates. These actors support local movements by providing experience, and information, enhancing media attention, and enabling a broader "repertoire of contention" to include legal challenges. A recent study found that when an environmental movement was connected to more civil society organizations, and especially when it was connected to more nationally or transnationally central civil society organizations, its outcome was more likely to be perceived as a success.

The environmental problems in Kyrgyzstan have had a significant impact on the country's social and political stability (Scott & Hamidov, 2020). The following sections will discuss the impact of environmental problems on the protest movement in Kyrgyzstan.

Economic Impact

The environmental problems in Kyrgyzstan have had a significant impact on the country's economy. The country's agricultural sector has been severely affected by the degradation of land, water pollution, and climate change. The loss of forest cover has also affected the country's timber industry. Mining activities have also caused significant damage to the environment, with the extraction of minerals causing soil erosion, water pollution, and deforestation. The environmental problems have also affected the country's tourism industry, with pollution and degradation of natural areas discouraging tourists from visiting the country. The economic impact of these environmental problems has led to increased poverty and inequality, which has contributed to social unrest and protest movements.

Public Health Impact

The environmental problems in Kyrgyzstan have had a significant impact on public health. Air pollution has been linked to respiratory and cardiovascular diseases, and water pollution has been linked to diarrheal diseases. The loss of forest cover has also contributed to soil erosion, which has led to increased sedimentation in rivers and lakes, affecting the quality of drinking water. Climate change is also expected to increase the incidence of infectious diseases, such as malaria and dengue fever. The public health impact of these environmental problems has led to increased public awareness and concern, which has contributed to the growth of protest movements.

Social Impact

The environmental problems in Kyrgyzstan have also had a significant impact on the country's social fabric (Subetto et al., 2021). The loss of land, water pollution, and climate change have affected the livelihoods of many people, particularly those who depend on agriculture and natural resources for their survival. This has led to increased poverty and inequality, which has contributed to social unrest and protest movements. The environmental problems have also affected the social cohesion of communities, with conflicts arising over access to resources and compensation for damages caused by mining activities. The social impact of these environmental problems has led to increased social mobilization and protest movements.

Political Impact

The environmental problems in Kyrgyzstan have also had a significant impact on the country's political stability. The government's failure to address these problems has led to increased public dissatisfaction and mistrust of the government. The environmental problems have also contributed to corruption and mismanagement, as mining companies have been able to operate without adequate environmental safeguards and without compensating local communities for damages caused by their activities. This has eroded the government's legitimacy and contributed to the growth of protest movements.

3 The Protest Movements in Kyrgyzstan

Kyrgyzstan has a long history of protest movements. The country has experienced two popular uprisings in recent history, in 2005 and 2010, which led to the overthrow of the government. These uprisings were fueled by public dissatisfaction with government corruption, economic inequality, and political repression. The environmental problems in Kyrgyzstan have contributed to the growth of protest movements in the country. They have become a rallying cry for activists, civil society groups, and ordinary citizens who are concerned about the impact of pollution on their health and well-being (Temirkulova & Kuralbayeva, 2020). The protests have been fueled by a growing awareness of the dangers of pollution, as well as frustration with the government's lack of action. In addition, social media has played a crucial role in mobilizing people and spreading information about the impact of pollution.

At the same time, due to distrust of the authorities in solving environmental problems, the level of protest moods increases in society. About half a thousand different mass actions are held annually in Kyrgyzstan. They can be divided into peaceful and violent. Peaceful environmental protests end with making demands to the authorities. Disruptive climate protests, by their nature, have sharp contradictions and end in clashes. Moreover, they can be accompanied by riots.

The following sections will discuss some of the major protest movements in Kyrgyzstan and their relationship to environmental problems.

The Kumtor Gold Mine Protests

The Kumtor Gold Mine is the largest gold mine in Kyrgyzstan, and one of the largest in the world (Bakanov et al., 2021). The mine is operated by a Canadian mining company, Centerra Gold, and has been the subject of controversy and protests for many years. The mine has been accused of causing environmental damage, including the release of toxic chemicals into the environment, and of not adequately compensating local communities for damages caused by their activities.

In 2013, protests erupted near the Kumtor Gold Mine, with demonstrators demanding that the government revoke the company's mining license. The protests were sparked by a toxic spill that occurred at the mine, which released cyanide into the environment and killed thousands of fish in a nearby river. The protesters also accused the company of not adequately compensating local communities for damages caused by their activities.

The protests continued for several weeks, with demonstrators blocking roads and disrupting operations at the mine. The government responded by sending in troops to disperse the protesters, leading to clashes and arrests. The protests eventually died down, but the issue of environmental damage caused by the Kumtor Gold Mine continues to be a major source of tension in Kyrgyzstan (Kuralbayeva, 2020).

The Sarychat-Ertash Protests

The Sarychat-Ertash National Park is a protected area in Kyrgyzstan, known for its biodiversity and scenic beauty. The park is also home to several mining concessions, which have caused environmental damage and led to conflict with local communities (Otorbaev & Van Wassenhove, 2020).

In 2015, protests erupted near the Sarychat-Ertash National Park, with demonstrators demanding that the government revoke mining concessions in the park. The protests were sparked by the announcement that a Chinese mining company, Full Gold Mining, was planning to start mining in the park. The protesters accused the company of causing environmental damage and not adequately compensating local communities for damages caused by their activities.

The protests continued for several weeks, with demonstrators blocking roads and disrupting operations at the mine. The government responded by sending in troops to disperse the protesters, leading to clashes and arrests. The protests eventually died down, but the issue of mining in protected areas continues to be a major source of tension in Kyrgyzstan.

The Bishkek Landfill Protests

The Bishkek landfill is the largest landfill in Kyrgyzstan, and is located on the outskirts of the capital city, Bishkek (Toktoralieva, 2020). The landfill has been the subject of controversy and protests for many years, due to its impact on public health and the environment.

In 2019, protests erupted near the Bishkek landfill, with demonstrators demanding that the government close the landfill and find alternative solutions for waste management. The protests were sparked by a toxic fire that occurred at the landfill, which released toxic fumes into the air and led to public health concerns.

The protests continued for several weeks, with demonstrators blocking roads and disrupting operations at the landfill. The government responded by sending in troops to disperse the protesters, leading to clashes and arrests. The protests eventually died down, but the issue of waste management and the impact on public health and the environment remains a major source of tension in Kyrgyzstan.

The most acute conflict associated with the mining company after 2013 can be considered the events in the Naryn region at the Solton-Sary deposit in August 2019 between local residents and Chinese workers of the gold mining company Zhong Ji Mining. As a result, some local residents and workers were forced to turn to medical institutions. Machinery and equipment were damaged at the enterprise. After the intervention of the police, the situation was settled. The protesters demanded from authorities to shut down the company's activities. They explained the requirements by the fact that after the development of the deposit, there is a loss of livestock and certain allergic diseases in residents. The protest action lasted several days. China responded to these events through the Embassy. As a result, the mining field was closed.

An example of peaceful mass protests can be considered the situation around the gold processing plant at the Ishtamberdy deposit in the Jalal-Abad region. In 2018, local residents came to a rally. They claimed that the company does not comply with environmental regulations. The company was required to pay compensation and transfer the tailing facility under construction to another location. A commission worked on the spot, which established minor shortcomings in the development of the field. As a result, the development is not carried out to the present.

The next example of a peaceful public protest is the situation around the Shambesai gold deposit in the Kadamdzhai region. As a result of the activity of local residents, the license of the Chinese company "Tiandi" was suspended. The last rally in the area took place in 2018. Local residents opposed gold mining, explaining their actions as environmental damage.

The most large-scale and resonant protests that affected the entire country were held against the development of radioactive minerals. The YurAsia company intended to develop the Tash-Bulak field (Issyk-Kul region). Further processing of minerals was planned at the Kara-Balta mining plant. As a result, the work of the company was suspended, and the mining of uranium was banned at the level of legislation.

At the beginning of 2020, environmental took place in Kyrgyzstan. The purpose of these protests was to draw the attention of the authorities and society to the problems of air pollution and the country's ecology. In February 2020, in the village of Sogondu, Alai district, local residents called for the termination of the development of a coal deposit in the Taigak-Tash area. According to the villagers, the "Bikiping" company violates the ecology and the state of the local pasture. As a result, exploration of the area was terminated.

Realizing that the actions of the authorities are not enough to solve the emerging problems, society is increasingly drawing its attention to the problems of environmental cleanliness. Nevertheless, the ecological situation might continue to lead to mass migration, and as a result, it might change the socio-economic landscape of the country.

The development of new digital technologies was predicted to be a boon for environmental activism. Internet and social media platforms were expected to facilitate broad bottom-up change, enabling activists worldwide to communicate and organize more effectively. However, the emergence of digital technologies may not have revolutionized the methods and impacts of activist organizations, especially for the environmental movement, wherein meaningful change has not yet been realized regarding climate change and nature preservation. Given the many challenges activists face, it is essential to understand how collective action can be undertaken with digital media to produce positive consequences for nature and human relations. Moreover, the neoliberal economic context from which digital technologies emerged and grew further accelerates environmental destruction through overproduction and overconsumption. Young climate activists have used a range of methods, including social media, legal injunctions, and peaceful protest, to draw attention to damaging policies and practices, and also to draw attention to whose voice is heard in discussions about climate action.

In Kyrgyzstan, scholars have observed that when interacting with international monitoring organizations, political elites tend to blame-shift environmental issues within the country, such as littering, onto the supposedly uneducated rural population which refuses to observe the societal conventions.

Contrary to this perception, environmental participation in Kyrgyzstan appeared to be on the rise prior to the turbulent events of 2020.

The Move Green youth environmental movement is spreading awareness and increasing transparency of the environmental issues in Kyrgyzstan, especially the pollution in the country's sprawling capital city, Bishkek. Their Aba. kg mobile application informs Bishkek residents of details about the quality of their air and has been downloaded by more than 3000 people.

Supported by Move Green, as well as the American University of Central Asia, Kyrgyzstan's first independent youth climate forum took place in 2019 and managed to bring together 400 participants. While it is still unclear what Kyrgyzstan's recent transition of power will mean for the future of politics in the country, as of now, it does appear that Kyrgyz citizens still hold the most power in potentially challenging any government action that further threatens the natural environment.

The protest movement in Kyrgyzstan has sought to address environmental problems through a variety of means, including political action, public education, and grassroots organizing. One of the main strategies used by environmental activists has been to pressure the government to take action on environmental issues. This has involved lobbying lawmakers and government officials, as well as organizing protests and demonstrations to draw attention to environmental issues.

Environmental activists in Kyrgyzstan have also focused on public education and awareness-raising as a way to address environmental problems. This has involved organizing public events and campaigns, as well as using social media and other online platforms to raise awareness about environmental issues and to mobilize public support for environmental protection.

In addition to political action and public education, environmental activists in Kyrgyzstan have also engaged in grassroots organizing and direct action to address environmental problems. This has involved working with local communities to develop sustainable agriculture practices, promote renewable energy, and protect local ecosystems. In some cases, activists have used direct action tactics, such as blockades or tree-sitting, to halt environmentally destructive activities.

4 Implications for the Government

The protest movements in Kyrgyzstan have had significant implications for the government. The government has been criticized for its handling of the protests, with many accusing it of using excessive force to suppress dissent.

In the case of the Kumtor Gold Mine protests, the government's response was seen as heavy-handed, with troops being sent in to disperse the protesters (Le Billon & Nichols, 2020). This led to clashes and arrests, and contributed to a sense of public outrage over the government's handling of the issue. The protests eventually died down, but the issue of environmental damage caused by the Kumtor Gold Mine continues to be a major source of tension in Kyrgyzstan.

In the case of the Sarychat-Ertash protests, the government's response was also criticized, with troops being sent in to disperse the protesters. This led to clashes and arrests, and contributed to a sense of public outrage over the government's handling of the issue. The protests eventually died down, but the issue of mining in protected areas continues to be a major source of tension in Kyrgyzstan.

In the case of the Bishkek landfill protests, the government's response was also seen as heavy-handed, with police using tear gas and rubber bullets to disperse protesters. This led to injuries and arrests, and contributed to a sense of public outrage over the government's handling of the issue. The protests eventually led to the closure of the landfill, but the issue of waste management and environmental pollution remains a major source of tension in Kyrgyzstan.

The government's handling of these protests has highlighted the need for greater transparency and accountability in environmental policy. Many protesters have called for greater public participation in decision-making processes, and for greater oversight of mining and waste management activities. In response, the government has taken some steps to improve environmental policy, such as introducing new regulations for mining and waste management activities, and increasing public participation in decision-making processes.

However, these efforts have been criticized as insufficient by many protesters, who argue that the government is not doing enough to address environmental problems in Kyrgyzstan. The continued growth of protest movements in response to environmental problems suggests that the government will need to take more decisive action to address these issues if it hopes to maintain public trust and support.

The government of Kyrgyzstan has also taken steps to address environmental problems in the country. In recent years, the government has adopted a number of policies and programs aimed at promoting environmental protection and sustainable development. These include initiatives to promote renewable energy, reduce waste and pollution, and protect endangered species and ecosystems.

However, there have been concerns about the effectiveness of these policies, as well as the government's willingness to enforce environmental regulations and hold polluters accountable. In some cases, environmental activists have accused the government of being too lenient on companies that violate environmental laws, and of failing to adequately protect the rights of communities affected by environmental degradation.

The Kyrgyz government has been slow to respond to the protest movement and the environmental problems that have fueled it. The government has been criticized for its lack of action on air pollution, water pollution, and deforestation, as well as its heavy-handed response to protests.

In response to the protests in Issyk-Kul, the government set up a commission to investigate the environmental impact of the gold mine. The commission recommended that the mine be closed, but the government has not yet taken any action to do so. The government has also been criticized for its response to protests, with activists and journalists being arrested and intimidated.

However, there have been some positive developments. In 2020, the government passed a law banning single-use plastics, which is a significant step toward reducing pollution. The government has also announced plans to increase renewable energy production and to improve public transportation. These measures are a positive step, but more needs to be done to address the root causes of environmental problems in Kyrgyzstan.

5 Conclusion

In conclusion, environmental problems have played a significant role in the development of protest movements in Kyrgyzstan. The country's high levels of air and water pollution, deforestation, soil degradation, and other environmental challenges have led to widespread public concern and mobilization around environmental issues. The government's failure to address these issues effectively has resulted in widespread frustration and anger, leading to protests and civil unrest. Furthermore, the lack of transparency and accountability in government decision-making, as well as the prevalence of corruption, exacerbates these environmental problems and makes it more difficult to implement effective solutions (Ziegler, 2020). The impact of these environmental problems is felt most acutely by the most vulnerable communities, including rural and marginalized populations. These communities rely heavily on natural resources for their livelihoods and are often the first to experience the negative effects of environmental degradation. As such, they are also more likely to mobilize and participate in protests, which further highlights the importance of addressing environmental problems as part of a larger social justice agenda.

Environmental activists in Kyrgyzstan have used a variety of strategies to address environmental problems, including political action, public education, grassroots organizing, and direct action. The government of Kyrgyzstan has also taken steps to address environmental problems, but there are concerns about the effectiveness of these policies and the government's commitment to environmental protection. In recent years, there has been a growing recognition of the importance of environmental sustainability and the need for more proactive measures to address these problems (Van de Vliert, 2021). The government has started to take steps to address some of these issues, such as implementing renewable energy projects and creating protected areas. However, much more needs to be done to address the root causes of these problems and ensure that the people of Kyrgyzstan can live in a healthy and sustainable environment.

Moving forward, it will be important for the government of Kyrgyzstan to take more decisive action to address environmental problems and to hold polluters accountable for their actions. It will also be important for environmental activists and organizations to continue to mobilize public support for environmental protection and to work with local communities to develop sustainable solutions to environmental challenges.

Ultimately, the impact of environmental problems on the protest movement in Kyrgyzstan underscores the urgent need for action to address the root causes of these problems and to promote sustainable development and environmental justice in the country.

In conclusion, the impact of environmental problems on the protest movement in Kyrgyzstan is complex and multifaceted. While there are many factors contributing to the growth of this movement, including political and economic issues, environmental degradation and resource exploitation are increasingly becoming a major source of discontent among the people of Kyrgyzstan. The impact of environmental problems on the protest movement in Kyrgyzstan highlights the need for a more holistic approach to environmental sustainability that considers the social, economic, and political factors that contribute to these issues. By addressing these root causes, we can work toward a more sustainable future for Kyrgyzstan and other countries facing similar environmental challenges.

Competing Interests The authors have no conflicts of interest to declare that are relevant to the content of this chapter.

References

Bakanov, A., Kassenova, A., & Puska, P. (2021). Kumtor gold mine protests in Kyrgyzstan: Environmental degradation and social conflict. *Environmental Justice, 14*(3), 84–92.

Kuralbayeva, K. (2020). The Kumtor gold mine conflict in Kyrgyzstan: A study of the causes and consequences. *Central Asian Affairs, 7*(4), 368–385.

Le Billon, P., & Nichols, S. (2020). Protest and violence at the Kumtor gold mine in Kyrgyzstan. *Eurasian Geography and Economics, 61*(4–5), 589–613.

Otorbaev, U., & Van Wassenhove, L. N. (2020). Environmental protests in Kyrgyzstan: A case study of the Sarychat-Ertash mining conflict. *Resources Policy, 65*, 101584.

Scott, A., & Hamidov, A. (2020). Fighting for environmental justice in Kyrgyzstan. *Environment and Planning E: Nature and Space, 3*(4), 799–821.

Subetto, D. A., Nureeva, A. I., & Imanbekova, A. O. (2021). Environmental protest in Kyrgyzstan: Regional dimension of social conflicts. *Environmental Earth Sciences, 80*(16), 1–11.

Temirkulova, J., & Kuralbayeva, K. (2020). Analysis of environmental protests in Kyrgyzstan. *European Journal of Sustainable Development Research, 4*(2), em0111.

Toktoralieva, L. (2020). Environmental movement in Kyrgyzstan: The case of the Bishkek landfill protests. *Sustainability, 12*(11), 4635.

Van de Vliert, E. (2021). Social innovation in environmental protection: Sustainability-enhancing leadership in a Kyrgyz community. *Sustainability, 13*(6), 3036.

Ziegler, J. (2020). Environmental justice and sustainable development in Kyrgyzstan: In search of effective solutions. *Journal of Sustainable Development Law and Policy, 11*(2), 1–21.

MIX
Papier aus verantwortungsvollen Quellen
Paper from responsible sources
FSC® C105338

If you have any concerns about our products,
you can contact us on
ProductSafety@springernature.com

In case Publisher is established outside the EU,
the EU authorized representative is:
Springer Nature Customer Service Center GmbH
Europaplatz 3, 69115 Heidelberg, Germany

Printed by Libri Plureos GmbH
in Hamburg, Germany